# NAKED SPIRITUALITY

*A Life with God in 12 Simple Words*

*Brian D. McLaren*

HarperOne
*An Imprint of HarperCollinsPublishers*

HarperOne

NAKED SPIRITUALITY: *A Life with God in 12 Simple Words.* Copyright © 2011 by Brian D. McLaren. All rights reserved. Printed in the United States of America. No part of this book may be used or reproduced in any manner whatsoever without written permission except in the case of brief quotations embodied in critical articles and reviews. For information, address HarperCollins Publishers, 195 Broadway, New York, NY 10007.

HarperCollins books may be purchased for educational, business, or sales promotional use. For information, please e-mail the Special Markets Department at SPsales@harpercollins.com.

HarperCollins website: http://www.harpercollins.com

HarperCollins®, 🏰®, and HarperOne™ are
trademarks of HarperCollins Publishers

FIRST HARPERCOLLINS PAPERBACK EDITION PUBLISHED IN 2012

Library of Congress Cataloging-in-Publication Data
McLaren, Brian D.
Naked spirituality : a life with God in 12 simple words / by Brian D. McLaren. — 1st ed.
p. cm.
ISBN 978-0-06-185402-6
1. Spiritual life—Christianity. 2. Prayer—Christianity. 3. Christian life. I. Title.
BV4501.3.M327  2011
248.3'2—dc22    2010053599

15 16  RRD(C)  10 9 8 7 6 5 4 3

# Contents

# PART III
## *Perplexity: The Season of Spiritual Surviving*
### 141

# PART IV
## *Harmony: The Season of Spiritual Deepening*
### 187

# Preface

H<small>E WAS NAKED.</small>

In broad daylight. In church.

He had taken off all his clothing—in front of the local bishop, in front of his neighbors and peers, and in front of his angry father. He now stood before them all.

"I shall go naked to meet my naked Lord," he said.

We know him as St. Francis, but at that moment he was just Giovanni Francesco di Bernardone, a young man on trial in the portico of the church of Santa Maria Maggiore in Assisi, Italy. Standing there self-exposed, he must have seemed more like a candidate for involuntary hospitalization than elevation to sainthood.

His father was a prosperous merchant of fine fabrics, an appreciating commodity at the beginning of the thirteenth century, when dressing up was becoming more and more essential for those wishing to ascend the socioeconomic ladder. He had accused Francis of selling some of his merchandise to raise money for a church renovation project. Since that fabric had indeed been sold and the proceeds invested in Francis's mission, Francis had nothing to offer in restitution. So he gave his father everything he had, his money, the shirt off his back, and the rest of his garments, saying, "I give you not only my money, but also my clothes." In so doing, Francis stripped off this earthly identity and clothed himself in a more primal and primary identity as God's unclothed creature, God's naked and vulnerable child.

That wasn't Francis's only experience of public nakedness. Once, the story goes, Francis commanded his colleague Friar Ruffino to go preach in the Assisi church "naked, save only for thy breeches." When Friar Ruffino complied, Francis felt ashamed for issuing such an extreme command, so he went and joined him in naked preaching (we're not sure whether the "breeches" were included). Years later he stripped naked again and went out in the snow to make snowmen—this time in an attempt to deal with his sensual desires. One would imagine that the technique worked well enough at least for the time he was outdoors in the freezing cold.

Francis joined a long tradition of nakedness in the service of spirituality, stretching from the days of Samuel and Saul (1 Sam. 19), through Isaiah's three-year stint preaching nude (20:3), to Jesus himself. In the Sermon on the Mount, where Jesus talks about turning the other cheek and walking the second mile, he says that if someone takes you to court, suing you for your overcoat, you might as well give them your other clothes too (Matt. 5:38–41), implying (I think) that in so doing, your self-exposure will serve to expose the heartless greed of your opponent. Jesus lived out this teaching three years later when, by his exposure on the cross, he unmasked the brutality of the occupying Romans and the hypocrisy of the local religious establishment.

In a set of details both strange and poignant, Mark's Gospel tells us that before being crucified, Jesus was stripped of his clothes three times. After the first stripping, he was mockingly clothed in a purple cloak of royalty, in which he was derided, spat upon, and beaten. Then he was stripped a second time and reclothed in his own garments. Finally he was stripped once more, and the soldiers cast lots to see who would take home his outer garment, his inner garment, and maybe his sandals as bonus pay for their day's work. Hanging on that cross, contrary to our discreet religious art, Jesus was fully exposed. It wasn't until after Jesus was dead that a kind soul, Joseph of Arimathea, covered the naked corpse with a linen cloth (15:16–46).

Naked we came from the womb, Job said, and naked we shall depart this life, but in between, we clothe ourselves in a thousand fascinating ways. Think of the immense variety and meaning of clothing in human society—military uniforms, academic regalia, religious robes; clothing as status symbol, designer labels as the mark of belonging to an in-group; festive costumes to celebrate a holiday or season; prom dress, wedding gown, bikini, burka; white lab coat, faded blue jeans, bright green shirts or bold red jerseys to proclaim political protest or team loyalty. We all learn to speak verbal languages—English, Chinese, Spanish, and so on—but we all must become fluent in the finely nuanced languages of dress as well. If clothing means and expresses so much, then of course so does nakedness.

In his list of things for which there is a time and season, the sage of Ecclesiastes does not say, "A time to get dressed and a time to get naked," but there are indeed such times. Without nakedness, for example, you can't go under the bright light of surgery. And without nakedness you can't enter into the candlelight of intimacy.

This is a book about getting naked—not physically, but spiritually. It's about stripping away the symbols and status of public religion—the Sunday-dress version people often call "organized religion." And it's about attending to the well-being of the soul clothed only in naked human skin. As a result, it must be a vulnerable book, tender in tone, gentle in touch. You won't find much in the way of aggressive arguments here, but rather shy experience daring to step into the light. It's an honest book, and I hope a practical one too, perhaps with some awkward spiritual parallels to what they used to call a "marital manual."

You won't need to agree with all the planks of my theological platform. I am a Christian, and all I write flows from my experience in that rich tradition, but you may be of another tradition entirely or of no known tradition at all. Instead of seeking theological agreement, this book invites you to experiment with the naked experience of God that provides the raw material from which all worthwhile theology derives.

There's a lot of dirty theology out there, the religious counterpart to dirty politics and dirty business, I suppose. You might call it spiritual pornography—a kind of for-profit exploitative nakedness. It's found in many of the same places as physical pornography (the Internet and cable TV for starters), and it promises similar things: instant intimacy, fantasy and make-believe, private voyeurism and vicarious experience, communion without commitment. That's certainly not what we're after in these pages.

No, we're after a lost treasure as old as the story of the Garden of Eden: the possibility of being naked and not ashamed, naked before God and naked before one another too, so we have no need to cover up, to protect, to posture, to dress to impress, just the freedom to be who we are, what we are, as we are (see Gen. 2:25). At their best, religious and spiritual communities help us discover this pure and naked spiritual encounter. At their worst, they simply make us more ashamed, pressuring us to cover up more, pushing us to further enhance our image with the best designer labels and latest spiritual fads, weighing us down with layer upon layer of heavy, uncomfortable, pretentious, well-starched religiosity. As someone who has experienced some of the best and some of the worst of religion and spirituality, I hope this book will help you strip away distractions and discover that precious hidden treasure, that primal gift underneath.

# INTRODUCTION

So what do you do for a living?" you might ask, if we happened to sit next to each other on a flight, mutually ignoring the flight attendant's spiel about how to turn our seat cushion into a flotation device and what electronic devices we need to turn off before takeoff. "I'm an author," I might whisper, which might then prompt you to ask what I write books about. I'd probably reply, "I write books on spirituality, cultural change, and social issues," or something like that. More often than not, we'd end up getting into an interesting conversation that would last until well after we reached our cruising altitude. (Unless you want to take a nap—I promise I wouldn't bother you in that case.)

Since we haven't actually met, I have to imagine what you might tell me about yourself. I was a pastor for over twenty years, so I learned to be a good listener. If you're like a lot of people I meet, you might describe yourself as "more spiritual than religious." You're seeking meaning and depth in your life, maybe even a deeper experience of God, but you don't feel that traditional "organized religion" helps very much.

Or you might describe yourself as faithfully religious—a lifelong churchgoer, a paid or unpaid minister, a diligent seminarian or theologian, a hardworking pastor, parachurch worker, or priest. It may all be working beautifully for you, and you're ready to take the next step in your spiritual journey.

But you may feel you're on autopilot, going through the motions. You're keeping the religious treadmill spinning, but your soul is dry, thirsty, empty, tired. You may feel a little toasted, if not fully burned out. Too much guilt. Too many shoulds. Too much pressure. Too much activity and controversy without a clear sense of worthwhile outcomes. If that's the case, you may wish you could rediscover the deeper purpose of it all, the point, why you do what you do.

You might tell me that you have been engaging in some deep questioning and theological rethinking.[1] You can no longer live with the faith you inherited from your parents or constructed earlier in your life. As you sort through your dogma and doctrine, you've found yourself praying less, less thrilled about worship, scripture, or church attendance. You've been so focused on sorting and purging your theological theories that you've lost track of the spiritual practices that sustain an actual relationship with God. You may even wonder if such a thing is possible for someone like you.

You may have come to the point where even the word "God" is problematic for you. You are so dreadfully sick and tired of hearing God's name overused and abused that you'd rather not add to the commotion. You're tempted to compensate for all the noisy religious overstatement by speaking of God as seldom and softly as possible. As you've been going through this painful process of rethinking both your theology and your practice of faith, your experience of God may have gradually been evaporating from your life. As a result, God may be shrinking from a substantial Someone to a vague something, leaving a thin residue that is next to nothing. All that may remain for you is a theoretical concept, an esoteric principle, a distant abstraction that's eventually not worth talking about—or to.

You may be spiritually disappointed and wounded; you may feel God has abandoned you, turned on you, left you, and you don't know where to go next. You may be, perhaps without admitting it even to yourself, one of the increasing numbers of theologians, pastors, priests, and lifelong Christians who have practically become atheists because of long-standing disillusionment, unanswered questions, and unresolved pain. You may have been so skeptical and cynical for so long that now you're skeptical of skepticism and cynical about cynicism. You wonder if there could be a postskeptical faith, a postcynical hope, and maybe even a postatheist love.

You may be rebuilding after a faith collapse, or you may be embarking on your virgin voyage into faith and a spiritual life. Either way, you have no interest in fake spirituality, forced spirituality, hyped spirituality, inflated spirituality. You want to strip away all the layers of pretense and get down to naked reality. You "get" what Fr. Richard Rohr says:

**The goal of all spirituality is to lead the "naked person" to stand
trustfully before the naked God. The important thing is that
we're naked; in other words that we come without title, merit,
shame, or even demerit. All we can offer to God is who we
really are, which to all of us never seems like enough. I am sure
this is the way true lovers feel too.**[2]

Doctrinal correctness, institutional participation, and religious conformity won't suffice anymore. You need a life centered on simple,
doable, durable practices that will help you begin and sustain a naked
encounter with the holy mystery and pure loving presence that people
commonly call God.[3]

If we happened to meet—on a plane or train, at a party, or wherever—and if you expressed to me any of these kinds of struggles or
needs, this is the book I would have wanted to be able to give you
before we said good-bye. I wrote it because it's the kind of book I wish
someone had given to me at several points during my own spiritual
journey, when I was first getting started or when I hit some rough
patches of doubt or struggle.

All that's required to get started is a little tiny seed of faith—faith that
there's something or Someone out there (or "in here") worth searching
for. That might not seem like much, but I know it's enough.

# Chapter 1

# Spiritual Experiences and Spiritual Experience

I had been my whole life a bell, and I never knew it until at that moment I was lifted and struck.

ANNIE DILLARD[1]

I GREW UP IN A religious home. A full-dose, hard-core, shaken-together-and-my-cup-runneth-over, conservative, Bible-believing, Evangelical, fundamentalist Christian home. Christmas and Easter? Of course! Every Sunday morning? Obviously! Sunday school? Complete with memorizing Bible verses, singing Christian choruses, and competing in Bible Olympics! Holidays and Sundays were just the spiritual appetizers. For the main course, there was also church every Sunday night. And there was a Wednesday night prayer meeting too. And in the summer, Vacation Bible School and Christian summer camp. There were even occasional revival meetings that required attendance every night for a week—or two weeks, God help us. Then there were special kids and youth programs on top of everything else. If that weren't sufficient to save our souls from secularism, at every meal we bowed our heads for prayer—including when we went out to restaurants, which always made me squirm and then feel guilty for squirming.[2] And after dinner on most nights—a kind of spiritual dessert—my dad would have us read a daily devotional guide. And I haven't even mentioned prayers and Bible stories at bedtime.

You'd think with all that religion, I might have overdosed and become an atheist. Or at least an agnostic. And maybe I would have, except that underneath all the layers upon layers of religion, I discovered a living, breathing, naked spirituality.

For you, the discovery may have occurred at a twelve-step meeting. When you found yourself fighting for survival against a raging addiction, suddenly faith in higher power really mattered. You needed more than a dressed-up Sunday religion—you needed a naked spirituality that would help you get sane again.

Or it may have happened in a small fellowship group on a college campus, or on a retreat, or in a time of illness or bereavement, in the middle of a divorce, or maybe walking along a path in a forest. Maybe someone close to you was transformed before your eyes, and it turned out that their spiritual conversion was contagious. However it happened, what had been a concept or theory got translated into naked experience and real-life practice. You felt something. You knew something. You changed.

I think there is a kind of innate spirituality in young children; the primal connection of child to parent translates naturally into trust in God. But as we mature, our spirituality must mature too. Otherwise, that childlike connection will be lost along with childhood innocence. In my case, a more robust spirituality started sneaking up on me in my early teens. I had learned hundreds of Bible stories, memorized dozens of Bible verses, said thousands of prayers—including one called the "sinner's prayer," important to all fundamentalists. But around puberty, there were little inklings of a new space opening up in my psyche, a capacity for doubt and a capacity for a kind of experience that I had never had before. (It's interesting how intellectual and spiritual capacities seem to develop along with sexual ones.) I wasn't sure what I was looking for, but by the time I was sixteen, I was on the path of passionate spirituality.

I think I was fifteen when a seventeen-year-old fellow I met at summer camp told me the story of his dramatic conversion several months earlier. He had been slipping—or jumping—into a dangerous love affair with a drug called mescaline. His grades plummeted, and he dropped out of school. Then through a "straight" (in those days it meant non-drug-using) girlfriend he had "gotten saved." He was now clean and sober, studying the Bible, reenrolling in school, getting his life together. I saw something real in his life, something more robust and vigorous than I had experienced, and it left me a little envious.

Later that year, another friend invited me to a "discipleship group" made up of some college students who read the Bible, prayed, and talked about their spiritual growth. I didn't exactly fit in this group; they were older and smarter and more serious than I was, and I was already planning my escape from a hyperreligious life. But again, I saw something real in their lives, something I didn't have. If I ever did become a more spiritual person, I wanted to be like them, I thought.

Along with my attraction, I must admit I felt a lot of revulsion. To a teenager in the early 1970s, church culture seemed like a throwback to the 1950s—or the 1850s, or the 1750s, take your pick. To a guy interested in science, all the anti-evolution rhetoric seemed unnecessary, even a little silly. To a kid growing a scruffy beard and playing in a rock and roll band, the crew-cut, white-shirt-and-tie-clad, pro-war, anti-hippie churchy role models seemed singularly creepy—just as I must have seemed to them. I felt stuck in a religious twilight zone, not in, not out.

Right in the middle of all this ambivalence, some neighborhood buddies, similarly conflicted, I think, invited me on a weekend retreat with the youth group from their Southern Baptist church. And that's where spirituality snuck up and crashed upon me like an unexpected wave at the beach. The retreat leader sent us off on Saturday afternoon for an hour of silence during which we were supposed to pray. I climbed a tree—being a back-to-nature guy—only to discover that my perch was along an ant superhighway and that mosquitoes also liked the shade of that particular tree. But eventually, between swatting and scratching, I actually prayed. My prayer went something like this: "Dear God, before I die, I hope you will let me see the most beautiful sights, hear the most beautiful sounds, and feel the most beautiful feelings that life has to offer."

No, it wasn't an altruistic prayer asking God to end world hunger or war. No, it wasn't focused on repenting of my many sins, although, like any hormonally infused teenage boy, I had my share of things to feel guilty about. No, it wasn't a theological prayer affirming important tenets of faith. In fact, it was pretty adolescent, and some might say trite. But it was *my* prayer, honest and at least a little loftier than my occasional pleas for a cute girl in Spanish class to get a crush on me or for help on the algebra quiz I forgot to study for.

In spite of my sincerity, absolutely nothing happened. As the other fifty-seven or so minutes stretched on, I couldn't think of much else to say. I scratched mosquito bites, flicked ants off my legs, felt my butt go numb, and eventually climbed down the tree and wandered back to the retreat center for supper. There were evening activities, and then we were supposed to go to bed, I think. But somehow, a few friends and I snuck away to a hillside and found ourselves sitting under one of those sparkling autumn night skies. I walked several paces away from my friends and lay back in the grass, fingers interlocked behind my head, looking up, feeling strangely quiet and at peace. Something began to happen.

I had this feeling of being seen. Known. Named. Loved. By a Someone bigger than the sky that expanded above me. Young science geek that I was, I pictured myself lying on a little hill on a little continent on a little planet in a little solar system on the rim of a modest galaxy in a sea of billions of galaxies, and I felt that the great big Creator of the whole shebang was somehow noticing little tiny me. It was as if the whole sky were an eye, and all space were a heart, and I was being targeted as a focal point for attention and love. And the oddest thing happened as this realization sank in. I began to laugh. I wasn't guffawing, but I was laughing, at first gently, but eventually almost uncontrollably. Profound laughter surged from within me.

It wasn't a reactive laughter, the kind that erupts when you hear a good joke or see somebody do something ridiculous. It was more like an overflowing laughter, as if all that space I had been feeling opening up inside me was gradually filling up with pure happiness, and once it reached the rim, it spilled over in incandescent joy. "God loves me! Me! God! At this moment! I can feel it!"

The joy felt huge, so big that I got a little scared. My stomach started to hurt because I was laughing so hard. Not only had I never felt anything like this before; I had never heard of anything like this before. I started to feel as though I might burst apart, because the joy felt bigger than I could contain. I felt that my universe was turning upside down, and I might fall off the planet and out into the depths of space. I prayed again: "God, I don't think I can take much more of this. Maybe you'd better tone it down a little." Gradually the euphoria subsided, and I quietly moved back toward my friends.

While I had been having my private spiritual experience, they were having a spiritual experience of their own, one of a more social nature. I remember hearing one of them say to the others, "I love you guys. I really love you guys." And then they all started telling each other how much they appreciated each other—saying the kinds of gushy, sincere, vulnerable things that teenagers normally say only when they're graduating, at a funeral, or getting drunk. I don't think I said anything, but I know I felt caught up with them in something spiritually tangible— theologians would call it the Holy Spirit—and was bound together with my friends and with God. Soon most or all of us were all sniffling, moved to tears at the connection we were feeling—to each other and to God.

Then I remembered my prayer in the tree a couple hours earlier. Wham! It hit me. God had answered my prayer!

In the previous few minutes, I had seen the most beautiful thing that eyes can see: the glory of God shining in the radiance of creation. I had heard the most beautiful thing that ears can hear: friends telling friends that they love one another. And I had felt the most beautiful thing that any heart can ever feel: the love of God and the love of others. And at that, my sniffling turned into quiet sobs, again coming from a deep part of me I had never even been aware of before.

If my private laughter was chapter one of my first spiritual experience, and if those shared tears were chapter two, chapter three came later the same evening when I had a vision. I wouldn't have known to call it that at the time, but, looking back, I think that's what it was. I was praying again, and in my imagination I could see a pair of sandaled feet. I knew the Bible story about a sinful woman weeping at Jesus's feet, and it was as if I were being brought into that story not as an observer, but as a participant. I saw myself as a pool of water, of tears, spreading around Jesus's feet. I was filled with a profound desire to pour myself out for Jesus in simple, pure, selfless love. Whether or not I was a true Christian before that night, I don't know and it doesn't really matter.

But from that night on, I was a wholehearted lover of the Creator, a person thirsty for the Holy Spirit, and a devoted follower of Jesus. That was my triune baptism into spirituality.

I don't like to talk about these experiences much. Talking about them has a way of cheapening them. The memory of the experience itself gets replaced by the memory of telling the story about it. Eventually the experience itself all but disappears, and pretty soon the story being told has little connection to anything that actually happened. Meanwhile, a suspicious psychologist could, I'm sure, offer plausible explanations for what happened to my friends and me that night. There's a time and a place for that kind of scrutiny and analysis, and I don't see neurological, psychological, sociological, and spiritual categories as mutually exclusive.[3] But even so, sharing experiences like this can feel like casting one's heart before analytical critics, which is not a pleasant thing.

In spite of those misgivings, I've shared this dramatic experience for three reasons. First, I think it's important for you to know that I'm not writing about spirituality as a dispassionate observer. Since that starry night, I've been an insider to spirituality. And since that initial spiritual baptism, many other kinds of spiritual experiences have similarly snuck up and surprised me. Some of them have been equally dramatic, some more, most less, but still very meaningful. Sometimes they haven't come when I felt I needed them most, and others have felt like bounty poured upon bounty. They've never been an on-demand, push-button kind of thing for me. But usually, even when I'm in the middle of a tough and draining day or season, if I'm quiet for even a few seconds, I have been able to find that sacred space at the center of my life where there is at least a faint, quiet glimmer of that same joy, love, and unity that I experienced that night under the stars. My initiation into spirituality stuck, and it has persisted through life's many dangers, toils, and snares, as the old hymn says. So everything I write about spirituality today has been tested in the crucible of my own experience during the nearly forty years since that night.

Second, I want to distinguish the wine of spirituality from the wineskin of the religion in which I experienced it. That dramatic experience took place at a Southern Baptist retreat center, around the fringes of charismatic renewal, in the context of the Jesus Movement, in the broader context of conservative Evangelicalism—the same basic matrix, incidentally, that gave birth to the Religious Right. At the Bible studies, conferences, youth events, and religious festivals I began attending after that night, I would regularly hear sermons against evolution and for six-day creationism—sermons that never sat right with me. When I listened to Christian radio—as I did religiously—I would be warned against every approach to the Bible except fundamentalist literalism, about which I always had my doubts.

When I went to youth rallies, I would be told repeatedly that anyone who had not said the required "sinner's prayer" would miss out on the "abundant life" before death and would go straight to hell afterwards. Again, I always had misgivings about this dualism. When I went to church and Christian conferences, I was consistently taught why women shouldn't be leaders, why gay people should be stigmatized, and why liberals were anti-God, and although I probably nodded in agreement and maybe even voiced a flimsy "Amen" from time to time, I had my doubts. And to top it all off, in popular books and through little tracts and scary propaganda movies, I would be reminded that something called the Rapture would occur any day—so we shouldn't concern ourselves with social issues, but only focus on saving souls and helping them become born-again, Spirit-filled, elect, Evangelical Christians just like us.[4]

Now, almost four decades later, I cringe when I hear the teachings that were standard fare back then. I have discarded those theological wineskins, but I treasure more than ever the wine of the Spirit that was somehow conveyed to me through them. That suit of theological clothing doesn't fit me anymore, but the naked spirituality that sustains me today originally came to me dressed in it. I hope you can see that even if a particular style of religious clothing now feels stiff, tight, and ill-fitting for you—Roman Catholic or mainline Protestant, Evangelical or Pentecostal, Sunni or Shiite, Reform or Orthodox—the possibility of naked spirituality remains a live option.

Third, I want to acknowledge that dramatic spiritual experiences happen, but they are, by definition, pretty rare—otherwise they wouldn't seem dramatic. Beyond that, although they solve some problems, they can create others. Some people, for example, seem to develop an addiction to dramatic spiritual experiences that disrupts their life much as other addictions would. Most important, dramatic spiritual experiences simply aren't the point. Whatever the value of extraordinary dramatic *spiritual experiences,* to which some people seem more prone than others, I'm convinced that what matters most—and is available to everyone—is daily, ordinary *spiritual experience.* With or without dramatic experiences, we can all find, expand, and hold a quiet, sacred space at the center of our lives, a space where we experience vital connection to the living God. We can all learn to tap into the quiet current of sacredness and love that runs from the Creator through all creation. Dramatic experiences can awaken some of us to the reality of the spiritual life, but they are not sufficient to strengthen, sustain, and deepen us as truly spiritual people.

But how do we become *truly spiritual people?* How do we learn to strip away the superficialities so that, in Richard Rohr's terms, our naked souls can encounter the naked God? How do we nurture daily spiritual experience, with or without dramatic spiritual experiences? That's where spiritual practices come in, and that's what we will explore together in the pages ahead. We will root twelve essential spiritual practices in one simple word each. These twelve practices will not in any way be exhaustive, but they will be essential—essential for strengthening a vital, vigorous, naked spirituality.

# CHAPTER 2

## *"But I'm Spiritual"*

True religion helps us to grow, but pseudo-religion hinders growth, for it creates and maintains obstacles and barriers. Thus it is that much religion merely censors experience and does not liberate it, stifles human potential and does not allow it to blossom. Much religion is superficial and does not help the journey inwards, which is so necessary to spiritual health. There has to be a movement toward the still center, the depths of our being, where, according to the mystics, we find the presence of God.

KENNETH LEECH[1]

I STARTED AS RELIGIOUS AND then was plunged into spirituality that night under the stars. Others do the reverse, starting with spirituality and then exploring religion. But a lot of folks I meet feel a tension between spirituality and religion. "I'm not religious myself," they say, "but . . ." Why does the word "religious" almost demand to be followed up by a "but" for so many people?

To find out, when I hear "but I'm spiritual," I often follow up with a question: "I'm curious. What do you mean by 'spiritual'?"

Four answers come up again and again, and each rings true in my own experience. First, when people say "I'm spiritual," they mean that secular science, politics, and economics don't have all the answers for them. They believe life has a sacred dimension that can't be reduced to formulas, rules, and numbers. They believe we have hungers that can't be fed by facts alone, votes alone, or even the quasi-religious "invisible hand of the market" alone.

Second, they mean that organized religion doesn't have all the answers for them either.[2] They're concerned that religious institutions are complicit in too many of the world's problems, and that they lead their adherents on too many adventures in missing the point.

Third, the word "spiritual" signals for them an inner sensitivity to aliveness, meaning, and sacredness *in* the universe. They can't in good conscience assign God, heaven, meaning, values, souls, worship, the afterlife, and eternity to the sacred category and consign everything else—including bodies, sexuality, work, animals, plants, the earth, daily life, and history—to the profane. Instead of separating the two, instead of denying one in favor of the other, and instead of reducing one to the other, they want the former to infuse the latter, and the latter to be enlivened by the former. They want to marry God and creation, heaven and earth, soul and body, eternity and history, afterlife and life, not divorce them. They want to integrate both categories in a vital, intimate—can we say *naked*?—communion.[3]

Fourth, spiritual people seek practical ways to nourish that sense of integration and communion. It might be meditating, hiking on a wilderness trail, volunteering at a soup kitchen, doing yoga, going to art galleries, participating in festivals, or going on pilgrimages. It might be fasting, feasting, or having deep talks with a few friends. Whatever the specifics, spiritual people have—or at least wish they had—some set of moves, rhythms, habits, or practices that, to some degree at least, keep them from sleepwalking or going on autopilot, so they live with a greater sensitivity to the sacred aliveness and meaning that surround them.

The truth is that these four characteristics of spirituality are also at the heart of true religion, as the etymology, or origin, of the word "religion" makes clear. The root of the word is "lig-," which you see in the word "ligament." It means to connect, to join together, to unite, to bring everything together in one body or one wholeness. And of course "re" means "again." So you might say that good religion is about connecting us together again.[4] Most deeply, it is about binding us together into one body with God, acknowledging that different religious denominations and families have differing ways of describing and relating to God.[5] It is also about bonding and uniting us again with one another and with all creation—the trees and the mountains and the

animals, with the stars and space and wind. In this light, true religion
and naked spirituality are two names for the same thing: *seeking vital
connection.* And seeking vital connection, it turns out, is another name
for love.[6] So, we might say, both spirituality and religion are, at their
best, two names for "love."

In that light we can better understand the "but" in "I'm spiritual, but
not religious." What many experience in religious communities on a
popular level seems closer to the opposite of love. Religion as they experience it promotes conflict and selfishness rather than generosity and
otherliness. It teaches them to prioritize their own personal salvation
and religiosity over the well-being of others. It teaches practices and
beliefs that make some fear, dehumanize, and judge others, straining
or tearing the ligaments of creation instead of strengthening them. In
this way, religions can actually become antireligions, "de-ligamenting"
us instead of "re-ligamenting" us. Maybe if we name this kind of false
or unspiritual phenomenon "de-ligion" instead of "religion," we can
save the latter word for the traditions that enhance and support naked
spirituality.

That's why, in the end, I don't think we need to pit religion against
spirituality, any more than we would pit clothing against nakedness.
Nakedness is a good thing, and clothing is a good thing too. In the
middle of a blizzard, a parka and boots come in handy, just as sturdy
jeans and a long-sleeved flannel shirt do when you're walking through a
forest full of nettles and mosquitoes. The lack of appropriate clothing in
a hostile environment can kill you. So can the presence of inappropriate
clothing. So the issue isn't clothing versus nakedness, but appropriate
versus inappropriate ways to clothe nakedness. And we might say the
problem isn't religion, but rather inappropriate religion—religion that
doesn't serve, protect, enhance, or express the naked life within it.[7]

Jesus worked with these images of clothing and nakedness quite a
bit, especially in Matthew's Gospel. Dressing up a wolf in a sheepskin
doesn't change its ravenous nature any more than dressing up spiritually greedy or vicious people in religious garb does, he said (7:15). The
naked beauty of the "lilies of the field" surpasses the fine wardrobe of
King Solomon (6:28–29). Hypocrites use both their fancy religious
garb (23:5) and their flowery public prayers (6:5) to impress other

people, but God isn't impressed. In contrast, he urged his followers to go into the closet—the place where you undress and dress in private, the place where you are naked—to pray "in secret" (6:6). "Isn't the body more than clothing?" he asked (6:25), and we might similarly imagine him asking, "Isn't spirituality more than religiosity?"

In John's Gospel, Jesus explores the same theme with a variety of vivid images.[8] Imagine, for example, Jesus standing by a well in the blazing desert heat of a Middle Eastern day, sharing a drink of cool water with an unnamed woman who has since been known as the "woman at the well" (4:7–26). She was a lot like so many spiritual seekers today: confused and frustrated by the conflicting claims of what we're calling de-ligions. One of the hot-button de-ligious arguments in those days centered on which mountain was the most holy, which mountain worshippers were supposed to ascend for bona fide, certified worship. So she brings up this my-mountain-is-better-than-your-mountain controversy, inviting this itinerant rabbi to render his opinion on which group chose the right piece of topography.

Predictably (if you're familiar with Jesus's approach to de-ligious controversy), Jesus doesn't answer her question. Instead he says, in essence, "That's a surface question of de-ligion, but you're looking for something deeper and more satisfying: a cool drink of pure, life-giving, thirst-quenching spirituality. Dressed-up de-ligion divides people based on arguments about mountains, but it sends everybody away thirsty. Naked spirituality invites people to a deeper level and unites them there, and their spiritual thirst is fulfilled. God is Spirit, and those who approach God must come to God in a spiritual and authentic way."

So Jesus turns her attention away from a solid, external, fixed *mountain,* and helps her imagine instead a flowing, internal, spiritual *fountain,* like the one that sources the well beside which they stand. He asks her to think deeper—about *living water* that flows up from within you, wherever you are, on this mountain, on that mountain, or anywhere else. There are any number of mountains of de-ligion—systems that fracture communities socially into in-groups and out-groups, "us" and "them." But there's one fountain of Spirit, he suggests, accessible to everyone. De-ligious people argue endlessly about which mountain is higher and more scenic than the others. They stake their claim to this religious mountain or that one. They defend theirs and attack others. But naked spirituality is different. You don't argue about the fountain—you drink from it and experience its movement and flow within you. It's flowing under everyone's feet, as it were, and can well up in the soul. When you have the fountain flowing within you, you don't need to travel to some distant mountain to find what you're thirsty for.

*And you are restored to community*

Immediately before this encounter, Jesus had another conversation, this one by night rather than at midday, presumably indoors rather than outdoors, with a traditional religious man named Nicodemus instead of a marginally religious anonymous woman. Like a lot of religious people, Nicodemus was preoccupied with teachings and miracles. Jesus told him that this approach would get him nowhere. He needed to become like a little child and start learning about naked spirituality from square one. "You have to be born of . . . Spirit," he says (John 3:5).

This time, instead of comparing Spirit to water in the aquifer beneath their feet, he points out the window to the wind blowing free in the trees above them.[9] "Hear that?" he says. "God is like that. Wind. Spirit. Mysterious. Powerful. Wild and untamed and uncontained. Always moving. You can't see wind or nail it down or catch it in a bottle. That's how Spirit is." In both encounters, the pattern is amazingly similar: Jesus points away from de-ligion and toward Spirit. He leads people away from religious structures and controversies that divide people into in-groups and out-groups; instead, he leads people to a different space entirely, where we can all experience the same Spirit.[10] He does this sort of thing in John's Gospel again and again.[11]

In the episode that comes right before this encounter with Nicodemus, Jesus uses yet another dynamic image for Spirit (John 2:1–11). He is at a wedding banquet where the wine has run out—a big embarrassment for the groom and a big disappointment for the guests. Jesus points to six ceremonial stone jars, the kind that are used in religious purification ceremonies, each holding twenty to thirty gallons, and directs them to be filled with water. When the banquet organizer tastes a cup drawn from the stone jars, he is amazed; it's better wine than any that had been served previously. Spirit-wine that fills empty religious containers, and at a wedding banquet, a celebration of joy, love, and union—the symbolism is as delicious as the wine must have been!

Whatever imagery he uses—wine, wind, or wellsprings—it's clear that Jesus wants to focus on naked spirituality, not the religion that clothes it. In fact, when he shows up at the Temple, the headquarters of the regional religion, he stirs up so much trouble that Temple personnel begin plotting for him to be arrested and killed. The Temple, he says, has already become obsolete, and the Spirit will do just fine even if the Temple is destroyed (John 2:19–21; 4:21–24). It's the same for the movement that arises in his aftermath, as every page of the New Testament makes clear. It's all about Spirit. Sometimes New Testament writers depict us as entering into the Spirit, like a person plunged into a cleansing bath, like a ship launched into water, like a branch grafted into a vine, or like a person born into the wide world (Mark 1:8; 1 Cor. 12:13; John 3:5; 15:15). In other passages, the Spirit comes into us, like wine into a body, like sap into a branch, like breath into the lungs, like an inhabitant into a house (Eph. 5:18–19; John 14:23; 15:5; 20:22). Sometimes, marital imagery is used: we are united with the Spirit like a bride with a groom, and we become pregnant with Spirit-life that will be born through us into the world as good and beautiful works (see Rom. 7:1–6; Rev. 19:9, 21:2, 22:17).

A spiritual life is a Spirit life, a life in the Spirit, and Jesus's life and work come into proper focus when we realize his goal was not to start a new religion—and certainly not to create a new religion that would seek to compete with or persecute his own religion, Judaism! No, his goal was to fill with Spirit-wine the empty stone jars of religion—his own religion and any other one, I'd say. His goal wasn't to start a new religious argument about dogma-mountains; it was to fill hearts with Spirit-fountains. His goal wasn't to replace one group of powerful religious grown-ups (like Nicodemus) with another, but to help everyone become like little children through Spirit-birth.

When people say, "I'm not religious, but I'm spiritual," many of them, I think, see what Jesus saw, that the Spirit's realm of activity can't be limited to the sphere of religion in general, much less to any particular religion. The Spirit of God is the fine wine of justice, joy, and peace; the uncontained wind of creativity, comfort, and liberation; the living water of holiness, beauty, and love. Whenever people encounter justice, joy, peace, creativity, comfort, liberation, holiness, beauty, love, or any other good thing, they are in some way encountering the Spirit, or at least the signature or aftermath of the Spirit. The Spirit, then, is bigger than any particular religion or religion in general. Nobody has a monopoly on Spirit.

AND WE
need each
other.

Get that straight, and a thousand other things begin to fall into place. We can put ourselves into the sandals of that woman drawing water from that well, or Nicodemus hearing the wind in the trees, or the disciples tasting that wine drawn from those ceremonial stone jars. We might just dare to believe that we too can experience the water, the wind, and the wine.

# CHAPTER 3

# *Twelve Simple Words*

Better a single word spoken from a heart of love than a thousand
from a heart of indifference.

EVAGRIUS PONTICUS[1]

SPIRITUAL EXPERIENCES LIKE THE one that I had under the stars that
night are wonderful—but not very dependable, which raises the question of how we can experience a life with God day by day and moment
by moment, as a way of life. How can we build a naked life with God
that is rich in spiritual *experience,* with or without dramatic *experiences*? On this question both our ancient religious traditions and our
contemporary theories of education and human development agree: a
way of life is formed by practices. By practices, we mean doable habits
or rhythms that transform us, rewiring our brains, restoring our inner
ecology, renovating our inner architecture, expanding our capacities.
We mean actions within our power that help us become capable of
things currently beyond our power.[2]

Our ancient traditions and contemporary theories also agree that
there are personal and social dimensions to practices.[3] On a personal
level, practices have little or no impact on us unless we experiment with
them and learn to work with them over time. But in order to experiment with and participate in them, we need a community or society
that has embodied, refined, taught, preserved, and enhanced them generation by generation. So in order to learn a set of practices personally
and make fullest use of them, we must find a community that embodies
them socially.[4]

So, for example, I'm incapable of speaking Chinese today. But if I find a social group of fluent speakers, and in their company I begin practicing a single new word, phrase, or series of phrases day by day, I will one day be reasonably fluent myself. I'm incapable of running a marathon today. But if I find a group of runners who can teach me a time-tested training regimen, I can start with a half mile today. Then, in six months, following their regimen, I will be able to run all twenty-six miles. I'm incapable of playing violin today. But if I find a master violinist and join her circle of dedicated students, with some months or years of practice, I will someday be able to contribute to a band or orchestra and play an Irish jig or Mozart symphony.

Similarly, I may be incapable of accepting an insult without retaliation today. I may be incapable of remaining grateful in the midst of fatigue. I may be incapable of receiving attention for successful achievements without becoming conceited. I may be incapable of loving my enemies or seeing things from their point of view. I may be incapable of overcoming discrimination, resisting the urge to consume or pollute, or remaining patient under stress. I may be incapable of remembering that God loves me and knows my name, that God graciously accepts me apart from my performance, or that God loves and knows "the other" no less than me.

But what if there were some practices by which what is now spiritually impossible for me could actually become possible? What if there were practices that made space for the well of living water to flow, for the wind of the Spirit to blow, for the stone jars in my life to be filled with a nobler cause and a more meaningful, joyful purpose? What if there were communities that focused on embodying those practices, and what if they were ready to welcome me to learn among them?[5] Would I want to learn those practices and enter into those communities?

You might think, "Yes, I would want to. But I've wanted to learn to speak Chinese, run a marathon, and play the violin too, and I've never been able to discipline myself to engage in the necessary practices. So if these practices are going to require an hour a day or something, it's not likely I'll follow through, as much as I should, as much as I might wish I would."

The point is well taken. If the only people who can embark on a spiritual journey are those blessed with a lot of self-discipline and sufficient free time, many of us are in trouble. That's why we need simple, doable, durable practices that can be integrated into many things we are already doing . . . taking a walk, commuting, cooking or eating, resting in bed, relaxing at home, taking a break at work, waiting for an appointment, enjoying a hobby.

In the coming chapters, I would like to introduce you to twelve spiritual practices that have passed the *simple, doable,* and *durable* test for me. They are part of our ancient traditions, and they can provide twenty-first-century people like you and me with a basic curriculum for our spiritual novitiate. You can think of them as twelve stretches for runners, twelve moves in martial arts, twelve basic positions in yoga, or twelve warm-up exercises a musician might employ. You can do them in groups, and I hope you will, but you can begin on your own, in private, today. Like learning your first few chords on a guitar, you'll find it amazingly easy to begin to play with these practices. But like expanding on those basic chords in order to become a guitar virtuoso, you'll also find these twelve practices endlessly engaging and challenging.

I stumbled into this simple-doable-durable approach to the spiritual life over many years, and to some degree it arose out of frustration. For a while after my experience under the stars I enjoyed a kind of spiritual honeymoon. My problems seemed to be quickly resolved when I prayed; my questions were easily answered when someone showed me the right Bible verse. But that season of simplicity didn't last.

Eager to learn and grow spiritually, I started consuming books, sermons, and tapes (remember cassettes?) by the dozen, and many of them smuggled two dangerous words into my heart: "not enough." "You don't pray enough." "You don't study the Bible enough." "You don't share your faith enough." "You don't attend church enough." "You don't give enough money." And so on. To the degree that I believed God was as demanding as these teachers, authors, and preachers whose products I was eagerly consuming, I started to experience a kind of spiritual malpractice and malformation. When I thought I succeeded in doing enough, I would fall prey to spiritual pride. When I felt I wasn't doing enough, which happened more often, I would fall into vicious cycles of guilt and discouragement.

The tyranny of "not enough" ushered me firmly from that initial season of simplicity into a season of complexity. In order to be anybody in the religious communities to which I belonged, I needed to amass more and more Bible lore, so that if someone mentioned Zephaniah, Meribah, Meggido, Huldah, and Berea, I'd immediately know which were people and which were places, what era of biblical history they hailed from, and why they were important. But that was still not enough. I also needed to know the complexities of theology. I was raised in a school of theology known as Dispensationalism, which itself involves a good deal of complexity—detailed charts, time lines, arguments, and counterarguments. Then I was introduced to Calvinism, with its even more intricate complexities, and then to Pentecostalism, and so on. On top of being conversant with the complexities of the theological systems I ascribed to, I needed to understand alternative systems enough to refute them (which often meant misunderstanding those systems enough to caricature them). On top of that, each theological system included dozens of subsystems, each with its own fine nuances, intricacies, and bitter disputes: eschatology, apologetics, pneumatology, missiology, hermeneutics, and so on.

I applied myself diligently to each new challenge. And I became at least as complexity-competent as anybody I knew. But there were three problems with all this complexity. First, mastering more and more of it got really fatiguing. Since there was no end to the complexity, there was no end to the fatigue either. Second, I could see absolutely no correlation between the amount of theological complexity and the amount of spiritual vitality, Christlikeness, or fruitfulness in my life or in the lives of others. In fact, for a lot of people I met, the more they knew, the meaner they got. All their knowledge turned into ammunition, which just made them more dangerous and less pleasant to be around. Complexity, I concluded, was overrated.

That introduced me to a third stage in my spiritual life: perplexity. The perplexity only intensified when I became a pastor. Our little congregation had people from many different denominational backgrounds, each with their own brands of simplicity and complexity, each feeling frustrated that the others weren't "normal." Managing these competing assumptions and expectations was, on some days, downright maddening and miserable. The perplexity further intensified when we began welcoming a lot of people who were completely new to the faith. Did I want to baptize all these new spiritual seekers into a naive simplicity that I knew wouldn't last? Or did I school them in the complexity that I felt was little more than a rat race? Or would I mire them in the painful perplexity that I was experiencing? Jesus's haunting words to the Pharisees often came to mind: "You travel over land and sea to win a single convert, and when he becomes one, you make him twice as much a son of hell as you are" (Matt. 23:15, NIV). That wasn't exactly my idea of a great way to spend my life!

So, with increasing desperation, I kept looking for ways to jettison excess baggage. I kept trying to get down to the naked essence, something beyond the first three stages that distilled the best and stripped away the rest. I needed a new approach to spirituality for my own spiritual survival, but no less for the well-being of the people I was called to serve. Eventually I felt I had broken through to a fourth stage, which I later called harmony—because in it I could see the strengths as well as the limitations of earlier stages, and I could see that each stage had its own beauty. From that new vantage point, I felt I could see the first three stages with greater clarity—and empathy—than ever before.

Perhaps you already see what was so hard for me to realize back then, that my frustrations were teaching me exactly what I needed to understand to better help myself and others on the spiritual journey. I was learning—the hard way, no doubt—that there are predictable stages or seasons in the spiritual life. A period of relative coherence and stability was followed by a period of restlessness and turbulence, after which a new period of coherence and stability would unfold, followed by yet another period of restlessness, and so on. I came across a number of thinkers and theorists who had reached similar conclusions and mapped out these periods in various ways.[6] By integrating their scholarly work with reflection on my own experience as a spiritual person and as a pastor, I sketched out a four-stage framework that has been helpful to me and to many others for over two decades now: *Simplicity, Complexity, Perplexity,* and *Harmony*.

Some years later when I was exposed to the concept of spiritual practices (it was a radically new way of seeing things for me back then), I tried to correlate specific practices with the four stages or seasons in the spiritual life. Just as a child needs to master addition before subtraction, multiplication before division, and algebra before calculus, I felt there must be some natural sequence in which spiritual practices could best be acquired. I decided for both theological and pastoral reasons to focus on the private, personal practices that deepen our life with God. Eventually I settled on three practices for each stage, or twelve total, and they will be our focus in the coming pages.[7]

As I experimented with these practices in my own life and tried to teach them to others, I started lodging each practice in one simple word. Why one word? The honest answer is that in my own season of Stage Three, Perplexity, I couldn't manage much more than one word. I had become so tired of the words piled upon words that characterized Stage Two that one simple word for each practice seemed to lighten the burden and bring clarity to the chaos. As I deepened in Stage Four, I sensed the need to slow down the pace of my inner life, to live in a more contemplative way. One word slowed me down in a way that many could not. The more I taught this framework of practices and stages to others, the more I realized that people in Stage One—who want above all else to get things exactly right—could get one word exactly right. And people in Stage Two—who are all about mastering complex challenges—could see the whole framework as just the kind of challenge they were waiting for. So this framework of stages and practices offered something appropriate to people at each stage, even as it invited them to move forward when they were ready.

Here's the framework, with the twelve practices arranged in the four stages:[8]

**Simplicity:** The Springlike Season of Spiritual Awakening
> *Here:* The practice of invocation and presentation, awakening to the presence of God
> *Thanks:* The practice of gratitude and appreciation, awakening to the goodness of God
> *O:* The practice of worship and awe, awakening to the beauty and joy of God

**Complexity:** The Summerlike Season of Spiritual Strengthening
> *Sorry:* The practice of self-examination and confession, strengthening through failure

*Help:* The practice of expansion and petition, strengthening through weakness

*Please:* The practice of compassion and intercession, strengthening through empathy

**Perplexity:** The Autumnlike Season of Spiritual Surviving

*When:* The practice of aspiration, exasperation, and desperation, surviving through delay

*No:* The practice of rage and refusal, surviving through disillusionment

*Why:* The practice of lament and agony, surviving through abandonment

**Harmony:** The Winterlike Season of Spiritual Deepening

*Behold:* The practice of meditation and wonder, deepening by seeing

*Yes:* The practice of consecration and surrender, deepening by joining

*[ . . . ]:* The practice of contemplation and rest, deepening by being with

As you think of these four stages, you might imagine an ascending spiral that grows wider every year as you pass through spring/Simplicity, summer/Complexity, autumn/Perplexity, and winter/Harmony afresh.[9]

Although we're working within the metaphor of predictable patterns of the seasons, we must acknowledge that unpredictable storms also arise in each season. And although our calendars give the illusion that one season ends on a certain day and another begins the next day, we've all experienced those surprisingly mild days in winter and surprisingly cool days in summer, not to mention the nearly constant surprises of spring and fall. So there's unpredictability and surprise inherent in our simple framework of four seasons in the spiritual life.

Through these seasons we shape a spiritual life that is deep, honest, and strong. The point isn't to stay in spring or summer forever, nor is the point to get to (or through) winter as soon as possible, any more than the point of life is advancing from infancy to old age as soon as possible. No, the point is to live each stage well, to learn well what each day and season have to teach, to live and enjoy life, and bear the good fruits of a life with God through all of life's seasons.

By the time we've passed through these seasons a few times, these twelve practices become to the soul what the rhythms of breath, sleep, and pulse are to the body: constant, natural, life-giving, unconscious, effortless. Our spiritual life becomes our way of remaining awake to God and aliveness, our way of being at home in the universe with (as St. Francis said) brother sun and sister moon, brother fox and sister fire, connected and at peace with everything. Together, we and God are like an elderly couple, bound together through a lifetime of joy and heartache, holding hands with the one we love and with whom we have shared everything. (Or, like the fourteenth-century Persian mystic Hafiz said, we become like two giant fat people in a boat who keep bumping into each other and laughing.)[10] So little needs to be said as we sit together looking at the sea, watching the waves roll in. We start with one kind of simplicity, and we'll someday arrive at a second simplicity that has much in common with the first, but has been deepened, broadened, and strengthened through all we've experienced and endured in between.

*For me, stage theory requires for more research than a person's "heres what I did, as order must be right." then we have pervasive Developmental Disorders are possible. Glad these are possible.*

# PART I

# Simplicity: The Season of Spiritual Awakening

**M**ANY OF US HAVE memories of when our spiritual lives first came alive—the season of our "first love."[1] For example, in those initial months after my experience under the stars, I felt the Bible speak to me as never before. The simplest word or phrase would stir my soul. My weeks centered around Tuesday nights, the time of the "Jesus people" prayer-and-teaching gathering I attended with some friends. I started wearing a big wooden cross around my neck, and I carried a big, green Living Bible on top of my high-school books—in hopes that someone would ask me about either of them, so I could "bear witness" to my exuberant, contagious faith. I loved to insert "Praise the Lord!" into my speech as often as possible—which elicited "Amen!" from my Christian friends and surprise or annoyance from my other friends. Speaking of my Christian friends, we could often be found huddling in a stairwell or even the "smoking court" (a fixture of high schools back in those days)—not smoking, but praying for a miraculous intervention of some sort. And our prayers, it seemed to us, were answered way beyond the statistical norm. We seemed to "live and move and have our being" in the holy glow of God's presence. It was spiritual springtime, and we assumed it would never end.

Spring is an amazing mixture of fragility and vitality. Each new sprout is delicate, but what can compare with the combined power of millions of leaves bursting out, drawing energy from the sun? The first season of the spiritual life similarly combines tenderness and toughness as tiny seeds sprout and display the magnificent power of life and growth.

Just as all higher mathematics depends on learning basic arithmetic, and just as all more sophisticated music depends on mastering the basics of tempo, melody, and harmony, the spiritual life depends on learning well the essential lessons of this first season, Simplicity. If these lessons aren't learned well, practitioners will struggle in later seasons. But if in due time this season doesn't give way to the next, the spiritual life can grow stagnant and even toxic.[2] Nearly all of us in this dynamic season of Simplicity tend to share a number of characteristics. We see the world in simple dualist terms: *we* are the good guys who follow the good authority figures and we have the right answers; *they* are the bad guys who consciously or unconsciously fight on the wrong side of the cosmic struggle between good and evil. We feel a deep sense of identity and belonging in our in-group. This in-group loyalty is constantly reinforced by our Stage One leaders, who offer us clear, authoritative, black-and-white answers to every question of belief or behavior, reminding us of the great danger of being misled by *them* into accepting wrong answers or following the wrong rules. As a result, our relationships in this stage tend to be dependent or even codependent; we need our in-group and its confident, charismatic leaders to know who we are and what we're about. God, from this vantage point, is our ultimate Authority Figure, giving us simple truths to believe and simple rules to follow, leading us into battle against evil and blessing us by being ever on our side. This simple, dualist faith gives us great confidence.[3]

This confidence, of course, has a danger, as the old Bob Dylan classic "With God on Our Side" makes clear: "You don't count the dead when God's on your side." The same sense of identification with an in-group that generates a warm glow of belonging and motivates sacrificial action for *us* can sour into intolerance, hatred, and even violence toward *them*. And the same easy, black-and-white answers that comfort and reassure us now may later seem arrogant, naive, ignorant, and harmful, if we don't move beyond Simplicity in the fullness of time.

So what are the important and essential lessons of Simplicity, and how can we learn them well without getting stuck there long after the "fullness of time" has expired? Those questions lead us to the first three practices of naked spirituality: awakening, gratitude, and awe.

# CHAPTER 4

# Here: *Starting Right Now*

*The Practice of Invocation and Presentation:*
*Awakening to the Presence of God*
Alternate Words: *Now, You, Who, We, Open, Home*

You will find stability at the moment when you discover that God
is everywhere, that <u>you do not need to seek God elsewhere</u>, that
God is here, and if you do not find God here it is useless to go and
search elsewhere because it is not God that is absent from us, it
is we who are absent from God. . . . This is important because it
is only at the moment you recognize this that you can truly find
the fullness of the Kingdom of God in all its richness within you.

METROPOLITAN ANTHONY BLOOM[1]

IT WAS A SUNNY October afternoon twenty years ago. I was far away
from civilization, deep in the mountains of Pennsylvania, fishing for
native brook trout in a pristine valley, under a canopy of hemlocks and
white pines that spiced the air with their sweet scent. I had taken a few
days away at a retreat center for personal rest and recharging, hoping to
de-stress and let my soul revive a bit from the pressures of the ministry to which I was devoting my life. I was kneeling beside a freestone
stream, releasing a trout, admiring its beauty—the magical wash of
reds, grays, oranges, and whites that shimmered at the intersection of
clear mountain water and clear autumn light. Over the sounds of the
brook, I thought I heard a voice calling in the distance. I stopped and
listened, and then nothing.

"Maybe it was a dog barking," I thought. A few more times I thought I heard something, but when I paused, I heard over the running water only the calls of crickets and crows. A half hour later I had rounded a bend in the stream, and this time I knew I heard a human voice, a long, faraway shout, two tones, the first higher, the second lower. "Somebody must have lost a hunting dog," I thought. I couldn't think of any reason for anyone else to be this far out in the forest calling for somebody.

It was maybe another half hour later, a few more bends downstream, when I heard the voice again and realized that the name being called was my own. My heart started pounding. Nobody names a dog Brian, and nobody would have gone to this much trouble to find me unless there was something seriously wrong. Was it one of my parents? My wife in an accident? One of my kids? I scrambled up the bank, imagining a thousand tragedies, and once I mounted the dirt road that led up and out of the valley, I started yelling at full volume, my voice breaking: "Here!" I called. "I'm *here*!" A few minutes later, my pulse racing and my chest heaving, I came across an employee from the retreat center. A group of people had spread out across the area by car, on foot, and using off-road vehicles looking for me, he explained. "Your wife called. It's an emergency. She's at the hospital with your younger son."

That began a long adventure. In the coming days we learned that Trevor had a serious disease—either aplastic anemia or leukemia. As soon as the diagnosis came in—it was leukemia—we began treatment, which, thank God, effectively cured him three years later. But still today, when I'm walking in the woods, my heart skips a beat if I hear—or think I hear—someone calling in the distance. And that simple word *here* has taken on new meaning for me, whether I'm calling out to someone else—"Is anyone *here*?"—or whether I'm answering a call, "I'm *here*!"

I had a five-hour drive from the mountains to the hospital. As you can imagine, I cried and prayed the whole way. As that disorienting day gave way to another and another, something emerged through the chaotic emotions and disrupted schedules. My wife, Grace, and I knew that we were not alone, that our son was not alone, that our family was not alone. We knew that God was *here*, with us, even in *this, here*.

*Here* is the simple word by which we show up, respond to the one calling our name. *Here* is the way we name where we are—pleasant or unpleasant, desired or not—and declare ourselves present to God's presence. Before settling on *here* as the simple word in which to lodge our first spiritual practice, I considered several others. An obvious choice would have been "God" or "Lord" or "You." Direct address of the soul to its Source must surely come early in any exploration of the spiritual life. But something held me back from making these obvious choices, and I wasn't sure what it was. Now I think I know. When we begin by naming God, too often we assume that we know more about the one we're addressing than we may actually know. The name carries too much unacknowledged conceptual freight for us.

Author and literary critic C. S. Lewis tried to capture this danger in a poem he wrote called "Footnote to All Prayers." When we pray, he said, we bow toward God and refer to God with familiar symbols, like father, judge, king, and so on. In so doing, we may falsely assume that our idea of God is identical to God, that the real God "out there" is no bigger than and no different from the idea we have "in here" in our heads. Our cherished symbols, our familiar language, he warned, may carry the distortions of "our own unquiet thoughts" or the confining shape of a "folklore dream"—concepts of God that are partial at best, misleading at worst. We may forget that our best symbolic representations are in the end merely "frail images" of God, images that "cannot be the thing" that God is.[2] Whatever the reality actually is to which the word or name "God" points, we know that God's reality must always be far higher and greater and other than our concepts and images of God—even our best concepts and images. So if, like archers, we aim our arrow-prayers toward the bull's-eye of our conceptual target—at our limited ideas of God instead of beyond and above our ideas—our prayers will simply arc back down into the dirt. Our only hope is that God finds our arrows mid-flight and magnetically draws them to their intended destination. That hope in God's "magnetic mercy" inspires Lewis's poem-prayer.

So I decided to work with the simple word *here,* because it subverts the assumption that we have God named, figured out, and properly "targeted." Instead, it places us out in the woods, so to speak, calling out so that we can be found by the one seeking us: "*Here* I am, in the presence of a mystery. *Here* I am, in the presence of a Presence who transcends, surpasses, overflows, and exceeds every attempt at definition, description, and even conception. *Here* you are, whoever you are, however similar or dissimilar you are to my preconceived notions of you. May the real I and the real you become present to one another *here* and now."

Whether I feel I'm seeking God, calling out, "Is anybody here?" or whether I feel God is calling out to me and I respond, "Here I am!" I think the simple word *here* can do something amazingly comprehensive. Through it, I show up. I come out of hiding. I let myself be found. The teacher is taking attendance, and I tell the teacher that I'm present and ready to learn. This acknowledgment of mutual *here-ness* becomes the prelude to mutual *nearness*. Through mutual *presentation,* the soul and God open the way for deep connection.

There is an old theological term for this first practice of awakening, of becoming present to the Presence: *invocation.* The word suggests a summoning, but of course God isn't busy out in the backyard, needing to be called inside to meet us in the kitchen.[3] No, God has been with us all along, even though we may have been too busy or distracted, too groggy or sick, or simply too immature to notice. Through invocation, we are calling inward to our own souls, summoning ourselves to wake up, so we can attend to the Presence in whose attention we are held and in whom we live, move, and have our being.

*Here* can help awaken us to our own situation as well. Here I am at this point in history, within today's swirl of politics and economics, within epochal shifts in climate and plate tectonics, and within the ongoing drama of human civilization and its discontents. Here I am, at this point in my own story—as a child, a teenager, an adult, a senior citizen. Here I am, on this hill, on this grass, looking up at this sky. Here I am, on this unique day in the history of the universe, with that bird singing over there, those planes flying overhead, these plants springing up around me, each thing with its own unique luminosity. Here I am, in this predicament, in this catastrophe, in this boring afternoon, in this hospital bed with all this beeping, buzzing, humming equipment. Here I am, with all my problems and faults, all my embarrassments and mistakes, all my whirring conscious thoughts and all my subconscious rumblings and doubts. Here I am, walking down this aisle, taking this exam, in between these contractions, about to deliver this lecture, in the middle of this divorce, writing this book. I don't have to be somewhere else—right here is okay. In fact, it's the only place I can be to begin to awaken spiritually. *Here.* Now. Just as I am.[4]

Being present here where we are can actually be tougher than it seems. I'm always tempted to be partially somewhere else, to pretend I'm not where I am, who I am, how I am. I'm always tempted to pray elsewhere than here, to shift my weight into a kind of religious fantasyland, a doctrinal matrix, a state of emotional hype, some other kind of not-here in which to encounter God. But no. When we want our spirituality to be naked, simple, and authentic, we resist escapism, realizing that a God who cannot be found here is not really God. So we say, "Let's start *here.* Now."

That's not to say it's wrong to choose a special place as our *here.* Jesus frequently withdrew into the countryside, away from the crowds. The early Celts identified certain special "thin spaces," where the membrane between the visible world and the unseen world felt especially permeable to them. Leaders as diverse as Moses, the Buddha, the desert fathers, and Muhammad all recounted powerful spiritual experiences during times of withdrawal and solitude. To plug into the naked *here,* sometimes we need to unplug from the thousand distractions and demands that keep us not-here in fantasy or render us only half here in anxiety. To awaken to nonvirtual reality, we may need to unplug from the video game or website. To resituate ourselves in the down-to-earth presence of God, we may need to unplug from our heady isms, whether economic, political, or even theological.[5]

So withdrawal to a place less fraught with distraction and more hospitable to awakening makes sense. But the purpose of practicing a retreat to a thin-place *there* is so that eventually we can practice awakening *here,* wherever that may be. When we practice awakening to the here-ness of God in solitude or out in nature, we gradually learn to stay awake to God's here-ness in the midst of the crowds, the noise, and the rush and crush that threaten to derange us.

If I resist derangement in the hustle and hassle, I can be "reranged" and rearranged in what Richard Rohr calls the *naked now,* another way of saying the *naked here.*[6] If I can unplug from fantasy and bring the real me to the table, the real me as I am at this moment, then I can make room for the real God as well. Not just the God other people told me about. Not just the God I was told I had to believe in. Not just the God who is the projection of my wishes, "unquiet thoughts," or "folklore dreams." But the God who is here—as present as gravity, light, heat, friendship, hope, love—the real Presence, who is really present.

Just yesterday, this practice sustained me. I was on the subway in Washington, D.C. The seats were all taken, so I was standing, holding one of the support poles in the rumble and sway of commuting. I closed my eyes briefly and said, "*Here.* I'm here, God. You're here. We are here together." I simply tried to hold that awareness that here, now, in the commotion and clatter, I was with God. I held that here-ness as I exited the subway, ascended the escalator, weaved my way through crowds on sidewalks and crosswalks, and entered a meeting with lots of important people. In those situations, I often become more aware of their presence than God's, so as I walked into the meeting, I whispered, "*Here,* Lord. I'm here with you. You're here with me." When I found my seat, in between hellos and handshakes, I tried to stay centered in the presence of God, simply breathing, "*Here, here, here,*" in each *here* staying awake to God's presence above me, before me, behind me, beside me, beneath me, and within me, as the old Celtic blessing puts it.

When I just used the term "God" to name the Presence, I wasn't actually using a name, strictly speaking. "God" and "Lord," like "Father," "Mother," "Doctor," "Professor," or "Your Majesty," are titles, not names. Titles usually imply a relationship. Whenever I use a title to address God, I can awaken myself not only to God's presence, but also to my presence in a multifaceted relationship with God.

This is a precious thing to savor. It's deep, and huge. When I realize I am here with God our Creator, God our Father, the Lord my Shepherd, I am awakening to the relationships in which I live—as a creature in creation, as a child in a family, as a member of God's flock. But dare we move beyond this language of relationship? Dare we go even farther— to address God not simply by title, but even by name?

Dare we move from *here* to *who* and *you*? This is exactly the move a young zealot named Paul makes when he is knocked off his feet on the Damascus road. Paul shows the typical strengths of a Stage One pilgrim, deep in the season of Simplicity. Fueled by the anxieties and furies of de-ligion, he is out to imprison those who defy the religious system to which he is so desperately devoted. But along the way, he experiences a blinding light. Somehow, in that light he hears his own name, repeated twice. His response suggests that up until now, he has known exactly who God is and what life and religion are about, or at least he has thought so. But now, as he experiences a kind of new birth and new beginning in an actual encounter with the living God, he must let what he knew with such certainty be deconstructed and fall behind him. He must reopen the question: "Who are you, Lord?" This question is essential in the shift from de-ligion to deep religion, from religiosity to spirituality. We must hold that question open to God: *Who are you?* Without doing so, we will pray yet again to our image of God, our set of preconceived notions of God, our familiar boxed and framed conventions, and our comfortable stereotyped assumptions about God. By holding *who* before God, we open and present ourselves to the God beyond our notions, to the living *You* who is actually here.

This kind of awakening begins the transformation of a religious (or de-ligious or nonreligious) life into a spiritual life, a life with God—not later and elsewhere, but here and now. How much higher and wider and deeper and richer our lives become when we awaken to the presence of the real, wild, mysterious, living God, who is bigger than our tame concepts of God. As we sense an inward vocation from God and toward God, we can respond with presentation, saying, "Here I am, Lord. I present myself to you, presenting yourself to me." We begin to live with a perpetual *Here I am,* and *here you are,* in our hearts, inviting constant, vital connection, unbroken communion, lifelong friendship—starting right here, starting right now.

## Chapter 5

# Here: *Naming the Mystery*

The Logos, the Word . . . that informs the cosmos—all things great and small—is still spoken in sparrow song, wind sigh, and leaf fall. An electron is a single letter, an atom a complex word, a molecule a sentence, and a mockingbird an entire epistle in the great ongoing saga. The ocean still whispers the song that originated with the big bang. Listen to the longing in your heart for love and justice, and you may hear the sacred word. To live in a reverential manner is . . . to create an autobiography in which we tell the stories of the unique epiphanies that have informed our lives.

SAM KEEN[1]

THE BUSH IS BURNING, but it's not burning up. How could that be? That's the paradox Moses faces in Exodus 3 in one of the Bible's paradigmatic encounters of a human being with the mysterious Presence of God.[2]

Moses is tending sheep in the middle of nowhere one day and sees a common bush filled with uncommon fire. He is drawn to the flame, not necessarily out of reverence—he's at something of a spiritual low point when the encounter happens—but out of curiosity. It's fascinating that God would self-manifest in a flame, since by its very nature fire (like the wind, water, and wine we considered in Chapter 2) is mysterious, at once attractive and intriguing and in some ways scary and dangerous. It's equally fascinating that this extraordinary flame is fused with an ordinary bush. It's still more fascinating to think that the ordinary isn't destroyed by the extraordinary or, to put it differently, that this is a fire that doesn't consume; it burns but doesn't burn up—a curious paradox that draws Moses in.

Interestingly, the conversation begins not with Moses invoking God, but with God invoking Moses—by name. God doesn't say to Moses (as God does say to some other people in the Bible), "Attention, earthling!" or "Now hear this, human being!" Instead, Moses simply hears his own name—twice, in fact, just as did Paul centuries later—"Moses! Moses!" I wonder if Moses, out in the barren desert, felt as I did that day walking along the stream; I wonder if his heart pounded and his breath was taken away.

This story is deeply suggestive about our awakening to God. First, as we've seen, it suggests the uncontainable mystery and wonder of the Presence who calls to us.[3] Second, it suggests that as we approach God, we begin not as knowers, but as the known. We are named before we name, called before we call, spoken to before we speak. What feels like an initiative on our part turns out to be the response to a prior initiative taken by the one who calls us. So we are not, through our invocation, waking up God and getting God's attention. We are being awakened, and God is attracting our attention, and we respond to the one who was already *here,* but we didn't realize it.

Third, the story suggests that an encounter with God requires a response. Moses responds by presenting himself to the mysterious presence who has called his name. *Here I am,* in this sense, would mean "reporting for duty," and in-*vocation* would mean God's call for us to enter a vocation, or mission.

After cautioning Moses to keep his distance from the fire and to remove his sandals as a sign of being in a holy place, God then self-introduces in a fascinating way: "I am the God of your father, the God of Abraham, the God of Isaac, and the God of Jacob" (Exod. 3:6). God doesn't self-identify by giving God's personal name, but by naming persons Moses already knows. God shows up, we might say, behind familiar faces—the faces of Moses's own ancestors.

So then, in this encounter God first wants to be known through a dynamic image beyond words—a dancing flame that doesn't destroy what it fills. Then God wants to be known through a heritage, a tradition, a story, as if God is saying, "You are now encountering the one that your ancestors have encountered over many generations." Yes, God says, this is an unprecedented experience for you, but it is not unprecedented in history; it is your time now to enter into a conversation your ancestors participated in.[4] Might we hear the same message coming to us, here and now?

As the conversation unfolds, God gives Moses a mission and promises to be with him in its fulfillment. But Moses's response is surprising. He doesn't say, as we might expect, "Yes, Sir! Your wish is my command!" Instead, Moses—and this is really stunning, when you think about it—argues. During a paradigmatic experience of God one is capable of quarreling, questioning, debating, and doubting! This pattern, amazingly enough, holds true throughout the Bible. The experience of God is not normally so overwhelming that one is reduced to quivering mush; instead, it invites one to stand tall (though barefoot), to push back, to question, even to resist.[5]

At one point in the give and take, after God says, "Here's what I want you to do," Moses replies, basically, "No way. You have the wrong guy." Then, as if negotiating a business deal, Moses says, "Okay, suppose I do agree, and I go and tell people that God has sent me on a mission, but then people say, 'Which god? What's the name of the deity who sent you?' What do I say then?" Now Moses is asking for something beyond a title like "Father," "Mother," "Sir," "Your Honor," or "the God of your ancestors." Moses is asking, "What is your name? Your personal name? If I am Moses, who are you?"

Moses's experience echoes two experiences of his distant ancestor Jacob (Gen. 28:10–22; 32:22–32). Jacob also had an encounter with God—in a dream of a ladder to the sky instead of a vision of a burning bush in the desert. God self-introduced in the same way, "I am the LORD, the God of Abraham your father and the God of Isaac" (28:13) and similarly added a promise to be with Jacob. Many years later, Jacob had another encounter, again at night, this time with God strangely manifesting not from the top of a celestial ladder in the sky, and not from within a burning bush on the ground, but as a powerful assailant determined to overcome Jacob in a wrestling match. Jacob's impulse was the same as Moses's: to get this being's name! Interestingly, the mysterious nighttime wrestler did not capitulate, but instead turned the tables and demanded Jacob's name, and then, when Jacob acquiesced, changed Jacob's name to Israel.[6] Quite an interchange!

When we approach God through the awakening practice of *here,* we're entering into this primal drama of human beings encountering the one who knows them, who knows their names, and who can never be captured or pinned down in any single name. When we begin to pray, we too are Jacob wrestling, refusing to let go. We too are barefoot Moses, curious yet resistant and bargaining, grappling with mystery. And like Jacob and Moses, we will be changed through our encounter.

God's voice, still emanating from the burning bush, answers Moses, "I AM WHO I AM" (Exod. 3:14), an enigmatic name theologians are still pondering millennia later. What does the phrase mean? Perhaps it means, "I will be whoever I will be, Moses, so get used to the fact that you can't wrestle my identity down." Perhaps it means, "I am the essence of being itself." Perhaps it means, "None of your business! Who do you think you are to try to nail down my identity in a single word that your little brain can manipulate? I am who I am, and that's as much as you'll be able to grasp." Some scholars see a kind of future tense to the statement, as if God is saying, "I will be who I will be," or in other words, "I am the one you will gradually get to know, always at hand, but never in hand." I imagine it means all of these, and more.

This same tension—that God wants to be in dialogue with us, but yet God's full identity must always remain mysterious to us, above us, beyond us, ahead of us—is captured in the opening lines of the prayer Jesus taught his disciples. "Our Father in heaven" refers to God through a title, a title that implies relationship. God is our source and parent, God cares about us, we are part of God's family—and not just we as individuals, but all of us together, because we are taught to pray "Our Father," not "My Father in heaven."

But then Jesus teaches the disciples immediately to follow "Our Father" with the words, "hallowed be your name," or "may your name be revered." Quite certainly Jesus is here evoking the mysterious name "I AM WHO I AM," the elusive name that names truly by not naming concretely. If the first line evokes the possibility of a personal relationship and intimacy—"Our Father in heaven" (as does "the God of your father, . . . Abraham, . . . Isaac, and . . . Jacob")—then the second line evokes mystery and transcendence—"may your unspeakable name be held in reverence, the name I AM WHO I AM, I WILL BE WHO I WILL BE."

This sacred name for God, which occurs 6,828 times in the Hebrew scriptures, was considered so holy that it would rarely be spoken, a tradition I respect and try to follow myself (which explains why I am not offering an English transliteration of the Hebrew name). Many of Jesus's Jewish brothers and sisters through the centuries, to retain appropriate reverence for God's mysterious name, began to encode it in an alternative name. They created the code name "Jehovah" by mixing the four consonants of the holy name with the vowels of the word *Adonai,* which is a title of respect used for God and for powerful human beings too, like "My Lord" or "Sir" or "Your Majesty." In written English today, translators often render the name as "the LORD" (in capitals) or as "G-d." At points in this book where I am especially eager to remind us of G-d's otherness, G-d's definite undefinability, I will employ this practice as well.

One way or another, we are wise to retain this dynamism, so that reverential awe dances like a flame within us whenever we make the first move in the spiritual life, when we show up to G-d seeking mutual nearness in mutual here-ness, whether we say "Lord," "Our Father in heaven," or "Mysterious Presence." We must preserve this essential dynamic tension in addressing G-d, who names us accurately and knows us utterly, while acknowledging that we can neither fully know nor adequately contain the Divine Mystery in any name. Throughout the Bible—and the Qur'an and many other sacred writings too, by the way—we feel this tension in the spiritual life, this tension between naming God and not reducing G-d to a name, this tension between addressing God through a name, but never possessing G-d in a verbal or conceptual address, this electricity between what theologians call God's immanence, or accessibility, and G-d's transcendence, or complete otherness.

When people experience a breakdown in the spiritual life, it's often because they don't maintain this tension. If they resolve the tension on the side of transcendence or otherness, God becomes distant—at first a kind of remote deity, then a kind of abstract principle, then an impersonal cosmic force or energy—and eventually God may disappear entirely, leaving us in a world of numbers and equations without meaning or purpose. Moses's bush no longer burns; Jacob's ladder leans against a wall, and his mysterious assailant is just another mugger. We call out, but nobody is home.

If people resolve the tension on the side of immanence or nearness, G-d becomes too much the chum or mascot or even guard dog, a genie who comes obediently when summoned by the magic words. When this happens, prayer is like rubbing a magic lamp or commanding guard dogs to attack an intruder. One's religion starts looking a lot like superstition or witchcraft. And magical religions in this mode too easily turn homicidal and genocidal because, quite conveniently, "God" hates the same people its adherents hate and is happy to share their malice.

Naked spirituality differs from magical religion as love differs from lust. Where magical religion tries to harness cosmic powers so that "my will may be done," naked spirituality seeks to unleash my powers so that "God's will may be done." Where magical religion tries to possess God for one's own benefit, naked spirituality seeks to be yielded to God for God's will, the common good.

So our first simple word is truly significant. The posture of invocation and presentation, holding our hearts open with *here,* brings us into an essential, dynamic, and creative tension. This tension is essential for naked spirituality to break free from its husk like a seed in springtime. One name for this dynamic tension is *reverence.* Sometimes the Bible calls it "fear" as in the "fear of the Lord," but it's clear that "fear," when used this way, doesn't mean the kind of spiritual terrorism to which many people are subjected in fire-and-brimstone sermons and God-as-Terminator theology. (If "fear" in this context were intended to mean anxiety in the face of danger, why would God's first words to someone experiencing God almost always be, "Don't be afraid"? See, e.g., Gen. 26:24; Luke 1:30.) No, reverence or holy fear suggests this dynamic tension of being drawn to the beautiful and mysterious flame, while always remembering that the flame is powerful and transcendent beyond imagination. Reverence means wanting to avoid the dual dangers of thinking of the living God as a distant, impersonal, uncaring force or faceless principle, on the one hand, and reducing God to one's pet personal deity on a leash or genie in a bottle, on the other hand.

So how do we try to maintain this dynamic when we pray? One

answer becomes clear when we survey the invocations in any random selection of Psalms.

O God (79:1)
O Lord (79:5)
O God of our salvation (79:9)
O Shepherd of Israel (80:1)
O Lord God of hosts (80:4)
O Lord of hosts, my King and my God (84:3)
O God of Jacob (84:8)
O Lord, God of my salvation (88:1)
O Judge of the earth (94:2)

You'll notice the range of ways that God is addressed. First, whenever you see "Lord" (large and small capitals), it's a sign in English that the Hebrew name for God drawn from "I am who I am" is being used in the original text. You'll also notice that in addition to this mysterious name with all that it evokes of God's transcendence, the sacred poets invent scores of other names, a kind of torrent of images and metaphors for God: king, shepherd, rock, friend, father, co-worker, potter, shepherd, wind, breath, vine, farmer, and so on. Then, if that weren't enough, poets employ dozens of adjectives to name God; God is the Holy One, the Faithful One, the Everlasting One, the Almighty, the Eternal, and so on. Then there is a whole category of names in Hebrew that combine the two—joining the unutterable name for God with words or images that describe what God is or does for God's people: "the Lord my healer," "the Lord my provider," "the Lord our Creator," "the Lord our Banner," "the Lord our justice," and so on.

In Islam, similarly, there are ninety-nine names for God—stopping short of one hundred as if to say, "No name is sufficient, and all names together still fall short." Here are a few that I especially love:

The All-Compassionate
The All-Merciful
The Pure One
The Source of Peace

The Inspirer of Faith
The Guardian
The Creator
The Maker of Order
The Shaper of Beauty
The Forgiving
The Giver of All
The Sustainer
The Opener
The Knower of All

So our diverse traditions agree that to approach God with the dynamic tension of reverence, we need a wide repertoire of names and images for God, so that we can avoid getting stuck in a rut in referring to God. We need to move from image to image, name to name, and never settle exclusively on just one. So I may let an image like "God, my Rock" bring to mind God's unchanging dependability or God as a shelter from enemies. But then I must avoid the tendency to let God seem static and heavy rather than dynamic and free by adding another image—God as Spirit, blowing like wind over the waters of creation, for example. And then I can move to God as Parent, King, Shepherd, or Potter, as the Shaper of Beauty, the Opener, or the Source of Peace. By never letting my mind reduce God to one image or one name, I keep my mind opened up and awake rather than shut down and half asleep and, in so doing, I maintain reverence.

My own practice of reverent awakening or invocation often unfolds like this:

> O God, you are my light. . . . You are my Shepherd. . . . You are my Friend. . . . You are my Creator. . . . You are the Holy One. . . . You are the Shaper of Beauty. . . .

Sometimes I take this exercise a step farther, drawing from St. Francis's way of prayer.[7] I begin with *here* and move to *who, who* as a question that I then answer in a variety of ways. The prayer goes like this:

*Here I am, Lord. Here you are, Lord. Here we are together.*
  *(Pause.)*
*Who am I, Lord? Who are you, Lord? Who are we together?*
  *(Pause.)*

Simply opening the question is more important than closing in on any single answer. In fact, it's the multiplicity of answers that counts. On those restless nights when I am struggling with insomnia, I decide to stop spinning in my hamster wheels of worry and inquietude. I climb off the wheel and awaken myself to God's presence by using the prayer above. I move from *here* to *who,* letting answer after answer come to mind. Sometimes this exercise helps me fall asleep. Sometimes it doesn't. Either way, it's okay.

One night, my responses to this exercise came together in this simple song:

*O Lord, who are you? O Lord, who am I?*
*Who are we together?*
  *We are glowing fire in a burning bush.*
  *We are master and apprentice.*
  *We are lover and beloved*
  *Giving birth to a better world together.*
  *We are artist and work in progress.*
  *We are vine and fruitful branches.*
  *We are partners in this mission.*
  *We are builders of a brighter future.*
  *We are wind in swaying treetops.*
  *We are mother and her child.*
  *We are friends in conversation.*
  *We are dancers who move to joyful music.*
  *We are wide blue sea and leaping dolphin.*
  *We are warm spring sun and growing seeds.*
  *We are poet and living poetry.*
*We are singers who fill the earth with harmony.*

In a moment, I hope you'll put this book down and take a few deep breaths. Allow yourself to slow down and rest for a minute. As you feel your weight settle on a chair or on the ground, let the weight of your soul rest back on the presence and love of God. Just be *here*. You might want to hear, in your imagination, the living God calling your name, repeated twice as with Moses and Paul (and others in the Bible too), inviting you to reply, "*Here* I am." It might help you to repeat those words for a while, in rhythm with each breath. Simply present yourself to the Rock, the River, the Light, the Wind, the Shepherd, the Greatest, the Shaper of Beauty, the Merciful One, the Unnameable One, the Presence. "*Here* I am. *Here* you are. *Here* we are together." Try this now.

You may then want to let your *here* progress to *who*: "*Who* are you? *Who* am I? *Who* are we together?" Try this now. Try letting the question give you permission to let your understanding and experience of G-d expand, transcend, and surpass your current understandings and boundaries.

Hold the space with *here* and *who*. And then, if it feels right, try working with the word *home*. Affirm that to be here with God is to be at home, wherever you are. That home base or home space is simultaneously your soul (your space, where God is welcome) and heaven (God's space, where you are welcome).[8] The word *open* may also help you open yourself to God, and realize that God's embrace, God's front door, God's presence is also open to you, welcoming you. It may even help you to clench your fists, symbolizing how we are often tight and closed off to God's presence, bringing to mind the things that have had you uptight lately. Then you can gradually open them as you open your heart to God, and perhaps then *You* will be the most helpful simple word.

From that quiet, simple beginning, see what happens. See what unfolds. This is the beginning of naked spirituality.

Please don't just turn the page. Please don't simply keep reading. First, practice *here*.

CHAPTER 6

# Thanks: *The Happiness of Appreciation*

*The Practice of Gratitude and Appreciation:*
*Awakening to the Goodness of God*
Alternate Words: *Again, This, Dayenu*

If the only prayer you said in your whole life was "thank you,"
that would be sufficient.

MEISTER ECKHART[1]

I'M IN GUATEMALA. SOME friends and I are driving through the
countryside in an old car, no air-conditioning, the windows wide
open, until we see an approaching vehicle. Then we quickly roll up the
windows, so we won't be covered by the cloud of red dust that follows.
But within seconds, beads of sweat are forming on our foreheads and
upper lips, so we crank the windows down again. Up and down our
windows go as rusty buses, ramshackle pickups, and other old weather-
beaten cars approach and pass, mile after mile. We finally come to a
little town. We stop, turn off the engine, step out, stretch, and, as the
red dust settles and the noise of the road fades, we hear a new sound
off to the right, down through some scraggly trees, past a few bony,
wide-horned brown cows standing in the shadows chewing their cud.

Beyond the cows and just outside a few strands of barbed wire,
there's a stream and a little swimming hole sparkling in the full sunlight. In its brown waters a dozen children are splashing and wrestling.
Their laughter rises like music, a cloud of joy as real as the cloud of red

dust stirred by another car passing on the road behind us. I think, "I've seldom heard this much pure happiness in my life." We watch for a few minutes, smiles irrepressibly arising on our faces, and then decide to take a break and explore the town before continuing our journey. As I turn off to be on my own for a few minutes, I see the homes these children come from. They're small in size and modest in construction, but often painted the most dazzling colors, this one coral pink, the next aquamarine, the next tangerine orange, the one over there a light purple, peeling off in places, showing a royal blue underneath.

There are some dads sitting in the shadows of a few trees, cigarettes dangling under the bills of well-worn baseball caps, sharing stories, playing cards, nodding and smiling as we walk by. There are some moms squatting on front porches, peeling potatoes, washing dishes in plastic basins, nursing babies, shooing flies. I smell coffee roasting, mixed with the scent of a farm not far away. I hear a muted accordion and a flatulent trumpet from a broken radio speaker. I hear the sound of someone sawing a plank, a rooster crowing in the afternoon heat, a dog bark twice off in the distance, and everywhere the buzz of insects mixed with the jingling music of children's laughter in the background.

Maybe someday there will be televisions in every house, I imagine. Maybe someday there will be video games and DVD players. Maybe the hum of air conditioners and the roar of many cars. But I don't think there will ever be more happiness in the air than there is today.

What is this extraordinary happiness? Where does it come from? Back home, kids with a thousand times more wealth and security are bored and whining in their carpeted living rooms, not laughing and playing in brown creek water; back home, parents are stuck in traffic and worrying about a thousand things, not enjoying an ordinary day.

Walking through that town in Guatemala, I remind myself of something we all know but don't take seriously enough. It's not how much you have that brings happiness; it's how much you appreciate however much or little you have.[2] Again, it's not the amount of stuff you have that counts; it's the amount of *appreciation* you have that matters, and appreciation means "gratefully holding" rather than simply "having without gratitude."

Perhaps we need to update those famous lines from the American

Declaration of Independence that, along with being endowed by our Creator with certain inalienable rights that include "life, liberty, and the pursuit of happiness," we are encouraged by our Creator to slow down and appreciate the gift of life, to employ our liberty in service for others, and to gratefully cherish the happiness we already have. *Gratitude* may be the greatest secret to happiness there is. But if that's the case, wealth comes with a hidden danger, a threat to happiness. The more we have, the more we need to practice gratitude; otherwise, we will begin taking more and more of what we have for granted. If we habitually take more and more for granted, our ingratitude will eventually lead to unhappiness. And of course, if we have little, we will also need to practice gratitude, so our little that is greatly appreciated can count for more happiness than much that is little appreciated. So, well-off or poor, we all stand in utter need of great gratitude.

You have already anticipated, I imagine, why gratitude is so essential to naked spirituality. First, because spirituality in today's world is constantly under assault by consumerism, which claims that the source of joy is not in God or within, but in a new pair of shoes, a trip to southern France, or a new flat-screen TV. In relation to consumerism, gratitude could be called downright subversive. As I've detailed elsewhere, a lot of people spend a lot of money every day trying to keep you from being grateful.[3] They want you to think a lot more about what other people have than what you have, so you'll want more. They want you to think a lot more about what you don't have than what you do have, so you'll want more. And if you want more, you'll buy something from them, so they'll have more. But will they appreciate the money they gain from stimulating your greed? Probably not, because they too have been sucked into the whole "never enough" vortex of consumerism, so they're seldom grateful and therefore never satisfied—which keeps them needling you to give them more of your money.

Consumerism thus robs the soul of happiness while it sells the soul more stuff. But this petty larceny on the individual level leads to far greater crimes. Just think of where this sick, never-enough system drives us: to mountains stripped for gold or coal, to oceans plundered of fish and seas toxified with oil, to hillsides denuded of trees and wildlife, to fields scraped by bulldozers and paved with blacktop, so we can have yet another shopping mall (or storage facility) where we can buy (or store) more things we don't need and won't take time to appreciate. Habitats are thus stolen from other creatures, which means those creatures die and are stolen from other creatures that depend on them. Ecosystems that have developed over millions of years are tipped into disequilibrium and collapse. The cascade of extinction and imbalance rolls on like an avalanche or gushes out like an oil spill, stealing not just from the humans of today, but from the humans of forever. Economists tabulate the gross domestic product, but whose spreadsheet measures the gross domestic *destruct*—the losses extracted in advance from our great-grandchildren when wild elephants, giraffes, wood thrushes, gopher tortoises, sea turtles, chimpanzees, horseshoe crabs, and swordfish have gone the way of the dodo?

We could give another name to the insanity of ingratitude: addiction. Just as it takes more and more heroin or cocaine to deliver the same high, ingratitude continually turns yesterday's luxuries into today's necessities. More and more stuff is required to give the same fleeting feeling of satisfaction. And just as addiction ultimately leads through insanity to misery and even death as the addict "hits bottom," an economy driven by ingratitude—whether global, national, family, or personal—races through overextension toward collapse. That's why gratitude is important, not just as a personal practice, but also as a group practice—it is a kind of immunization against both personal and corporate addiction.

Gratitude is the spiritual practice that raises its fist in the face of this insanity; but that raised fist is actually a raised hand—reaching up in gratitude to God. The naked spirituality that fosters this kind of gratitude may, in the end, be the only thing that can save the planet. Consider that for a minute before moving on, okay?

If *here* suggests waking up and presenting ourselves to the presence of God, *thanks* means waking up to the presents of God, waking up to the abundant gifts of life with which we have already been blessed. Joni Mitchell had it right—or almost right—in her song "Big Yellow Taxi." You don't know what you've got till it's gone, unless you practice gratitude.

When I was still a teenager, my friend Mary—one of the people who shared that dramatic experience on the hill that night under the stars—asked me, "How much money would you give to keep your eyesight if you knew you were going blind?"

"A lot," I answered. "Everything."

Then she asked, "What if it was your ability to walk—if you had a disease that would leave you wheelchair-bound unless you could pay for a cure. How much would you spend?"

"Everything," I said. "I'd liquidate everything I own and go as far into debt as I could to save my mobility."

"How about your hearing?"

"The same," I answered.

"How about your sanity—your mental health, your intelligence?"

Finally I asked, "What's your point?"

"I'm just trying to save you from BYTS—the Big Yellow Taxi Syndrome," she said, evoking the newly released Joni Mitchell song. "If you were to lose any one of these abilities, you would pay millions of dollars to recover it, so each one is worth millions of dollars to you. You would rather have the ability to see or hear or move or think than tens of millions of dollars in the bank. Well," she smiled and gave me a little shove, "you have them! Which means you're better off than a multimillionaire! You have to know what you've got before it's gone."

That's not a bad place to start with gratitude, with our own bodies. When I want to practice thanks, I can start with my toes—which, by the way, are underrated until you break one, as I did recently, and then you realize, limping, how much you depend on all ten every day. So I can be grateful for working toes, then for working feet, then for mobile ankles, then for strong calves, then well-lubricated knees, and so on. Each part of my body that functions—that doesn't wrack me with pain, that makes possible other benefits and pleasures—can be counted, enjoyed with gratitude, not taken for granted.

Then, I can continue my practice of gratitude with physical possessions. I can start outdoors, with the landscaping I enjoy, the pleasure of having a yard, the trees on my property that bring me such joy; then the car in my driveway, with all its features: good mileage, a good sound system, air-conditioning, and so on. Then I can work my way room by room through my house, from basement to attic. Recalling my friend

Mary's mental exercise, I can imagine my home being leveled by a tornado or flood and see myself sifting through the wreckage to find one shirt, salvage one photo, or rescue one piece of furniture. How glad I would be to have that one thing! In my gratitude exercise, I realize that I do have all these things, and I can turn to God to share my joy.

I can then extend my practice of gratitude to my family, each member, one by one. As I shared previously, one of my adult children survived cancer as a boy, and so my wife and I experienced, day after day, the realization that the child we had that day might be gone from us a year later. Although cancer took a lot from us, by stimulating gratitude and treating the Big Yellow Taxi Syndrome it gave us far more than it took.

From my body to my possessions to my family, I can continue my practice of gratitude by moving out to other people—friends, mentors, colleagues. Then I can take it a step farther—institutions like the courts, the police and other security forces, government and its many important duties, sports organizations, the music industry, entertainment. Every week or so, I'll hear a song by one of my favorite musicians—Bob Dylan, Joni Mitchell, Bruce Cockburn, David Wilcox, Keith Jarrett—or I'll see a comedy routine by Steve Martin or Stephen Colbert or Jon Stewart, or I'll watch a great movie or enjoy a good sporting event, and I'll breathe out a simple *thanks:* "Thanks, God, for the chance to be alive at the same time as these amazing people, to enjoy their talents, to watch their development over time. Thanks."

My practice of gratitude can continue expanding outward, to those elephants and giraffes, those wood thrushes and horseshoe crabs who are my neighbors on this planet. Mountains, rivers, oceans, continents, I can ponder each one while holding *thanks* open to God like a hand.

The other night I was experiencing a bout of insomnia, so this is just what I did. I brought the blessings of my life to mind, one by one. I didn't name them; I just pictured them while holding *thanks* open before God. I pictured what I had eaten for dinner a few hours earlier. Then I pictured the farmers who made it. Then I thought of all farmers everywhere, my mind quickly imagining scenes of rice paddies and wheat fields and vineyards and ranches and aquaculture ponds, from America to China to Argentina to Russia to Uganda to Canada. Then

I pictured the blessings of soil and sun and rain, which got me thinking about the water cycle and sunlight and the solar system and the galaxy.

And soon my mind was dazzled with a sense of the one big thing we call the universe, and—this might sound silly, but it might not—I felt a profound gratitude not just for the gifts that pertain to me and my life here and now, but for the gift of everything, everywhere, always. Instead of seeing the universe and its many gifts revolving around me as, sad to say, I normally do, for a few minutes I saw myself as one gift within the larger gift that we call creation. And I felt thankful not just that certain gifts are part of my life, but more; I felt thankful that my life can be part of this bigger gift, this sacred Given-ness. I'm fifty-four years old, and I don't think I ever felt that kind of great big gratitude until the other night. There was a kind of ecstasy to it, a deep delight and weighty joy that stayed with me as I drifted off to sleep, and remains with me now.

You can be still be grateful and still be greedy. The world can w/ injustice feel still resound and you don't have to feel responsible.

# CHAPTER 7

# Thanks: Dayenu—*Enough and More, and More*

Never let yourself think that because God has given you many
things to do for Him . . . pressing routine jobs, a life full up with
duties and demands of a very practical sort—that all these need
separate you from communion with Him. God is always coming
to you in the Sacrament of the Present Moment. Meet and receive
Him there with gratitude in that sacrament; however unexpected
its outward form may be receive Him in every sight and sound,
joy, pain, opportunity and sacrifice.

EVELYN UNDERHILL[1]

EVERY TIME YOU EAT, drink, or draw a breath, you are demonstrat-
ing that you are not a self-contained unit. Your skin might give you
a sense of boundaries, but in reality you are interconnected not only
with others, but with all creation. You are an organism in an environment, vitally connected and utterly dependent on resources outside
yourself—elements and minerals; chemical, biological, geological and
even astrophysical processes; friends, family, mentors, public servants;
ecological, social, political, and economic systems. Your story flows
from and into a million other stories; it's hard to know where your story
ends and others begin. At a funeral, when the officiant says, "From dust
you came, and to dust you shall return," he or she could just as easily
have said, "From stardust you came, and to stardust you shall return,"
because even earth's dust has a story beyond itself. Ingratitude makes
us foolishly forget the fragility of our skin and proudly deny our inter-

dependency and interconnectedness. If true spirituality and authentic religion are about vital interconnectedness, you can see how essential the practice of gratitude must be.

Jesus addressed gratitude again and again in his teachings, directly and indirectly. In the prayer he taught his disciples, for example, he offered these simple but revolutionary words that acknowledge our dependence: "Give us this day our daily bread." The phrase evokes the journey of Jesus's ancestors through the wilderness under Moses's leadership in about 1400 BCE. It reminds people of those days when they had to travel light, because they were always on the move, when each day they had to collect manna, bread for that day. Nothing could be stored for the next day on their journey, so each day was lived in utter dependence on God's provision, and nothing could be taken for granted.

Their journey was a journey of liberation. They were being liberated from slavery in Egypt, where they had been dehumanized and exploited, so that their elite Egyptian slave drivers could build their own never-enough system. It was also a journey of discipline. They were learning values on the journey that would form their national character when they finally settled down—so they wouldn't become either slaves or slave drivers in the future.[2] When we awaken to the addictive slavery of our contemporary never-enough system, we too want to go on a journey of liberation, and we too want to develop a humility of character enriched by daily dependence and daily gratitude, true thankfulness for our daily bread.

We are well insulated from this daily dependence and the gratitude it engenders. Bank accounts, insurance policies, even daily conveniences like refrigerators and air conditioners—they all build in us a sense of independence and invulnerability. But think a little deeper, and you see how thin the illusion of security can be. What if the sun stopped shining tomorrow? How long would any of us last, no matter how much money we had in the bank? What if the ocean currents shifted and the weather patterns changed? What if terrorists stopped the electricity from flowing or brought down the Internet for a few weeks or months? What if an epidemic broke out that stopped first air travel, then car and truck travel? How vulnerable would we feel then? So Jesus's prayer teaches us to travel light, to realize that, as his follower Paul would later say, if we have food and clothing, we have enough (1 Tim. 6:8), which means we have plenty to celebrate.

Jesus reinforces the same theme elsewhere in his Sermon on the Mount (Matt. 6:25–33). He reminds us that we can't keep our hair from turning gray (or falling out, about which I'm an expert). Nor can we add a day to our lives or an inch to our height—no matter how much we exercise our anxiety. Like the sparrows flying overhead or the day lilies blooming beside the roadway, we live within creaturely limits, and we depend for our survival on resources outside ourselves. This awareness of our creaturely limitations, dependence, and vulnerability doesn't make us less happy, Jesus suggests; it actually increases our happiness. It liberates us from the addictive drives of the never-enough system: more food, more drink, more clothes—always more, more, more. It liberates us to see ourselves as God's beloved creatures within God's creation instead of as self-made consumers in a self-made economic system.

In those simple words, "Give us this day our daily bread," Jesus invites us to radical nonconformity, which means radical liberation from the never-enough system. If we seek to fulfill God's dream for creation rather than our own little egocentric ambition to have more, more, more, he says, "all these things" that we need will come to us (Matt. 6:33; this is, I believe, the core meaning of this verse).

Now, that's not a promise of an easy life, because in many other places Jesus makes it clear that a life lived to fulfill God's dream for creation will involve suffering. But even here, Jesus implies that there is reason for gratitude. You see it in the Beatitudes, Jesus's eightfold way of happiness (Matt. 5:3–12). There is a blessing in poverty, he says; to the degree you miss out on the never-enough system, you partake of God's dream. There is a blessing in the pain of loss, because in your grief you experience God's comfort. There is blessing in being unsatisfied about the injustice in our world, he says; as God's justice comes more and more, you will feel more and more fulfilled. There is even blessing in being persecuted for doing what is just and good; as you enter into the heroic experience of God's prophets, you show yourself to be on God's side.

With these counterintuitive sayings and others like them, Jesus enrolls us in advanced classes in the school of gratitude. He shows us the disadvantages of advantages, and the advantages of disadvantages. He will make this paradox most dramatic through his own death; his suffering and crucifixion will eventually bring hope and freedom to all humanity, hope and freedom that could come no other way. Here is the deepest lesson of gratitude, then. We are to be grateful not just in the good times, but also in the bad times; to be grateful not just in plenty, but also in need; to maintain thankfulness not just in laughter, but also through tears and sorrow. One of Jesus's followers says that we should even rejoice in trials, because through trials come patience, character, wisdom (James 1:2–3). And another says, "I have learned to be content with whatever I have" (Phil. 4:11), so he can instruct, "Give thanks in all circumstances" (1 Thess. 5:18).

The words "in all circumstances" shouldn't be confused with "for all circumstances," of course. But neither should they be thinned to mean "in easy circumstances." Even in pain, we can find a place of gratitude, a place where alongside the agony of loss we still count and appreciate what remains.

Perhaps it becomes clear, in this light, how the attitude of gratitude is more valuable than any insurance policy. You may lose your job, but you can still be grateful for what you have left. You may lose popularity, but you can still be grateful for what you have left. You may lose a loved one, or facet after facet of your physical health, but you can still be grateful for what you have left. And what if you lose more, and more, and more, if bad goes to worse? Perhaps at some point, all of us are reduced to despair, but my hunch is—and I hope I never need to prove this in my own life, but I may, any of us may—having lost everything, one may still be able to hold on to one's attitude, one's practiced habit of gratitude, of turning to God in Job-like agony and saying, "For this breath, *thanks.* For this tear, *thanks.* For this memory of something I used to enjoy but now have lost, *thanks.* For this ability not simply to rage over what has been taken, but to celebrate what was once given, *thanks.*"

If we seek for other words to stand alongside the simple word *thanks* in expressing gratitude, I think one would be *again,* because one of the greatest obstacles to gratitude is the sheer bounty of God's generosity. Day after day we are given sunlight, water, air, breath, food, drink, family, friends, work, rest, sight, hearing, and a million other blessings, again and again, and our great temptation is to take them for granted. So when I notice that I've been taking these gifts for granted—a sure sign of which is that I'm moaning and groaning and complaining a lot—I rededicate myself to the practice of gratitude: "*Again,* God, *again* you have blessed me. *Again,* I savor this gift. *Again* I appreciate. *Again* I say thanks. *Again. Again.*"

Another word might be *this.* *This* day. *This* kiss. *This* view. *This* meal, *this* taste, *this* breath, *this* moment, *this* song. Instead of letting these treasures pass by as if they were nothing or as if we were unconscious of their beauty and wonder, we pause and savor them, and we lift our joy and appreciation up to God in gratitude. Because if God created these wonders, and if God created us with the capacity to enjoy them, what could be better than to enjoy them *with God?* Isn't that what gratitude is, in its purest sense, joining God in the enjoyment of the goodness of creation—the goodness that was celebrated in the first sentences of the book of Genesis, and the goodness that surrounds us now, in *this,* and *this,* and *this, again* and *again?*

For one more alternative word we can borrow from the Hebrew: *dayenu.* The word is from a Jewish song that has been a key part of the Passover celebration for over a thousand years. It means, "It would have been enough," and it functions within the retelling of the story of God's goodness over the generations:

> *If God had brought us out of Egypt,* dayenu—*it would have been enough.*
>
> *If God had split the sea for us,* dayenu—*it would have been enough.*
>
> *If God had led us through on dry land,* dayenu—*it would have been enough.*
>
> *If God had provided for our needs in the wilderness for forty years,* dayenu—*it would have been enough.*
>
> *If God had fed us manna,* dayenu—*it would have been enough.*
>
> *If God had given us Shabbat,* dayenu—*it would have been enough.*

*If God had led us to Mount Sinai,* dayenu—*it would have been*
*enough.*

*If God had given us the Torah,* dayenu—*it would have been enough.*

Singing this song fills one with a <u>sense of surplus</u>, of being super-
abundantly blessed, of being saturated with good things, of one's cup
being full and running over. And it fills one with a corresponding appreciation of God's unlimited generosity: *"Dayenu*—but there's more!
*Dayenu*—but there's more! And more, and more! Thanks be to God!"

I've been thinking these thoughts as I wander through this town in
Guatemala. I get back to our dusty car and I lean against the trunk,
waiting for my companions. I realize the little swimming hole is now
empty. A few white ducks sit placidly on the rocks where the children
were laughing an hour ago. The kids have gone home to dinner. Smoke
is rising from dozens of cooking fires around town, and I smell chicken
and onions cooking. A dog barks, a rooster crows, I take a deep breath,
and I am smiling without even meaning to. I feel full, and buoyant,
and alive. Something in me wants to sing. I'm too inhibited to dance
here alongside the road in the golden late-day sun, but I nod my head
and sway a little to the song I hear from a nearby radio. Life with God
is good. This day, this moment is good. I feel the vital connection.
"Thank you, Lord," I whisper. "Thank you, Lord. *Again* and *again,* for
*this* and *this* and *this. Dayenu. Dayenu. Thanks. Thanks."*

# CHAPTER 8

# O: *Practicing Jubilation*

*The Practice of Worship and Awe: Awakening
to the Beauty and Joy of God*
Alternate Words: *Hallelujah, Glory, Amen, How*

Oh, these vast, calm measureless mountain days in whose light
every thing seems equally divine, opening a thousand windows to
show us God. . . . These blessed mountains are so compactly filled
with God's beauty [that] the whole body seems to feel beauty
when exposed to it as it feels the campfire or sunshine, entering
not by the eyes alone, but equally through all one's flesh like radiant heat, making a passionate ecstatic pleasure-glow not explain-
able. . . . A few minutes ago every tree was excited, bowing to the
roaring storm, waving, swirling, tossing their branches in glorious
enthusiasm like worship. But though to the outer ear these trees
are now silent, their songs never cease. Every hidden cell is throb-
bing with music and life, every fiber thrilling like harp strings,
while incense is ever flowing from the balsam bells and leaves.
No wonder the hills and groves were God's first temples, and the
more they are cut down and hewn into cathedrals and churches,
the farther off and dimmer seems the Lord himself.

ADAPTED FROM JOHN MUIR[1]

I'M ON A FLIGHT home from Africa. My carry-on bags are packed
tight with wrinkled, dusty clothing plus some gifts from my friends
there, and my heart feels even more densely packed with memories to
add to those of previous journeys. Among the strongest, sweetest, and

most mysterious memories for me on these trips home is the experience of joining African friends in worship.

Imagine a dirt floor and no walls, but wooden posts supporting rough-hewn rafters that in turn support a vast tin roof that shades about a thousand cheap plastic lawn chairs—mostly white, some green—arranged in rows. In front, there's a rough wooden stage covered with random pieces of carpet and linoleum tacked or duct-taped together. A ramshackle sound system hums a little, background to the sounds of sparrows chirping and magpies scrapping in the sun outside. The place is empty now, but for the last few hours it has been rocking with joy. Old ladies and little kids clapped their hands, and smiles flashed like cameras at a celebrity event. The impossibly bright and varied colors of women's dresses swayed and swirled like so many flags, and dust rose from dancing feet in the rising heat. And the singing—harmony, echo, rhythm, call and response, punctuated by shouts and ululations. If you've ever worked up a sweat celebrating the goodness of God and life and love as they do in an African Pentecostal church, you know what I'm talking about, and if you haven't, I hope you someday will.[2]

I preached today, so for over a half hour I had a bird's-eye view of the congregation. An older man in the front row had one leg, probably a victim of a land mine during the last civil war. Another man had a patch over one eye and scars malforming his mouth, probably machete wounds from the same ugly period of violence. Many of the women were nursing babies, and for many of those mothers I'm sure sixteen years haven't yet passed since they themselves were babies. The worshippers' clothing was clean and bright—which always amazes me in a dusty place like this, especially because I know that nearly all these folks live in shacks or houses with dirt floors. But I also noticed that many outfits looked a little loose, because these are thin people who live on a dollar or two a day, often subsisting on a single meal a day and often depositing into their metabolic banks insufficient calories to compensate for withdrawals made by HIV and related diseases.

I have worshipped in the world's great cathedrals, and I love the grandeur, glory, reverence, dignity, and history that wash over me there. But these tin roofs, these dirt floors, these smells of sweat and cooking fires, these animating rhythms and swaying bodies and resonant voices, these mark for me *worship* at its most sublime. It's this simple, passionate, primal Pentecostal worship that speaks most deeply to my soul, whether it's in Africa, Latin America, or Asia or among the rural or urban poor in my own country. Why is it this way? Why are the most blessed often the most restrained in their worship, and why are those who have the least in terms of health, wealth, and safety the most ready to "make a joyful noise" and "sing for joy to the Lord"?

Is it because they relate to God primarily from their heart rather than their head? Is it because necessity has forced the poor to discover the practice of intentional celebration, the cultivation of disciplined delight? Could it be that our accumulation of possessions and protections coat our souls like rubber gloves, so that we touch, but do not feel? Could the growl of our roaring machinery and the glare of our bright screens and flashing signs relocate us among those with ears that do not hear, those with eyes that do not see? In this way, is the call to worship a summons to the half dead, half asleep, and half numb to strip down, step out, and draw near to the one thing money not only cannot buy, but may actually rob us of? Could it be that the conceptualized and formalized worship of the "developed world" is actually designed to inhibit and control rather than foment joy?

Author-activist Barbara Ehrenreich suggests this very thing. Empires and dictatorships maintain social control, she says, by converting (or subverting) the energy of jubilant dancing into regimented marching.[3] Pews in churches, she explains, are a rather late architectural innovation, added in the Middle Ages to inhibit the dancing that apparently broke out from time to time (think medieval European Pentecostals). Straight lines, orderly rows, military conformity—these suit the civilized state better than spontaneous outbreaks of collective joy. But, she says, rigid conformity and emotional inhibition stultify the human spirit, and so occasionally people defy the authorities and dare to dance. They create what author Kester Brewin describes as Temporary Autonomous Zones (TAZs), places where the normal patterns of hegemony and homogeneity are broken.[4] True, TAZs like Woodstock, Burning Man, Carnival, Mardi Gras, and many rock concerts and music festivals can be occasions for drunkenness and debauchery. But they can also be expressions, Ehrenreich says, of the human need for jubilation, of the human right to freedom, and even of the sacred quest for vital connection.

Perhaps the original experience of a TAZ was a holiday in its original sense, that is, a holy day, when we transcend the normal patterns of hegemony and homogeneity, labor and domination, and we get a tiny taste of the way life is supposed to be. We engage in holy play, godly partying, sacred merriment. These "holy TAZs" are, I believe, spiritual festivals of worship, where we make an empowering and vital connection to the "joy of the Lord."[5]

That, I think, is what I savor about my experiences of worship among "pure" or "primal" (as opposed to hyped-up and manipulated) Pentecostals, whether in other countries or my own. If our first simple word awakens us to the presence of God and the second to the presents or gifts of God, our third simple word awakens us to the heart of God, which is—consider this—characterized by an essential, unconquerable, boundless, radiant, wonderful, infinite, exuberant, generous, glorious joy. I know that comes as a shock to many of us.

Many of us associate God with cranky nuns with hands on hips or stern preachers with pursed lips nearly bursting with fury because we were *chewing gum in church*. We see God as a stern and controlling parent who was watching with simmering rage from the window when we were experiencing the thrill of our first kiss in a car in the driveway. Or we see God as a terrifying judge who has been counting our life's infractions and will inevitably charge us, mercilessly judge us, and eternally punish us for our guilt.

But the scandalous truth, known by mystics throughout history and affirmed in the pages of our sacred texts, is that when we connect with God, it is as if we are plugging our souls into a pure current of high-voltage joy. The joy that surprised me under the stars in my teens was exactly what the ancient psalmist knew (16:11), that God is a joyful being and to enter or awaken to God's presence is to enjoy a bracing jolt of invigorating delight followed by increasing levels of unending pleasure. Yes, there is indeed a place for quiet reverence, the dignity of robes, and the noble tranquility of marble columns and pipe organs. But my suspicion is that among the barefoot poor, we learn something that the well-heeled seldom discover—that God is joyful, and God's joy is contagious. When we tap into the joy of the Lord, when we step into the pure joy that burns like a billion galaxies in the heart of God, we'll soon find ourselves shouting, dancing, singing, leaping, clapping, swaying, laughing, and otherwise jubilating and celebrating.

Doesn't it make sense, then, for me to define worship as joining in the eternal, joyful celebration that erupts continuously among Father, Son, and Holy Spirit? Is it any wonder that Jesus, describing the kingdom of God, conceived of it as party, feast, banquet, festival? Could it be that the kingdom of God is the ultimate TAZ, the ultimate liberation from the normal oppressive patterns of hegemony and homogeneity?

If we entered the sacred connection with the words *here* and *thanks,* what one word can capture the joy of worship and holiday?[6] It would have to be a word of wonder, thrill, ecstasy, and—paradoxically—speechlessness. It would have to be a speech act that acknowledges the limits of speech.

A prime candidate would be that simple word "hallelujah." The word is beautiful, almost musical. Though drawn from the Hebrew, it is recognized in nearly every language today. In Hebrew it means "Praise G-d, all you people!" It expresses a vast range of worshipful emotion from exuberant joyful celebration to tender, grateful adoration. The word "glory" would also be a prime candidate, simultaneously evoking visual brightness, weighty substance, social splendor, and more. Maybe the word "amen" would also serve, since it is a way of responding to a moment of revelation or insight by saying, "Yes, that's right!" or "Right on!" or "I agree!" or "I second the emotion!"

But there's another word, even more primal and simple, in which we could lodge the sacred connection of worship. We've seen the word already, but passed it over without comment when we looked earlier at the many names given to God in the Psalms, the simple, primal interjection or exclamation O. This shortest of all words turns out to be one of the most amazing, because it can express the widest range of emotion. The exclamation "Ouch!" expresses the feeling of pain. "Wow!" expresses delight or pleasure or surprise. "Ugh!" expresses distaste. And what does *O* express?

*O* erupts from within us almost involuntarily and uncontrollably, expressing our reaction to almost any deep or powerful emotion. It may be awe in the presence of beauty—"O! What a glorious sunrise!" It may be gratitude in the presence of generosity—"O! What a kind gift!" It may be relief in the presence of comfort—"O! I'm so glad you're here!" It may be surprise—"O! I didn't realize you were standing there all along." It may even be agony that reaches out for empathy—"O! My head is pounding!" or "O! My heart is breaking!"

For our purposes, this little interjection of one letter, so tiny yet so challenging to define, can hold the joyful, amazing, loving wonder of awe, worship, and jubilation, to express what surpasses normal speech:

> O come, let us sing to the LORD;
> let us make a joyful noise to the rock of our salvation! (Ps. 95:1)

> O come, let us worship and bow down,
> let us kneel before the LORD, our Maker. (95:6)

> O magnify the LORD with me,
> and let us exalt God's name together. (34:3)

The form of the letter itself—a circle encompassing empty space— seems to beg us to fill it with all the emotion and thought we can muster. And this, I believe, explains why the word O arises so frequently in worship. Worship is an act of the whole being, uniting intellect with emotion, integrating reason with feeling, combining thought with affection, summoning both our brain's hemispheres and all our brain's layers and capacities in a joint eruption of joyful love and loving joy.

According to our best scientific estimate, matter, energy, space, and time big-banged into existence about 13.7 billion years ago. Then about 8.4 billion years ago, our planet formed. Then about 3.8 billion years ago, the first living cells formed in earth's warm seas. By about 0.6 billion years ago, the first somatic brains began functioning; reptile brains developed about 0.3 billion years ago, and mammalian brains about 0.2 billion years ago. And primitive hominid brains? They appeared about 0.0025 billion years ago, and modern humans appeared only 0.0002 billion years ago. And as for signs of religious sensibilities—cave paintings and ritual burials—they didn't appear until 0.00003 billion years ago, the blink of an eye in deep time.

So when we come to the spiritual practice of awe, whether expressed in a Pentecostal dance in Africa or a soaring cathedral in Europe, we're talking about a very young art, and we human beings are, on earth at least, its early pioneers. We are just beginning to unite brain and body, voice and movement, architecture and liturgy, word and music in this joyful discipline of drawing near to the joy of the Lord.

These young human brains of ours, it turns out, flowered into two hemispheres, each with its own strengths when it comes to worship. The desire to create analytical systems of belief clearly is a cortical function—probably originating in the left hemisphere—through which we apply our rational intelligence to questions of origin, destiny, personal and social morality, and divinity. The impulse to create works of art to celebrate and glorify God—temples, cantatas, poetry, icons, gardens—no doubt comes largely from the right side of the human brain. And the capacity for love in its most profound dimensions—*caritas,* altruism, generosity, humanitarianism toward our fellow creatures, and worship and love of God—would seem to arise within the highest capacities of both hemispheres working together.

The left-side analytical brain looks at a sunset and thinks about the spectra of light, ponders refraction, and conceptualizes the rotation of the earth in relation to the sun. Or it looks at a forest and names the trees, situates it in the conceptual scheme of forest succession, and estimates the profit from harvesting its lumber or converting it into a theme park. Or it looks at a feeble old woman on a hospital bed and estimates her age, looks for symptoms of disease, notices a thousand details that might help in making an accurate diagnosis, and predicts chances of survival. This left brain is abuzz with words, observations, calculations, theories, judgments, analyses.

But something happens when we expand from the left to the right brain. The hum and buzz of the cortical data stream stop dominating. We rise from the busy dissection of analysis to the calm union of appreciation. We move from aggressive reasoning to receptive understanding. From knowing about to knowing-in-relationship. From facts to meaning. From taking things apart to seeing things whole. From knowledge to love, from prose to poetry, and from invocation and thanksgiving to the awe of worship.[7]

Whole-brained worship, in this way, must include the humble acknowledgment that "more is going on than I realize." The busy left brain feels the digital thrill of being able to name, define, compare, contrast, analyze, dissect, categorize, and so on. But eventually it reaches its limits and invites the right brain into partnership. The right brain replies, as it were, "Yes, yes, very good analysis, and all that is true and of some real value. But no matter how much you chatter on about many things, you'll never comprehend the whole. You'll never get the big picture. So step back now, and let's together acknowledge the beyond-ness, the more-ness, the more-than-we-can-grasp-ness of what lies before us." When this sense of awe and wonder is directed not just at the sunset, a forest, a mountain, or the night sky, but through and with and beyond them to the source of all good things, wide-eyed wonder becomes joyful worship. Worship, then, we might say, is the highest exercise of all the parts of our multiform brain. No wonder the psalmist says, "Bless the LORD, O my soul, and all that is within me, bless God's holy name" (103:1).

But there's a problem. If we're not careful, our left and lower brains will reassert themselves and reduce our understanding of God down from the level of wholehearted, whole-brained, all-that-is-within-me worship. Soon we start worshipping the thin cortical God we conceptualize in our left hemisphere. Or we start idolizing the warm, sentimental God who suits our mammalian brains, who embodies the familiar, cozy sentiments of our little troop or tribe. Or, worse yet, we descend into our reptilian brains and kneel before a reptilian God who is driven to fight, vanquish, dominate, assimilate, or destroy the people we dislike having in our marked territory.

That's why, when we engage with the subject of worship, we must ask what kind or image of God are we worshipping, which is related to the question of which brain (or part of the brain) are we employing in worship. Andrew Newberg and Mark Robert Waldman explore this question at length in their book *How God Changes Your Brain,* and Michael Gerson summarizes their findings like this:

Contemplating a loving God strengthens portions of our brain—particularly the frontal lobes and the anterior cingulate—where empathy and reason reside. Contemplating a wrathful God empowers the limbic system, which is "filled with aggression and fear." It is a sobering concept: The God we choose to love changes us into his image, whether he exists or not.

For Newberg, this is not a simple critique of religious fundamentalism—a phenomenon varied in its beliefs and motivations. It is a criticism of any institution that allies ideology or faith with anger and selfishness. "The enemy is not religion," writes Newberg, "the enemy is anger, hostility, intolerance, separatism, extreme idealism, and prejudicial fear—be it secular, religious, or political."[8]

Worship is the practice of uniting all that is within us to celebrate the joyful goodness of God—and for us that must not be a reptilian and mammalian God of "anger, hostility, intolerance, separatism, extreme idealism, and prejudicial fear," but rather the God described poetically by the apostle John like this:

> This is the message we have heard from him and proclaim to you, that God is light and in God there is no darkness at all. . . . Beloved, let us love one another, because love is from God; everyone who loves is born of God and knows God. Whoever does not love does not know God, for God is love. . . . God is love, and those who abide in love abide in God, and God abides in them. . . . We love because God first loved us. . . . Those who love God must love their brothers and sisters also." (1 John 1:5; 4:7–8, 16, 19, 21)

To worship is to exercise the highest capacities we have. It exercises the parts of our brains that transcend the reptilian, the mammalian, and even the merely human. It invites us to contemplate the glorious, transcendent living God of love and, in so doing, to experience transformation into that image ourselves. This, it turns out, is a good and supremely joyful thing.

CHAPTER 9

# O: *Not Just a Word—A Way of Life*

Holy One of Blessing,
Your presence
Fills creation.
You have kept us alive,
You have sustained us,
You have brought us
To this moment.

SHECHEHEYANU, TRADITIONAL HEBREW PRAYER[1]

WHEN HUMAN BEINGS ENTER into the joyful celebration of the glory of God and the goodness of God's gift of life, normal prose breaks into poetry, normal voices break into song, normal postures break into dancing, and people don't simply become more religious—they become more alive.

You can feel this dynamic in the ancient Hebrew Psalms:

*The LORD is my strength and my shield;*
*in God my heart trusts,*
*so I am helped, and my heart exults,*
*and with my song I give thanks to God. (28:7)*

*Praise the LORD!*
*Praise God in God's sanctuary;*
*praise God in God's mighty firmament!*
*Praise God for God's mighty deeds;*
*praise God according to God's surpassing greatness!*

*Praise God with trumpet sound;*
*praise God with lute and harp!*
*Praise God with tambourine and dance;*
*praise God with strings and pipe!*
*Praise God with clanging cymbals;*
*praise God with loud clashing cymbals!*
*Let everything that breathes praise the LORD!*
*Praise the LORD! (150:1–6)*

It's ironic, I think, that at the moment we get a glimpse into the goodness, greatness, beauty, and glory of God, we simultaneously seek words to celebrate what we have seen—and we know that no words can do it justice. So we grasp for strong, sturdy words like "goodness," "greatness," "beauty," "glory," and we reach still higher for our loftiest words, like "wonder," "sovereignty," "power," "holiness." And still we feel they fall short. So we then seek to describe by negation, using prefixes and suffixes like "in-," "un-," and "-less"—"infinite," "limitless," "boundless," "endless," "unfailing," "unblemished," and so on. And still we are unsatisfied. So we reach for metaphors and similes, the tools of the poetic trade, and we summon our imagination to action. And when they fail us, we reach for riddle and paradox, as did St. Bonaventure, an early disciple of St. Francis whose words I adapted for a song:

**You are within all things, but not enclosed. You are outside
all things, but not excluded. You are above all things, but not
aloof. You are below all things, but not debased. Your center
is everywhere. You have no circumference. Your fullness is
everywhere.**

Even now, however inspired we feel, however our "tongue becomes the pen of a ready scribe" (Ps. 45:1), still we aren't satisfied. So we bring in the sound effects of nature—crashing waves, thunder, wind in trees, waterfalls—but still we're falling short. So we add every sound we can create in human music—from tubas to piccolos, from drum kits to screaming lead guitars, from congas to steel drums to dulcimers to banjos to violins. And then we add gesture, dance, leaping, maybe even some "holy rolling." And that's not enough, so we reach into architecture. And storytelling. And drama. And painting. And sculpture. Still unsatisfied, we add ritual and vestment, incense and stained glass. We even invent new instruments, new media, on screens and through speakers seeking to express our tiny glimpse of the glorious wonder that radiates from God. And never for a moment, after all we've said, sang, danced, and done, do we feel that we have overstated or even done justice to the glimpse of beauty, holiness, glory, love, power, kindness, purity, complexity, simplicity, depth, height, and infinitude with which we have been graced.

A moment like this comes in what many consider Paul's magnum opus, his letter to the Romans. The letter is interpreted in widely varying ways, the commonest conventional approach perhaps being to read it as a treatise on the theological theme known as "justification by faith." I greatly appreciate this doctrine, but I have become convinced that this isn't actually the theme of the letter.[2] I now understand the theme to be this: *all human beings, regardless of their status as religious insiders or outsiders, are invited into the new community of God*.

This thesis raised a big problem in Paul's day, though. The dividing wall between insiders and outsiders was high and thick, topped with razor wire and guarded by aggressive clerical rottweilers. In order to assert that the wall must come down, that all people must be welcomed as equals through the good news of Jesus, Paul has some "'splainin' to do." And that's what he does for the first eleven chapters. I don't, however, read those eleven chapters as one long linear argument. I read them as a succession of short arguments, analogies, metaphors, and logical experiments, like switchbacks by which a trekker zigzags up a mountain. Paul tries one tack, then another. One analogy works for a while, but then breaks down, so he switches to another metaphor, only to have that one hit a brick wall as well.

After eleven chapters of this, it's as if he is taken by surprise by the end of a sentence that begins, "For God has imprisoned all in disobedience . . ." When he concludes, "so that God may be merciful to all" (11:32), something in Paul seems to snap. His own Spirit-led conclusion seems to have gotten out ahead of him, leaping out and surprising him with its grandeur at the climactic moment. The good news, it turns out, is even better than he imagined. His line of reasoning has seemed to take on a life of its own, rising like a tsunami and carrying him to a higher and bigger appreciation of the gospel than he ever had before. (As a writer and preacher, I have experienced this myself. It's an amazing thing.) So his normal syntax breaks like a thin fishing line, and worship explodes like a sailfish heaving itself up from the sea in a wild leap of defiance and joy. And there it is—our little word *O*:

> *O the depth of the riches and wisdom and knowledge of God!*
> *How unsearchable are his judgments and inscrutable his ways!*
> *For who has known the mind of the Lord?*
> *Or who has been his counselor?*
> *Or who has given a gift to him, to receive a gift in return?*
> *For from him and through him and to him are all things.*
> *To him be the glory forever. Amen. (11:33–36)*

Explanation gives way to exclamation, reasoned answer to rhetorical question. As the wave of wonder crashes on the shore, Paul gets control of himself again. He tries to shake himself back into normal prose and pulls himself together to offer this conclusion in the next verse: "Okay, now that we've gotten a breathtaking glimpse of this amazing, explosive, overwhelming mercy of God, I want you to join me in worship, not by offering a sheep or bull as a sacrifice as in the old Temple system, and not even by going to church and singing, clapping, kneeling, or dancing for hours on end. I want you to worship God by offering your whole lives, all you have and are, as an offering of worship to God."

For Paul, then, the *O* of worship translates naturally and immediately into a way of life, life lived not for self-interest (which Paul often calls "the flesh," "the old self," or "the old humanity"), but for the common good or, in Paul's words, "faith working through love" (Gal. 5:6) and "serving one another in love" (5:13, NIV). This is remarkable, really. We might be less surprised if Paul had said, "In view of God's mercies, I demand that you spend at least one hour per day in church services or one hour on your knees, reciting prayers to God." But no, the tsunami of God's grace inspires us to express our worship not simply

Problem w/ Chapter: he's using too very techniques just told don't convey work what?

in religious activities, but in real life, through love for one another. The prayer of worship that leaps up in a simple *O* must be translated into the gracious eloquence of a good, kind, and just life, in the grammar and syntax of everyday relationships.

How can we infuse our daily lives with the poetry, song, and dance of worship and praise? I've tried to maintain several disciplines of worship in my life through the years, each involving a way to render my whole life a living sacrifice:

1. *Give God the first greeting every morning.* As I emerge from sleep into awareness, even before my eyes are open, I try to turn my attention to God, moving from *here* to *thanks* to worship: "O Lord! Good morning! Here I am, with you for a new day, and here you are, with me as always. Thank you, Living God, for this fresh install-ment in the gracious gift of life! O Lord! I worship you for who you are, gracious and compassionate, just and good, holy and forgiving, almighty and gentle."

2. *Give God the first thanks at every meal.* I believe the old practice of pausing to thank God before meals is a wise and good one. It reminds me of my creatureliness; like the birds of the air and the flowers of the field, I am dependent on God for my daily suste-nance. The simple act of table grace can certainly be practiced on mindless autopilot, but when it is done mindfully, with awareness, it can connect me at least three times a day with the Creator, who supplies soil and sunlight and rain to maintain the miraculous web of life, of which I am part. And true gratitude to God will also produce gratitude to my fellow creatures—wheat stalk, apple tree, and corn plant; chicken, salmon, and cattle; farmer, agricultural researcher, truck driver, grocer, and cashier too. Closing your eyes is fine, but I often think it's even better to pray with open eyes, noticing the rich brown texture of whole wheat bread, the robust green of lettuce, the bold red of a tomato, the clearness of water.

3. *Give God the first response to every pleasure.* You've probably had the same experience I have of being somewhere alone, witnessing some beautiful thing—a sunrise, an act of kindness, a rainbow, the Milky Way—and wishing your spouse or a friend were there to share it

with you. We often forget that, although another human being may not be present, our Creator is, and we can learn to share our joy with God. In so doing, we may come to feel that the opposite is in fact happening as well, that in this moment, God is sharing God's joy with us. The living God is the Creator of spinning galaxies and fluttering butterflies and towering mountain ranges and leaping whales and whirling subatomic particles. God is the giver of both good foods and the taste buds to enjoy them. God is the maker of the coral reefs of Costa Rica and Australia and the forests of Siberia and Tasmania and everywhere in between. And right now, at this moment, God sees and enjoys every glimmer of sunlight passing through the water on all the magical colors of every purple parrotfish and emerald angelfish and crimson wrasse and jade goby and red blenny and orange clownfish and blue damselfish and yellow tang. Imagine, then, the joy of God, as God sees how wonderful these things are, and God savors their goodness, and God takes pleasure in them as artists take holy pride in their creations.[3] In worship, we take notice too, appreciating the art, and the Artist. In this way we share in God's joy, and add to it through our spontaneous *O* of worship.

With practice, it becomes natural and instinctive to turn to God as our first response to all experiences of pleasure or beauty— the cardinal whistling outside the window this morning, the way sunlight comes through the blinds, the simple green of grass and its smell when freshly cut. Each one becomes like a church bell beckoning us to pray, "*O* Glory to God!" But at various seasons of my life, when because of depression, pressure, or pain these spontaneous expressions of praise are not forthcoming, I have been helped greatly through fixed-hour prayer, using various traditions to turn my attention several times each day to the goodness, wonder, and beauty of God. And when I am dull or down, not appreciating the goodness of the moment, I can at least employ my memory for past pleasures, even the pleasures whose loss might be causing sadness in the present.[4]

4. *Give God the first consideration in your weekly schedule.* It has been my practice not only to begin each day with private worship, but

also to plan each week around a special time of gathered worship where gifted people, drawing from rich liturgical traditions, guide a community of worshippers to ponder and celebrate the goodness of God in song, prayer, sermon, silence, and more. For me, first and foremost, this is what gathered worship is about. It's not about satisfying the demands of scrupulous religious consumers, but about helping people continue to taste and see the goodness of the Lord, letting their private O of daily personal worship harmonize with that of others to produce a glorious symphony of gathered worship. True, in some of our churches what happens on Sundays is lackluster and sometimes downright depressing, and in other churches what happens is noisy and showy and maybe a little tacky. But my guess is that just about anywhere, if we have the right eyes to see, there is great value in gathering for worship—whether it's on Sunday, Saturday, or whenever; whether it's in a glorious cathedral or temple, a spacious megachurch facility, or a small local chapel, synagogue, or mosque; whether it's in a humble storefront, in a coffee shop or pub, or around a kitchen table.

5. *Make God the first supervisor or customer for all work.* "Just as you did it for one of the least of these, . . . you did it to me" (Matt. 25:40), Jesus said, and that attitude can infuse all our work with new meaning. The apostle Paul was getting at the same thing when he said, "Whatever your task, put yourselves into it, as done for the Lord; . . . you serve the Lord Christ" (Col. 3:24). So the chef whose life has been offered to God as a living sacrifice of worship seeks to prepare each meal as if Christ were her customer, and the teacher teaches as if each student were the Lord. Similarly, the gardener, the computer programmer, the project manager, the administrative assistant, the politician, the salesperson, and the banker seek to serve, honor, and worship God as they water, program, manage, assist, govern, sell, and invest. They make their work sacred in this way, and my guess is, both their supervisors and their customers and clients will feel a difference.

6. *Give God the first part of every paycheck.* I think it is best to see giving not simply as an act of duty to my faith community—although that's a legitimate dimension of giving—but even more as an act

of worshipping God. When we are counting our blessings, having freely received enough and more than enough, we find it natural to freely give; when we're running on the never-enough addictive rat wheel, the generous impulse rarely if ever arises.

7. *Give God the joy of your creativity.* Since God is at heart a joyful creator, and since you are made in the image of God, you no doubt have found (or will find) some ways you enjoy being creative. Maybe you write poetry, play the guitar, garden, or cook. Maybe you design furniture, work with landscapes, sculpt, paint, take photographs, sketch portraits, or do collage. Maybe you dance, climb mountains, build birdhouses, or arrange flowers. Probably, in whatever you do, you apologize: "It's not very good." "I'm just an amateur." "I never took any lessons." "I really do it just for myself." My guess is that you do this for the same reason I do. I really love my creative pursuits, they are unspeakably precious to me, and the thought of their being evaluated, criticized, or even mocked by others is so distressing that I decide to preempt the criticism of others with my own disparagement.

Let me make this suggestion, to you and to myself. Let's apologize less and create more. Let's think of creating for the approval of others less, and for the pleasure of God more. Think of the little girl who draws a picture for her mother. She uses crayons to compose crude stick figures—a blue person, a red car, a green and brown tree, a purple house, a yellow sun with squiggly lines radiating out from it. And what does her mother do? Critique it? No, she uses magnets to display it on the refrigerator, where it may stay until the girl graduates from high school. What if God is more like that mother than the critics we fear? What could give our Creator more pleasure than our creative offerings?

I remember, as a father, feeling pure delight as my children ran free at a playground with their friends, completely unaware of me because they were so taken up with the joy of play and playmates. But when they saw me sitting quietly on the bench, ran over, and threw their arms around me, my delight was enriched all the more. And when they would climb the slide or the jungle gym and shout, "Dad, watch this!" I remember thinking that I would like very much to live this way with God: showing off, not in an egotistical way, but rather, humbly, generously, and with childlike abandon, seeking to bring pleasure to the One who gave me life. This, to me, is worship—not just words, but a creative way of life.

How fascinating that worshipping the Creator thus exercises the imagination and so drives us to creativity. Soon, in response to God's creativity and goodness, we fashion good works of art of our own, from Handel's *Messiah* to Bob Dylan's "Every Grain of Sand," from grand cathedrals that all can see to a poem written in a private journal for no eyes other than God's. The *O* of worship leads us to reach for a pen, paintbrush, garden tool, or guitar, an instinctive creative urge that reminds us that we are created in God's imaginative image. When we get a glimpse of God's creative glory, we ourselves become more creative and glorious ourselves.

The first sentence of the previous paragraph suggests that if we seek one more word to partner with *O* or *hallelujah* in the expression of worship, *how* is an excellent option. *How* functions in a fascinating way in the grammar of praise. Many of us experience it in the old hymn "How Great Thou Art." It spans question and exclamation and expands our imagination—"How wonderful?" "How wonderful!" "How kind?" "How kind!" "How glorious?" "How glorious!"

To be surrounded by so much goodness, beauty, and wonder and not to celebrate, to be given so much, but to fail to appreciate the source—wouldn't that spoil us? This realization helps explain why the Bible (and other spiritual literature) overflows with exhortations to worship. It is not that God is insecure and narcissistic, requiring frequent affirmations to be saved from depression or a fit of rage. Nor is it that God is dominating and sociopathic, capable of happiness only when others are groveling in deference. No, God wants *us* to be saved from being spoiled, self-centered, inflated, and distorted with a sense of entitlement. It is for our good, not God's, that worship is so important. Psalm 149 creates just this kind of scenario. It calls people to create a TAZ, to erupt in jubilation, to sing, dance, bang tambourines, and pluck stringed instruments in praise of God. And then it affirms that God takes pleasure in us as we take pleasure in God. God joins us in joy, and we join in God's joy. In jubilation we strengthen the vital connection.

Yes, there are problems to be faced. Yes, in the pages ahead, as in the days ahead, there are prayers of complexity and struggle, prayers of perplexity and lament, prayers of confession and desperation, agony and terror. Yes, there is a time to cry and groan in rage as well as a time to laugh and dance in joy. To these dimensions of the spiritual life we will turn presently. But before we go there, don't you agree we are wise to establish this baseline of spirituality as simple, pure, deep happiness in a life with God—of spirituality as a joyful awakening to the God who is *here,* near, with us, the One in whose presence we live and in whose attention and care we are held? Of spirituality as an overflowing *thanks* as we awaken to what can so easily and tragically be taken for granted? Of spirituality as a pregnant O that arises when we see the wonders of creation and trace in them the signature of the Artist from whom all good things flow? Of spirituality as the essential joie de vivre, shared with the One in whom both joy and life originate, the One in whom all good things freely play, and the One from whom and to whom all good things flow like sparks rising or rivers running?

So, in a moment put this book aside. Let your mind ponder good and great and wonderful things, things you love. As each comes before you, simply hold it in a spirit of wonder, in the simple word O. And then take that wonder and love for the thing and expand it out to the Source, the giver, the designer of all goodness, all greatness. Let your mind with all its capacities and your heart and imagination with all their powers see how good and great G-d must be, and in that awareness, let your O resound to God—silently, within you, or aloud as a groan or shout or song.

And if the urge strikes you, put on some music and dance!

# PART II

# Complexity: The Season of Spiritual Strengthening

T HERE'S A WAY TO do this." That's what I remember saying to myself again and again as I entered the season of Complexity. How was I to find God's will for my life? Change bad habits? Avoid or repair conflict? Become more well liked or effective? Find a mate and build a healthy family? Somewhere were people who knew how, and if I could find them, I'd learn their checklist, no matter how complex, and I'd master their techniques, no matter how difficult. I became an avid devotee of conferences and workshops at this stage—as I still am today. I scribbled copious notes on sermons and eagerly listened to religious broadcasts, wanting to glean every practical tip and memorize any step-by-step plan that might help me in my spiritual journey. Even today, decades later, I'm building on strengths I developed during my first journey through Stage Two.

When we're in Stage Two, we don't leave Stage One behind. We build upon it in three new movements of the soul. Without these three new skills or strengths, we remain dependent and immature, but with them we learn increasing independence. Whether it's praying, reading and interpreting the Bible, sharing our faith with others, fulfilling a ministry in the church, or simply handling the inevitable complexities of life, in Stage Two our goal is to be able to say, "I can do it myself. I can handle it. I know how."

Our focus now shifts from right versus wrong to effective versus ineffective. To the degree we feel we have orthodoxy (right belief) nailed down, we now turn to orthopraxy (right behavior). To our core of dualism we now add a new layer of pragmatism. The world is still divided between good and evil, but now good people are identified less as the correct and more as the effective, less as the ones who get things right and more as the ones who get things done. If the greatest sin of Simplicity was being wrong, now in Complexity the greatest sin is being apathetic or ineffective. If we previously were attracted to leaders who told us how to be and do *right,* now we are drawn to leaders who show us how to be and do *well.* If Stage One leaders taught us the rules of the game, Stage Two leaders now coach us in how to win it. (Right now, Stage Two readers are saying, "Yes. That's exactly why I bought this book!") We're no longer satisfied to be part of the right in-group; we now seek identity as part of a winning team. Within that team, we want to play our part well.

And that is our great strength as Stage Two people—we share the can-do, "Yes, we can!" spirit. Of course, as with every stage, we can get comfortable here and refuse to move on when this season has run its course. When reality refuses to comply with our complex schemes, strategies, and techniques, we can blame reality and go into denial rather than question some of our assumptions. Stage Two is, after all, a really enjoyable time in life, and saying good-bye to it is so painful that many people never do.

But for those of us just entering Stage Two, there's no need to think about letting it go. Right now, there are skills to master, goals to achieve, challenges to conquer. At the age of eighteen, those challenges might include choosing a college major or navigating the complexities of romance. At twenty, they may involve a relationship that needs to be nurtured, a career choice, or finding a cause to work for. At thirty and forty, they might entail raising children, handling new opportunities at work, or caring for an unhappy spouse or an unwell marriage. At fifty and sixty, life's challenges might include aging parents or fading dreams, health setbacks or new freedoms. At seventy, eighty, and ninety, they might involve surviving a surgery, coping with grief, planning for the next holiday with the grandchildren, or preparing for death. Whatever the challenges, Stage Two is about learning three essential practices that help us survive and thrive, not cave in or give up.

What are those practices? First is the ability to self-examine, admit mistakes, and process failure. Second is the habit of acknowledging our personal weaknesses and limitations and seeking wisdom, strength, and skill beyond our own. And third is the ability to empathize with others in their pain.

If Simplicity resembles springtime in its fragility and vitality, Complexity resembles summer—a time of hard work and getting things done during long sunny days.

# CHAPTER 10

# Sorry: *Holier Than Myself?*

*The Practice of Self-Examination and*
*Confession: Strengthening Through Failure*
Alternate Words: *Regret, Mercy*

*also Confess strengths!*
*tell truth of selves.*
*Must be corporate*
*not just solo.*

If there is such a thing as human perfection, it seems to emerge precisely from how we handle the imperfection that is everywhere, especially our own.

RICHARD ROHR[1]

I HAVE A FRIEND WE'LL call Carlos, who for many years was, like me, a pastor. He is one of the strong, kind, and holy people I've been privileged to know in my life. We see each other too seldom, but however long the absence, we pick up again where we left off. Over the years, Carlos has been a touchstone of spiritual authenticity for me. We have been confidants and friends to one another in some of our personal struggles. We have also had some monumental laughs together and played a couple of gut-busting practical jokes on each other.

Once I invited Carlos to speak at a weekend retreat for the leaders of the church I served. I won't go into the practical jokes that we played on each other that weekend, even though they were pretty funny and involved rubber snakes and showers. During a serious moment at the retreat, he said something to our little group that has stayed with me ever since. "A secret to the spiritual life," he said, "is desiring to actually be more spiritual than you appear to be." Then he added, "The secret to hypocrisy is desiring to appear more spiritual than you actually are."

*don't let left hand know...*

Maintain pretentions
to claim spirituality
to claim publicly

People like Carlos and me, who for most of our lives have gotten paid to be spiritual leaders, live constantly in the orange alert of spiritual danger: it is perpetually tempting for us to desire to appear more spiritual than we are. But I think any person who is part of a faith community of some sort also faces this danger. Forget keeping up with the Joneses; I'm projecting a false Jones image that I want others to think is real, and I'm struggling to keep up with that. Forget "holier than thou"; I'm seeking to appear holier than *moi*. That kind of pretense piles layers of clothing and cosmetics on naked spirituality, which makes our next practice all the more important.

The fact is, we are all hypocrites to some degree. None of us want to be known for our worst moments. Sometimes, like too many religious leaders of recent years (who, as religious broadcasters, were rewarded for projecting an image), we preach most loudly and passionately against the sins to which we are most subject—hiding our secrets out in the open, so to speak, fighting our personal demons "in here" under the guise of fighting culture wars "out there." Sometimes, we find the best way to keep guilt at bay over our own inconsistencies is to pour guilt on others. As we do so, our souls go dark and dangerous, as do the religious communities we lead.

That's why another friend of mine, Gareth, says we all need to come out.[2] Reflecting on our agonized and often dysfunctional religious controversies about homosexuality in recent years, he says that the gay community is doing an invaluable service for everyone, gay or straight. By admitting they're homosexual, gay people are leading the way for the rest of us to admit simply that we're *sexual*. When we pretend we aren't, when we hide our sexuality in shame and secrecy, we create a dark, damp culture where shame and self-hatred grow like mold, a disconnected culture of tragic pretense and inauthenticity. Another friend, Mark, says that we should put a sign just inside the front door of all our churches: "Let's pretend!" This way, we'll at least be honest about our dishonesty!

We've been considering the spiritual life in the season of Simplicity. Life is indeed simple in many ways, but it is also more than simple. There are shades of gray between our black-and-white extremes, layers and folds of complexity under every simple surface. And nowhere must we face that complexity more directly than when we deal with our own behavior. You're singing in a choir—maybe it's Handel's *Messiah*. Your eye catches the eye of another singer, and soon your imagination is writing a mental screenplay for a torrid affair even as your vocal chords and lips form the words, "Hallelujah! Hallelujah! For the Lord God Omnipotent reigneth." You're working in a slum in Africa, helping orphans whose parents have died of HIV/AIDS; you're there at your own expense, there on your own vacation time, and you're thinking about how you can post a blog about your experience to puff up your image in front of your friends back home. You're writing a book on building a life with God and at the same time you're wondering how it will sell and what status it will gain you in the eyes of your loyal readers and hostile critics. (Wonder who that is.)

Carlos is right. We all can be seduced by the appeal of appearing more spiritual than we actually are. Mark is right. We're all pretenders, all religious broadcasters, all of us false prophets projecting an image by which we hope to rake in profits—financial, social, relational, spiritual. Gareth is right. We all need to come out of the closet. We don't have to hide the real us—the sexual us, the insecure us, the doubtful us, the angry us, the complex, different, tempted, actual human us.

Novelist and essayist C. S. Lewis used to ask, "What is the most significant conversation you have every day?"

People would respond piously, "Your conversation with God, of course."

"No," Lewis would reply. "It's the conversation you have with yourself before you speak to God, because in that conversation with yourself, you decide whether you are going to be honest and authentic with God, or whether you are going to meet God with a false face, a mask, an act, a pretense."

The practice of *self-examination* and *confession* acknowledges the tragic gap between our appearance and our actuality. Through confession, we say, "God, I will not hide anything from you. You know already. Pretending in your presence is pure and pathetic insanity. I want to be who I am in your presence."

When I utter the simple words, "I'm *sorry*," I'm saying, "I acknowledge what you already know."[3] When I confess to God my secrets, the truths about which I fear rejection, I am rejecting de-ligion—which always involves a disconnection between who I really am and who I project myself to be. When I hold up to God the regrets and remorse I would otherwise try to hide in order to project a happy, likeable, and "spiritual" image, my "I am who I am" can resonate with God's "I am who I am." When I try to appear no holier, stronger, or better than I actually am, I keep the vital connection intact, unsevered.

Two powerful moments in the Hebrew scriptures have tutored me in the art of confession. First, in Psalm 32, King David reflects on his experience of doing wrong, refusing to admit it for a time, and then finally confessing his wrong and receiving forgiveness. It seems to have been written, as was Psalm 51, in the aftermath of a sordid period in David's life that began with an act of adultery. Adultery would be transgression enough, but the man whose wife David has taken has been one of his most trusted colleagues, a general in David's army. So David's adultery is also a betrayal of friendship and collegiality. Worse still, when David finds the woman is pregnant, he conspires to cover up the affair by having the general come back from the front lines to have relations with her, in hopes that the general will think the child is his own. When the general's loyalty to his troops frustrates David's cover-up plan, David conspires—successfully—to have the general sent to the front lines, where he will be killed. Then he takes the woman as his wife, and his cover-up appears to have worked perfectly.

Until, that is, a pesky prophet comes and exposes David's unconscionable behavior. So David has experienced the great grief of exposed wrongdoing and the even greater relief of coming clean. "Happy are those," he says, "whose transgression is forgiven, whose sin is covered" (32:1). By "covered," he doesn't mean *kept in secrecy,* because he then contrasts the happiness of coming clean with the misery of living in secrecy: "While I kept silence, . . . my strength was dried up as by the heat of summer" (32:3–4). The energy required to cover up, to broadcast a false, inflated image, David suggests, depletes the soul, creating a sick internal environment, a kind of moral HIV. Ironically, when he stops covering up his sin, his sin is covered—like a bill, like a debt, like an enemy attack—as if God says, "Don't worry. I've got you covered," covered by mercy, covered by grace.

If one manages to maintain the cover-up and keep broadcasting the fraudulent image, one becomes, if not acutely feverish, at least chronically numb—"calloused" is an image often used in the Bible, or "stiff-necked" or "hard-hearted." The projected image (what psychologist Paul Tournier called the "personage") becomes disconnected from the inner person, the appearance from reality.[4] No wonder the ancient Hebrews had a proverb that said, "Keep your heart with all vigilance, for from it flow the springs of life" (Prov. 4:23). No wonder they were taught to pray:

> *Search me, O God, and know my heart;*
> *test me and know my thoughts.*
> *See if there is any wicked way in me,*
> *and lead me in the way everlasting. (Ps. 139:23–24)*

No wonder they built into their annual calendar holy days of repentance, when all the members of the community of faith would pause to examine themselves, acknowledge their faults, individually and as a community, and come clean. No wonder they practiced elaborate rituals of sacrifice through which they dramatized the brutality of sin by sacrificing an innocent animal, which then became the main course in a ritual meal of reconciliation.[5]

The conscience is like a moral nerve for the soul. It's like a pain receptor that warns us of moral danger. Self-examination keeps our moral nerves from going numb; it keeps our moral skin sensitive and not calloused. "Something is wrong!" our conscience shouts. "You're burning yourself morally!" it screams. "Your integrity is being bruised or broken!" it cries. "You're feverish, infected, unwell!" it shouts. The pain of a sensitive conscience finds relief when we stop, self-examine, and say the same thing about our wrong that God would say. By awakening us to the moral danger of what we are becoming, confession allows us to choose a better path of becoming.

True, the conscience can become hyperactive, obsessive, self-destructive, like a watchdog that turns on its master with the same fury it has been trained to focus on an intruder. Just as we need to be protected *by* our conscience from integrity loss and character decay, we need to be protected *from* our conscience at times, from the destructive self-flagellation and the simmering self-hatred it can foster. The practice of self-examination and confession provides a way of calling off the guard dog, dealing with the danger, silencing the conscience's alarm bell, and moving on.

What applies to us as individuals applies to us in groups too, because not all of our faults and wrongs are simply personal. Sometimes they are transpersonal or social, not just embedded in the habits of individuals, but ingrained in the patterns of church, denomination, tribe, nation, or civilization. Personal actions like lying, breaking marriage vows, dishonoring parents, coveting, stealing, seeking revenge, and other personal sins can combine to create social weather patterns from which new categories of evil emerge—tornados of social injustice and economic oppression, hurricanes of racism and class or caste consciousness, heat waves of homophobia or patriarchy, blinding blizzards of systemic evil. These social weather patterns can last for generations, in turn creating personal behavior patterns in millions of individuals who have no idea they are being controlled or possessed by invisible forces larger than themselves.[6] We see these systemic problems identified in another instructive moment of confession from the Bible. It comes in the aftermath of an invasion into the Israelite homeland that occurred about 586 BCE. To understand the moment, let's imaginatively enter it.

# CHAPTER 11

# Sorry: *Unleashing Our Own Becoming*

> Jokingly but with a great deal of seriousness, [Father Damascus would] say, "Don't worry about purifying your motives. Simply know that they aren't pure, and proceed."
>
> BROTHER DAVID STEINDL-RAST[1]

THE ISRAELITES WERE IN a terrible situation. Decades ago, a brutal enemy destroyed the defenses of their capital city. An invading army captured and deported the "best and brightest" of their people. Since then, under occupation, they had struggled against forgetting their history, losing their identity, and being assimilated into the enemy culture. For decades, their once glorious capital city remained desolate, looted, in ruins.

Then in 444 BCE, one of the deportees gained permission to organize a rebuilding team and return to the capital city. They arrived in the city and assessed the damage. It was extensive, but the team leader realized that there was even more damage than met the eye. He knew that you can repair walls externally, but you must also heal the people internally. You can rebuild physical infrastructures, but you must also rebuild internal structures of character and identity and the social structures of justice and trust. The experience of conquest, occupation, exile, and domination had broken the people, and the visible ruins of the city were in many ways a metaphor for their damaged inner identity—not just as individuals, but as a people, as a community. Their corporate soul lay violated and in ruins just like their capital city.

So, as the city was physically restored brick by brick, wall by wall, and street by street, their leaders gathered the people together in a solemn assembly. The day began with exactly the kind of invocation, thanksgiving, and worship we have already considered, and then it moved to confession. As the day progressed, their leaders retold their story, beginning with their ancient ancestor Abraham. They recounted the various episodes of their journey as a people, from God's calling of Abraham to his settling in a new homeland, from the first exile and enslavement in Egypt to the Exodus, from wandering in the wilderness to resettling in their homeland. In each episode, God was with them, faithfully helping them survive and thrive. And then came the word "but." God had done so much for them, _but_ they had failed to live as they should. And so they confessed their sins to the Lord (Neh. 9:6–37).

How different is this kind of public acknowledgment from what normally happens in our communities and nations as we recount our past! We typically shrink our faults to invisibility and inflate our virtues to grandiosity in a public orgy of religious supremacy, patriotic nationalism, and corporate denial. But on that day of solemn assembly, it was different. The ancient Hebrews, under Nehemiah's leadership, came clean about their faults and did not indulge in self-defense, self-flattering excuses, or saving of face. Yes, they had a glorious past, _but_ their history also had a darker side. Thankfully, there was a second "but" after the first one, creating a compound syntax that seems perennially essential for public mental and moral health: God blessed them, _but_ they were repeatedly unfaithful, _but_ even then God remained gracious, forgiving, and compassionate to them. The only reason they survived was the compound grace of God that contradicts even their own contradiction of God's original grace. A portion of their corporate confession reads:

> But they and our ancestors acted presumptuously and stiffened their necks and did not obey your commandments; they refused to obey, and were not mindful of the wonders you performed among them; but they stiffened their necks and determined to return to their slavery in Egypt. But you are a God ready to forgive, gracious and merciful, slow to anger and abounding in

*[margin handwritten notes: "Dourette, not Mosaic" and "More Evangelical than monthic."]*

steadfast love, and you did not forsake them. Even when they had cast an image of a calf for themselves and said, "This is your God who brought you up out of Egypt," and had committed great blasphemies. (Neh. 9:16–18)

The symmetrical pattern of infidelity, forgiveness, and new infidelity repeated itself, not just once more, but again and again. But it was bracketed by an even larger symmetry: the people were consistently unfaithful to God, but God was utterly faithful to them. They abandoned God, but God did not abandon them. The people gathered in Jerusalem that day define for us the essence of social confession. They came out of the closet as a people, told their true story, and came clean about their history—the glorious parts and the shameful parts, the grace of God and their own repeated shabby and disgusting betrayal of that grace. There is no sugarcoating here; the document has the feel of business memo or legal brief, seeking to tell the truth, the whole truth, and nothing but the truth. Just as David was honest about himself and his sin, they were honest about themselves and their sin over many generations. This balance is important for us, especially us in the West, where centuries of social and theological individualism have blinded us to many of the realities of social sin, from the historic social sins of our forbears to the contemporary sins of the ecclesial, economic, and political systems in which we are all complicit to some degree.

This blindness (itself a kind of social sin) explains why in many churches in my childhood people could passionately confess certain personal sins (within polite categories)—dishonesty, greed, jealousy, and so on—but remain absolutely oblivious to our racism, anti-Semitism, Islamophobia, environmental irresponsibility, homophobia, nationalism, and denominational pride—not to mention the sins of our ancestors that created the structures of privilege we took for granted. If Nehemiah's contemporaries were leading us in prayer today, imagine the issues and groups they would name in American history: ethnic cleansing of Native peoples and enslavement of kidnapped Africans; discrimination against Irish and Italian Catholic immigrants and Jews; group profiling of Germans, Japanese, and now Latin Americans; McCarthyism; segregation; the death of civilians in Hiroshima and Nagasaki; denial of the vote to women and tolerance for domestic violence; mountaintop removal and climate change; oil spills and toxic waste; corporate plunder; the disproportionate recruiting for military service among the poor; preemptive and elective wars. What would corporate repentance for these kinds of sins feel like? What effects would flow from it?

There is, to be sure, an opposite kind of blindness, where people freely confess social sins of racism, chauvinism, homophobia, and consumerism, but keep their personal sins in the closet—whether it's a cruel way of treating one's spouse, neglect of one's children, drinking too much, sexually harassing subordinates, or whatever. And to be sure, nearly all of us are willing to confess sins in general; after all, who wants to appear so arrogant as to claim perfection? But we hesitate a bit more when things start getting specific socially or personally, when we feel that the real "me" or the real "us" may be brought out of the closet and into the light, exposing us as less holy than we normally try to appear.

Now I'm not a great fan of airing one's dirty laundry in public. I've been in so-called revival meetings where people were pressured or cajoled to a kind of lurid self-exposure that I think was both psychologically damaging and spiritually oppressive in the long run, even if it was cathartic in the moment. I have no desire to hear—or remember—the details of anyone's drunken orgies, private sexual behaviors, or long-standing personal grudges. But I do believe we all need to be completely candid with God in private. And sometimes, whether it's with a trusted priest, spiritual director, sponsor in a recovery program, or a circle of close friends, we need to bring other human beings into our secrecy too. "You're only as sick as your secrets," they say in the world of recovery from addiction.

Sharing our secrets with another human being as well as with God helps us in several ways. First, until I dare to share with you some secret, I am certain that I'm the only person so twisted and crooked and pathetic. But quite often, after I share my secret with you, you will tell me that you have the same problem, that you've made similar mistakes, and in our shared confession we both learn that we truly are not alone. We're all a mess, and honesty, like misery, loves company. Second, when I dare to share and you dare to respond with compassion rather than with judgment and rejection, your mercy and continuing acceptance can make visible for me the good news that previously seemed beyond belief for me. Experiencing mercy and grace from you, someone both present and visible to me, I can believe in mercy and grace from God, who is present but not visible to me. I realize I am in a safe presence, a presence in which I don't need to pretend, because I am accepted by grace just as I am. In your gracious presence, I experience God's gracious presence.

And then, third, comes the great surprise. In an environment of grace—human and divine—I find myself free, free to continue failing if I must, but also free to start doing better if I can. I am no longer expending the energy of broadcasting a false image; I am no longer being drained by the constant anxiety of possibly being exposed for what I really am. That previously wasted energy can now be redirected into actually living a better, fuller life.

This pretense-free environment of grace strikes the coup de grace to our furtive and pretentious patterns of behavior. In it, we are freed from being focused on what we are trying to escape or avoid. Graceless environments say, in essence, "Don't even *think* of the number 13." But inevitably, the harder we try to avoid thinking about the number 13, the more we *do* think about it. So imagine the tense teenage guy, infused with hormones, thinking, "I have to avoid lustful thoughts. I have to avoid thinking of cleavage. I have to avoid thinking of slender legs. I have to avoid . . ." You know exactly where this commuter train of thought will lead the poor guy. But in an environment of grace, avoidance of sin stops being the focus, and other things—generosity, creativity, fun, learning, whatever—can occupy our attention, so we sin less by thinking less about sinning. We can now yield to the good temptation of better things.[2]

Being able to be frank with God and others about our wrongs, failures, sins, faults, and other shameful secrets does justice to the nature of the universe we live in, a place where good things can quickly become perverted or polluted and where evil things can be healed and restored. Through confession, we stop deluding ourselves about being cozy residents of a secure status. In a status mind-set, we say, "I'm a good person." This can be a pretty slippery place to stand, because it can lead us to say, "I am very proud to be a good person," which can then lead us to become proud, which generally means we are no longer such good people. And sadly, we are generally the last to know, because we are still enthusiastically congratulating ourselves—against increasing evidence—on our status as a good person.[3]

Confession replaces a status mind-set with a becoming mind-set, a way of thinking that proves much less susceptible to self-delusion and self-limitation. Tutored in the simple word *sorry,* I remember that, whatever I was yesterday, I could be something different tomorrow, for better or worse. When I habitually confess my secrets and express my regrets to God over things I have done, I am able to cut the umbilical cord between the me who confesses and the me who did the thing I'm confessing. I'm acknowledging that I am already different from that person, because I am not denying what I did, and I am not defending it or excusing it. I'm saying, "I no longer want to be the kind of person who does those things, nor do I want to be the kind of person who covers up doing those things. I want to become a different kind of person."

So let's bring all this down to street level. Someone hurts you. Someone does you wrong. No doubt about it, that person is wrong for doing so.[4] So what do you do? You start holding a grudge. You feel bitter, rehearse their hurt, and nurse your wound. You feel superior. You refuse to forgive. As a result, your inner ecology begins to change; your inner climate warms in some ways and cools in others. And slowly, evil gets its hooks into you; you're becoming a worse person than you were before. Outwardly, everything's okay, and nobody notices. But inwardly, the metal of your character is rusting. The wood of your personality is rotting, and termites are tunneling. Slowly, subtly, your inner being is being weakened.

But then through the regular practice of self-examination and confession you do an internal home inspection. You realize what's happening, and you express regret. What the other person did was indeed hurtful, but your response to the wound has also been unwise; rather than disinfecting the wound, you've been careless and allowed it to become infected. The wound wasn't your fault, but the infection is. The simple word *sorry* opens the way for you to interrupt and reverse the moral decay under way within you.[5]

Just as sin is social as well as personal, so communities need to practice spiritual home inspection just as individuals do. Think of a religion or denomination that becomes preoccupied, as so many do, with
the doctrinal errors in other religions or denominations. Soon they
are congratulating themselves for their purity and correctness. Then
they are going out of their way to attack others whom they judge as
heretics or infidels. They suspect and reject people and wound or ruin
their reputations in the inquisition process. Sometimes, their slander-
ous words lead to cruel and even murderous actions. If you've never
studied the history of religious torture, you should, for it will help you
see that a religious status mind-set can lead to horrific atrocities done
in the name of God. Without the discipline of communal confession,
religions can switch sides as Peter did in the Gospel story (Matt. 16),
speaking through the inspiration of the Holy Spirit one minute and
through an unholy spirit the next, being called a rock one minute and
a stumbling block the next. What's true of religions or denominations is equally true for nations. How often do our nations practice
the self-delusion of exceptionalism rather than self-examination and
confession?

So confession, because it is directed first and foremost toward God,
helps us affirm the truth of our own becoming—helping us become
better and sweeter and humbler, not worse and bitter and more arrogant. And no less important, it also helps us affirm the truth that God is
gracious and compassionate, slow to anger and abounding in love, full
of mercy, faithful and just, forgiving our sin and cleansing us from all
that is wrong with us, eager to lead us from darkness into light.

The power of confession surges in a stunning scene near the end
of the underappreciated film *The Big Kahuna*.[6] Danny DeVito plays a
character named Phil Cooper. He is far from perfect, but he has learned
to acknowledge the truth about himself, keeping intact the vital connection between who he is and who he projects himself to be. Another
character, Bob Walker, is arrogantly and naively religious—perhaps
we would say he borders on de-ligious. Bob sees himself as a righteous
man, free of major flaws and, so, free of regrets. But Phil sees Bob differently; he warns Bob that until he learns the value of regret, he will
always lack true character. Here's their interchange:

PHIL: The question is, do you have any character at all? And if
you want my honest opinion, Bob, you do not. For the simple
reason that you don't regret anything yet.

BOB: Are you saying I won't have any character unless I do
something I regret?

PHIL: No, Bob. I'm saying you've already done plenty of things
to regret. You just don't know what they are. It's when you
discover them. When you see the folly in something you've
done, and you wish you had to do it over. But you know you
can't, because it's too late. So you pick that thing up and you
carry it with you. To remind you that life goes on. The world
will spin without you. You really don't matter in the end.
Then will you attain character. Because honesty will reach
out from inside and tattoo itself all across your face.

I mentioned my friend Carlos earlier. Phil's words help me understand one of the things I respect so much about him. He has regrets,
but he has held them up to the light, and honesty has tattooed itself all
across his face. The simple word *sorry* helps us carry our regret in the
presence of God, where it will not destroy us, but will become an essential nutrient in the growth of true character. Pity the soul who never
learns—or refuses or forgets how—to say *sorry*.

The word *sorry*, I'm aware, can quickly feel used up and cheap.[7] So as
part of my practice of confession, I try to name my wrongs in a single,
simple, specific, direct word: pride, lust, resentment, defensiveness,
unkindness, harshness, bitterness, greed, revenge, passive aggression,
passivity, exaggeration, lie, half-truth, cowardice, avoidance, and so
on. In this way, I've learned to hold open my regret in God's presence,
slowly lifting my wrongs up from the shadows into full exposure, as
it were—not running from them, denying them, minimizing them,
or making excuses about them. I discover two things as I do so. First,
I see why God's presence is described as light, and why God is even
identified with light (1 John 1:5). It is only in the light of truth, honesty,
justice, integrity, holiness, and purity that my wrongs are fully exposed.
But thank God, there is more. The light of God is not only true and just
and holy; it is also infinitely gracious, kind, merciful.[8]

And that's another alternative word that helps me in the practice of confession: _mercy_. If I name my wrong as I exhale, I can hold the word _mercy_ as I inhale. Breathing out regret, breathing in mercy—this is the life-sustaining rhythm of naked spirituality—stripping away my spiritual costume so I can stand before God as I am.

I obviously have a lot to say about confession. Sinner that I am, I can't live a moment without it. The fact that this is one of this book's longest chapters tells you something important about me—as does the fact that the subject of confession will spill over into the next chapter. Do not be impressed if I have spoken eloquently and at length about confession. Just know that I am more like you than you might imagine. Together, let us sinners confess our wrongs to the Lord. *Lord, have mercy.*

_Are all regrets = sins?_

_Hunh? I'm not supposed to believe you are like me?_

# CHAPTER 12

# Help: *Spiritual Jujitsu*

*The Practice of Expansion and Petition:*
*Strengthening Through Weakness*
Alternate Words: *Guidance, Strength, Wisdom, Patience*

The acknowledgment of our weakness is the first step in repairing
our loss.

THOMAS À KEMPIS

I N THE PREVIOUS CHAPTER, we saw how through self-examination
and confession we can sabotage our failures, sins, weaknesses, and
wrongs before they sabotage us. When we confess our sins, we re-
connect with humility and honesty—"truth in the inward being," as
David put it when he confessed his sins (Ps. 51:6). We have lost some
innocence, but have at least gained some humility and honesty—and,
one hopes, some compassion too, since we are now more likely to be
sympathetic to others who blow it in their lives, as we have in our own.
Perhaps humility, honesty, and compassion constitute a kind of second
innocence, an innocence without naiveté, you might say.

The grace of God works on our failures like jujitsu, a weaponless
martial art that turns the force of the attacker back on the attacker. In
so doing, grace connects us with God and others more powerfully than
untested innocence ever could have done. Instead of being connected
to God through performance—"Look how well I am doing!"—confession connects us to God through God's grace—"Look how much I've
been forgiven!" It's hard to imagine a more powerful word than *sorry.*

But *help* comes close. Our next spiritual practice, centered in this simple plea, works with a similar kind of jujitsu. When we call out for help, we are bound more powerfully to God through our needs and weaknesses, our unfulfilled hopes and dreams, and our anxieties and problems than we ever could have been through our joys, successes, and strengths alone. Because this practice involves expanding our resource base beyond our own limited capacities, we can call it *expansion*. Because it involves making a plea to God for help, we can call it *petition* as well. Whatever we call it, *help* represents a move from self-reliance to God-reliance, and that's a step in the right direction.

Now, petition means, in the most general way, prayers addressed to God by me and for me. This may sound selfish, and sometimes it is; there is an immature kind of petition that renders God my personal assistant or fixer or genie, the omnipotent enforcer of my will on earth. This immature petition can become a parody of the Lord's Prayer: "May my will be done in reality as it is in my selfish fantasies." This immature kind of petition is to be expected from immature people, whom we all are in many ways; we want God to adjust and remake the universe for our convenience and benefit. A large percentage of my petitions are of this sort:

> I'm running late, most often due to bad planning on my part, and I petition God for no traffic or a close-in parking space.

> My wife is angry or disappointed with me about something, so I pray that God will change her heart—that way, I won't have to deal with whatever it is in me that's bothering her.

> I'm afraid to confront an interpersonal problem, so I pray that God will solve it for me.

> I've said yes to too many things, so I ask God for extra strength to accomplish all of them.

I'm sure God understands these requests, and I think that some of them are mercifully granted. But I'm also sure that God is not interested in enabling me to stay immature forever by rewarding my bad planning, my insensitivity to my wife, my aversion to conflict, or my inability to set priorities and stick with them. As I mature, I notice that my prayers shift more and more in this direction:

"Lord, I'm running late again, and once again, it's because I thought I could get just two or three extra things done. Please, Lord, help me develop wisdom so that I won't be so prone to tackle too much in too short a time. And when I walk into the meeting late, help me not make any excuses, but take full responsibility for inconveniencing my colleagues."

"Lord, my wife is upset with me. Please help me to understand what's bothering her and to respond with compassion and love. And please help me learn to anticipate and meet her needs rather than frustrate her, as I so often do."

"Lord, I have a problem with Sam. I need to speak frankly with him about it. Please help me to tell the truth and not hold back, but help me to do it cleanly, without bitterness or hurt."

"Lord, once again I've taken on too much. Now I'm exhausted. Help me, Lord, to remember that you are the God who created Sabbath, that you want me to live a life that balances good work with adequate rest. Please liberate me from the fears and insecurities that are like a slave driver, always demanding more of me, never letting me say, 'No, I can't.' Help me to settle into the healthy rhythm that you set for me, for your yoke is easy and your burden is light."

I'm sure you see the difference. Immature petition tries to convince God to remake the world in our image for our convenience and ease, but mature petition asks God to remake us in God's own image, so that we can expand our capacity to respond to the world as it is. Immature petition asks God to give us an easier world with fewer annoying jerks to contend with, and mature petition asks God to help us become stronger, kinder people—and less annoying to our neighbors.[1]

Now someone is probably asking, "Well, if you want to be a stronger, kinder person, why ask God? Why not just buck up and be more independent? Isn't the very act of petition a kind of surrender to weakness?" I'm sure, for some people, that may be the case. But there are at least two problems with this independent approach.

First, what happens when we really are floundering in water over our head? Do we proudly pretend we're stronger than we actually are? Doesn't it make sense to cry out for help? Isn't it better to be humbly dependent and survive than to be proudly independent and drown? And second, what happens when our independence becomes pathological? Couldn't it be that life is engineered to be so hard that we eventually have to admit our powerlessness and ask for help beyond ourselves—help from others, help from God? Could it be that the old Beatles song was right—that it's immature to never need help in any way? Couldn't independence be not the ending point, but an adolescent transition period between childish dependence and mature interdependence? If we succeed in being independent, never needing God's help, couldn't that simply mean that we haven't tried anything very significant or challenging? Could it mean that we've never experienced the miracle of synergy with God, where we find God's strength flowing through us?

Most of the anxiety we face can be reduced to the fear that *life might bring us more than we can handle.* Maybe we'll fail, or if not fail, at least embarrass ourselves on the way to a second-best success. Maybe things we can't control will sneak in and control us. And maybe, as a result, our lives will not have a happy ending.

Sooner or later we need to accept two truths that both the book of Genesis and the theory of evolution teach us: *life isn't supposed to be easy, and struggle can lead to growth.* In Genesis, God creates a universe characterized neither by fully ordered stasis nor complete chaos, but rather by order and chaos in dynamic tension. In that matrix, we experience the stresses of struggle, change, and competition that challenge us to evolve, to grow, to become.

Consider what's missing in the good creation of Genesis 1. The earth is not fully populated; the Creator leaves room for procreation by all creatures. The creatures of earth are <u>not named</u>; God gives human beings the honor of naming things. Animals <u>wait to be domesticated and bred</u> for undiscovered traits. <u>Crops</u> wait to be discovered and planted. Seas, mountains, deserts, glaciers, and forests wait to be <u>explored</u>. Music and city life, dance and technology all wait to be created. The stresses of change, struggle, and competition draw us to <u>seize all of these possibilities and thus develop new strengths</u>. So again and again we are told in scripture, in dozens of different ways, that the hardships life throws at us are not intended by God to destroy us, but to strengthen us.

The apostle Paul says that we <u>celebrate our sufferings</u>, because they produce in us <u>endurance</u>, which in turn produces <u>character</u>, which in turn produces <u>hope</u>, which in turn makes us receptive to the outpouring of <u>God's love in our hearts</u> (Rom. 5:3–5). He says that the <u>weaker we become outwardly, the more we can be renewed inwardly</u>, and that our struggles, which he describes as lightweight and temporary, produce in us a <u>durable glory</u>, which he describes as weighty and eternal (2 Cor. 4:16–18). He calls suffering a privilege (Phil. 1:29) that allows us to have more and more of the "mind that was in Christ Jesus" in us (Phil. 2:5).

The apostle James, as we have seen already, says we should receive trials into our lives with joy, because, again, trials work like a fertilizer for the growth of character (1:2–4). <u>Without trials, we would be morally sterile, lacking qualities</u> like endurance, maturity, and wisdom. A similar process is sketched out by the apostle Peter. In Christ's suffering, Peter says, we find an example for enduring our own (1 Pet. 2:20–21). Without having to survive life's struggles, we would miss a critical chapter in the overarching story of our spiritual development, which he describes as a cumulative process that begins with faith, and then adds goodness, then knowledge, and then self-control, and then continues through endurance—which presupposes trials—and culminates in godliness, mutual affection, and love (2 Pet. 1:5–7).

There are days, of course, when we wish there could be some other system. We wish there could be a way of developing patience without delay, courage without danger, forgiveness without offense, generosity without need, skill without discipline, endurance without fatigue, persistence without obstacles, strength without resistance, virtue without temptation, and strong love without hard-to-love people. But it turns out that there is no other way. The Creator has created the right kind of universe to produce these beautiful qualities in us creatures. And among these beautiful qualities is interdependence—the ability to reach out beyond ourselves, to ask for help from others and from God, and to offer help as we are able. The whole shebang is rigged for mutuality, for vital connection.

The theory of evolution teaches the same lesson. If survival were easy, species wouldn't develop new adaptive features. If survival were stress-free, there wouldn't be 20,000 species of butterflies, 300 species of turtles, or 18,937 species of birds (at last count). In fact, there would be no butterflies, turtles, or birds at all, because it was stress, struggle, challenge, and change that prompted the first living things—slimy blobs in a tide pool somewhere—to diversify, specialize, adapt, and develop into the wonders that surround us and include us now. Seen in this light, evolution isn't a grim theory of "nature red in tooth and claw"; it depicts the planet as a veritable laboratory for innovations in beauty and diversity, fitness and adaptability, complexity and harmony.[2] It renders the earth a studio for the creative development of interdependence in ecosystems or societies of life. Put beauty, diversity, complexity, and harmonious interdependence together and you have something very close to the biblical concepts of "glory" and *shalom*.

So both science and faith tell us that we find ourselves in a universe whose preset conditions challenge us to ongoing growth, development, and connection. The cry for help, I propose, is what keeps us in the game. When we cry out for help, we reach out for resources and capacities we don't yet have. We dare to desire strength sufficient to meet life's challenges, instead of wishing for the challenges to shrink to our current levels of capacity. By crying *help*, we choose expansion rather than contraction, advance rather than retreat.

Clearly, we could make the opposite choice, to contract and opt out of our challenges entirely. If the challenges were to get too great for our taste, we could roll over and die—quickly through suicide or more gradually through addiction, despair, capitulation, or escape. We could refuse to develop the virtues that life's challenges evoke

This, I finally agree with

Good what would they feel? co. full claim.

Brian Not me! feminist never encountered theologians?

from us and instead choose vice as our coping strategy. If the test is hard, we could cheat instead of study. If the truth is unpopular, we could cover it up or twist it rather than tell it straight. If a colleague is unkind or incompetent, we could hate and reject instead of forgiving and understanding. If our neighbor is ignorant, we could mock instead of gently instructing. If a nation is different from and noncompliant with our nation's wishes, we could dominate or exterminate rather than negotiate and reconcile. If a vow becomes inconvenient, we could break it rather than keep it. If there are those who stand in the way of our ambition, we could crush rather than respect them. If there are those who oppose us, we could run and hide rather than stand and face them with courage.

We can and often do choose the shabbier of these options. But even when we degenerate instead of evolve, even when our hearts have contracted into an angry, ugly little fist, even then it's not too late. We can still have a change of heart. We can feel, from our place of contraction, a higher call to a better, more expansive way of life. Through confession (*sorry*) we can reverse our current trajectory, and then through petition (*help*) we can expand and grow again. Through that single simple word, we can partner with God to turn each challenge into an opportunity for growth.

We see this growth in the life of Jesus.[3] Shortly before his arrest, he is at the most stressful moment of his life to date, and he knows that one fork in the road will take him to even greater agony: torture, mockery, rejection, crucifixion, and death. So he goes to a garden—evocative because it recalls the story of Eden, the scene of the original crime in which humanity contracted rather than expanded. There Jesus cries out in petition: "Father, if you are willing, remove this cup from me; yet, not my will but yours be done" (Luke 22:42).

Simple words, a simple petition, but unfathomably deep: "I don't want to drink this cup of poison. I don't want to throw myself into a raging current that will dash me upon the rocks of human ignorance, hatred, cruelty, and violence. I don't want my thirty-three years of life and my three years of ministry to end like this—sweat, whips, bruises, welts, tearing tendons, labored breathing, and my blood dripping down onto the stones. But if doing so will unleash new possibilities for good, possibilities that you, God, desire to be unleashed in the world, then I will drink the cup and expand to meet the challenge."

Was Jesus's prayer answered? No and yes. The first half wasn't. God did not adjust the world to make Jesus's life more comfortable. But the second half was. God's will was done, and the consequences of Jesus's surrender to God's will that night continue to spread across time and space like ripples across a pond. Jesus did not receive a reprieve, a pass, a "get out of suffering free" card. Nor did he take the path of independence, shutting God out and choosing his own will instead. No, in weakness, in vulnerability, from the edge of the abyss, he reached out to God for help. And he received the strength to go forward and drink the cup of suffering. This is petition in its most mature and majestic form.

Was Jesus in error to start his prayer with a request for the cup to pass from him? Would it have been better for him only to surrender to God's will? I don't think so, and here's why.

The great commandment, articulated most famously by Jesus, but also celebrated in Judaism, Islam, Buddhism, and other traditions, calls us to love our neighbor as ourselves. The command presupposes a right and healthy way of loving ourselves. Petition is essential to this wise and healthy practice of love for oneself. Jesus's plea for the cup to pass was an expression of that healthy love for oneself. If Jesus had stopped there, yes, he would have fallen short. But he didn't. His prayer beautifully integrated love for himself ("May this cup pass from me") and love for God and others ("May your will be done").

This integration isn't as easy as it might at first appear. Many years ago, I had a spiritual epiphany one morning that showed me how far away I was from a proper love for myself. I was jogging—something I do not for the love of exercise, but to avoid putting on weight. Whenever I jog, my muscles and lungs nag me constantly. They say, "Okay, that's enough of this. You've proven your point. Let's just walk now. In fact, let's go over to Dunkin' Donuts and buy a couple of chocolate crème–filled donuts to reward you for your good behavior." Not very helpful self-talk!

The best way to distract myself from the chattering voices of my muscles and lungs was to listen to recorded lectures and sermons on my Walkman (an old device you can probably still see in a museum somewhere). Anyway, I was running and listening to a lecture, and the speaker quoted Abraham Lincoln, who said these words:

> I desire to so conduct the affairs of this administration that if, at the end, . . . I have lost every friend on earth, I shall have one friend left, and that friend shall be down inside me.

As I heard those words, it was as if the Spirit took them and pierced me to the core with them. Out of that deepest part of me, I felt a sob erupt. I had to stop running for a few minutes and found myself hunched over in the middle of the trail, feeling that in some mysterious way God was speaking to me and it was a matter of life and death that I listen. And the message that came to me was the realization that, deep down inside of me, I had an enemy, not a friend.

If a friend made a mistake, I would tell him it was okay, that nobody's perfect. But when I made a mistake, I would constantly beat myself up and mercilessly take myself to task. If a friend was working too hard, I would tell him to relax, to take a day off and go fishing or play a round of golf. But down inside me was a cruel taskmaster who was never satisfied. If a friend had some weaknesses, I would be gracious and compassionate. But not so with myself. And so that day I felt the Spirit using a quote from Abraham Lincoln (taken completely out of context) to tell me that if I was going to last, I actually needed to follow Jesus's words about loving others as myself, which required me to first be a friend to myself.

Some time later, I came across a quote from St. Bernard of Clairvaux, who talked about the three stages of love. In the first stage, we love God for our own sake, for what God can do for us. In the second stage, we love God for God's own sake, for who God is in God's own character and glory and beauty. It's hard to imagine anything better than that, but Bernard said in the third stage, we love ourselves for God's sake. We join with God in seeing ourselves in a gracious and compassionate light.

This is what petition is for. Through the practice of petition, you learn to stand with God and see yourself as needy, weak, limited, imperfect, edgy, stressed, driven, frightened, or troubled. But you don't criticize, condemn, chide, or reject yourself. Rather, you join God in God's desire for your own expansion and well-being. You join God in wanting the best for you, and in that light you make your request for your friend, yourself.

## CHAPTER 13

# Help: *Tapping into the Current of Power*

Prayer is what the brain does or wants to do to transcend the boundaries of the self, to sense a connection with what lies beyond the praying self.

KEN WILSON[1]

OVER A DECADE AGO, millions of people bought and read a book that made a bold promise about the value of petition. *The Prayer of Jabez: Breaking Through to the Blessed Life* began like this: "Dear Reader, I want to teach you how to pray a daring prayer that God always answers."[2] Along with bringing in millions of dollars in sales, the book stirred up a lot of controversy. It panders, some said, to the name-it-and-claim-it kind of petition often associated with the "prosperity gospel," a kind of get-rich-quick approach to petition that maintains that the only thing keeping poor people poor and sick people sick is their own failure to pray the right formulas with sufficient faith. It reduces God to a kind of genie, some said, forced to do our will by our clever mastery of a magic formula. No, others said, the book is simply a celebration of petition.

The book focuses on a marginal character mentioned in passing in a hard-to-translate passage (1 Chron. 4:7–10). The NRSV renders it like this:

The sons of Helah: Zereth, Izhar, and Ethnan. Koz became the father of Anub, Zobebah, and of the families of Aharhel son of Harum. Jabez was honored more than his brothers; and his

mother named him Jabez, saying, "Because I bore him in pain."
Jabez called on the God of Israel, saying, "Oh that you would
bless me and enlarge my border, and that your hand might be
with me, and keep me from hurt and harm!" And God granted
what he asked.

In this case, I think the NKJV has a better—or at least more interesting—translation of the last verse of the passage; it's the one used in
the book:

> And Jabez called on the God of Israel saying, "Oh, that You
> would bless me indeed, and enlarge my territory, that Your hand
> would be with me, and that You would keep me from evil, that I
> may not cause pain!" So God granted him what he requested.

The plot of this mininarrative seems to focus on Jabez's identity. He
is honored even though his mother dishonored him with a name meaning "pain." (We might imagine a mother today naming her child Headache, Nausea, or Cramps.) Cursed with this unflattering name—and,
we might imagine, not particularly blessed to have a mother who would
name her child in this way—Jabez doesn't want to become a victim of
the situation into which he was born. So he asks God to overcome the
misfortune of his name.

I don't take this as a selfish prayer. I take this as a liberating petition:
"Liberate me, God, from the way I have been labeled by my mother.
Liberate me to enjoy life in its fullness." As is often the case in Hebrew
literature, the basic prayer is rendered twice, in parallel form. First, it is
rendered in the positive: "Bless me, enlarge my landholdings, let your
hand be with me." And then it is rendered in the negative: "Keep me
from evil, that I may not cause pain." And this last line, I think, is the
key to the whole prayer.

Jabez seems to be saying, "I caused my mother pain at birth. She
named me Pain in response. And that name has hurt me. But I don't
want to keep the chain reaction going. I don't want to pay the pain forward and do to others what was done to me. So, God, please bless me,
enlarge my borders, and let your hand be with me, so that I can stop

the cycle of pain. Bless me so that I may be a blessing to others rather than a source of pain to them."

Seen in this way, Jabez is echoing the primal calling of Abraham and of all people of true faith, recorded in Genesis 12. God says to Abraham, "I will make of you a great nation, and I will bless you, and make your name great." But that's not all. Interwoven with these promises of blessing to Abraham and his descendants are these extended promises: "You will be a blessing. . . . In you all the families of the earth shall be blessed" (vv. 2–3).

So in petition, like Jabez, we expand beyond selfishness to otherliness, beyond pain to blessing: "Bless me, not just so I can be blessed, but more, so I can be a blessing to others. Heal me, not just so I can be healed, but more, so I can be a healer for others. Provide for me, not just so that I can be comfortable, but more, so that I can provide for others and bring comfort to them too. Bless me and keep me from harm, so that I will not cause pain to others, but will instead be a source of joy for them."

With this expanded understanding of petition, <u>I'm not at all discouraging you from asking God for blessings for yourself.</u> I'm encouraging you to do so. In fact, I would say that you have a moral responsibility to do so. Why? Because if you don't, you'll become anxious and preoccupied with your needs and wants. If you feel that all your happiness and safety depends on you, you will be increasingly self-focused. More and more of your energies will curve inward as you become increasingly self-absorbed. The story of your life will shrink to "me worrying about me for my sake." But by practicing petition, by referring your anxieties to God through the simple prayer *help,* your life story will expand to "me trusting God to take care of me, so I can focus on others for God's sake."

In that light, it's clear why both Jesus and Paul saw anxiety as such a destructive force (see Matt. 6:25–34; Phil. 4:4–9). <u>Anxiety is the black hole that sucks everything into itself.</u> So, both Jesus and Paul say, "Don't be anxious." Paul continues, "By prayer and petition, translate your anxieties into requests to God. And what will God do? Remake the world according to your desires? No. But God will change you, because you will be invaded—not by what you fear, but by the peace of God, a peace that soars above all comprehension. This peace will be like a border guard securing your hearts and minds, keeping your thoughts in the mature mind-set of Jesus, the liberating king" (paraphrase of Phil. 4:6–7, echoing 2:5).

There's a powerful secret in these words. The very act of translating anxieties into requests serves to disempower our anxieties and empower us. To put it simply, through petition we *reframe the situation* and *rename our need.*

How do we reframe the situation? Anxiety tempts us to catastrophize, to inflate every risk into a potential cataclysm. Soon, surrounded by possible catastrophes on all sides, we shrink into the primitive mind. We sink into reptilian scripts that limit our options to three: fight, flee, or freeze.[3] Through petition, we reframe our anxieties into opportunities for growth, calling to mind the joint lesson of Genesis and the theory of evolution from the previous chapter.

This reframing enables us to rename our need. For example, the reptilian brain might shout that we need to fight: "I must vanquish all who oppose or threaten me!" But we can instead request *compassion* to understand our antagonists, *mercy* to forgive them, *wisdom* to communicate with them, and *determination* to work toward reconciliation with them. The reptilian brain might scream that we need to flee: "This situation is stressful! I need to get out of here!" But we can instead request *patience* to endure the situation, *insight* into why we are so reactive, and *creativity* to transform our response into something more productive. The reptilian brain might whisper that we need to freeze: "Somebody is mad at me. I'd better keep my head down, lay low, and stay out of sight." But we can instead request the *courage* to stand tall, the *humility* to accept being misunderstood, and the *resilience* to get back up again after being knocked down.

Anxieties can gray the whole sky like cloud cover or descend on our whole horizon like fog. When we rename our anxieties, in a sense we distill them into requests. What covered the whole sky can now be contained in a couple of buckets. So when we're suffering from anxiety, we can begin by simply holding the word *help* before God, letting that one word bring focus to the chaos of our racing thoughts. Once we feel that our mind has dropped out of the frantic zone and into a spirit of connection with God, we can let the general word *help* go and in its place hold more specific words that name what we need, thereby condensing the cloud of vague anxiety into a bucket of substantial request. So we might hold the word *guidance* before God. Or *patience*. Or *courage*. Or *resilience*. Or *boundaries, mercy, compassion, determination, healing, calm, freedom, wisdom,* or *peace*.

For me, the fog of anxiety sometimes grows so thick that I can hardly concentrate enough to go through this reframing and renaming process. That's one of many reasons I often find it helpful to write my prayers.[4] The act of writing helps me concentrate, so I don't drift from the road of petition back onto the shoulder of worry or over into the ditch of catastrophizing.

When I write my petitions, I often find it helpful to separate them into minor and major leagues.[5] Sometimes, I'm so preoccupied with little things that I miss the big things, and sometimes, it's the reverse. So I often write at the top of a page in my journal (or type at the top of a page on my laptop) "LITTLE THINGS." Then I list every little frustration or problem that comes to mind, leaving some space between each one. Then, I go back to each item and write a prayer starting with the word *help*. My page might look like this:

Meeting with my boss: "Help me, Lord, to focus on his feelings and not react, whatever he says. Help me draw out his concerns and practice active listening."

Finances: "Help me, Lord, to put that money I wasted on that lawn maintenance service behind me, and help me make some good decisions about decreasing our monthly expenses. Especially help me be firm when I call the cable company and reduce that bill."

Weight: "Help me, Lord, to get back on track with my diet. Help me throw out that bag of chips, even though it's only half empty. I don't need the rest of it!"

Car: "Help me, Lord, to stop worrying about that funny sound in the rear tires. Help me make the call today to schedule getting the brakes checked."

Once I've cleared away the little frustrations and anxieties that are nagging at me, on another page I write "BIG THINGS." On this page, I try to get to some of the broader and deeper issues that are causing me stress. My page might begin like this:

Schedule/priorities: "Help me, Lord, to be less driven by the need to say yes to every request that comes my way. Help me be a good manager of myself; I would never keep piling more and more duties on an employee, but this is exactly what I do to myself. Help me get to the root of why I keep doing this. Is it the fear of disappointing other people? Is it a need to be liked or a fear of being criticized if I say no? Help me, Lord, to stop being a slave to the opinions of me held by other people, and help me to discern and live by wise priorities instead."

Office: "Help me, Lord, to understand and respond to the tense feeling in my office these days. Help me not blame my boss or co-workers, and help me not slip into the 'fix it' mode without first getting to the real issues. It feels as if we go in cycles, and here we are again. Help me . . ."

Resentment: "Lord, I notice a growing resentment in my heart toward Bernard. I realize I'm still feeling wounded by what I was told that he said about me last week. I feel betrayed. Help me to see him as a critical friend, not an enemy."

Anxiety isn't the only struggle that drives us to petition. We also need to practice petition when we're hurt or wounded by others. In a way, this is the flip side of confession. Confession deals with the times we do wrong to others, but hurt-related petition deals with the times others do wrong to us. I've noticed that many churches have a prayer of confession each week, but I have never (yet) heard a regular prayer of woundedness in a church, a prayer by which we acknowledge and process the pain of being hurt, insulted, taken for granted, presumed upon, inconvenienced, betrayed, or otherwise mistreated by other people. Since being wounded or sinned against is a terribly common experience, I suspect we need to pay more attention to it. In fact, being wronged is directly linked in the Lord's Prayer to the reality of doing wrong; we pray, "forgive us our sins *as we forgive those who sin against us.*"

Fr. Richard Rohr says it well: *Pain that isn't processed is passed on. Pain that isn't transformed is transmitted.* So we need to process our woundedness with God, and that processing begins by naming the pain and holding it—as we've been holding each of our simple words—in God's presence:

**Betrayed. Insulted. Taken advantage of. Lied to. Forgotten. Used. Abused. Belittled. Passed over. Cheated. Mocked. Snubbed. Robbed. Vandalized. Misunderstood. Misinterpreted. Excluded. Disrespected. Ripped off. Confused. Misled.**

It's important not to rush this process. We need to feel our feelings, to let the pain actually catch up with us, to drop out of the rat race of suppressing or denying being hurt. I've found that it takes less energy to feel and process my pain than it does to suppress it or run away from it. So, just as through confession we name our own wrongs and feel regret, through petition we name and feel the pain that results from the wrongs of others. And just as we rename our anxieties as requests to God, we translate our pain into requests:

*[handwritten note: And the anger please]*

**Comfort. Encouragement. Reassurance. Companionship. Vindication. Appreciation. Boundaries. Acknowledgment.**

*[handwritten note: Really? Please - don't get there too quickly!]*

It's important to note that we are not naming what we need the *person who wronged us* to do for us. If we focus on what we wish the antagonist would do to make us feel better, we unintentionally arm the antagonist with still more power to hurt us. Instead, in this naming, we are turning from the antagonist to God, focusing on what we need God to do for us. We're opening our soul to receive healing from God's ever present, ever generous Spirit.

Along with anxieties and hurts, we also bring our disappointments to God. If anxieties focus on what *might happen,* and hurts focus on what *has happened,* disappointments focus on what *has not happened.* Again, as the saying goes, revealing your feeling is the beginning of healing, so simply acknowledging or naming our disappointment to God is an important move. This is especially important because many of us, if we don't bring our disappointment to God, will blame our disappointment on God, thus alienating ourselves from our best hope of comfort and strength. Again, if we condense the cloud of disappointment into a name and a request, we take a step forward in maturity and faith:

> "I didn't get that job, and I was really hoping for it. Now I'm *crushed* with *disappointment*. But I'm not giving up. I'm still trusting in you, God. Something else will come my way in time. Help me persevere."

> "I had hoped this was the relationship that would lead to marriage. But now we've broken up, and I feel *heartbroken* and *deflated*. I bring my pain to you, God. Help me heal."

> "I was hoping this treatment would kill the tumor, or at least shrink it. But the reports say otherwise, and I'm deep in a pit of *despair*. Help me accept this *shattering blow,* Lord, and not be wiped out by it."

Whether we're dealing with anxieties, wounds, disappointments, or other needs or struggles, there is enormous power in simple, strong words—the words by which we name our pain and then translate it into a request to God. *Help* is the door into this vital practice of petition, through which we expand beyond our own capacities and resources to God's.

Sometimes we experience dramatic answers to our prayers for help. I think of one of the worst days of my life, when I was visiting the girl I loved and to whom I was engaged. When she told me she wasn't sure about our relationship and wanted to break the engagement, I was so brokenhearted that I simply walked out of her house. With nowhere to go, I walked the streets of her city, knowing nobody, feeling utterly alone and dejected. I could muster little more—to be honest—than a string of curse words, not cursing her, but cursing my terrible situation. But sandwiched between my muttered profanities, I also managed to send up the simple word *help,* hoping Somebody would hear.

After walking for what seemed like hours, and having left my watch at my ex-fiancée's home, I asked a man doing yard work if he knew what time it was. After telling me, he then asked, "Are you okay? Do you need to talk?" When I fumbled for the right words, he said, "When I saw you walking along the sidewalk, I felt like God was telling me you needed a friend." And so a few minutes later, I was sitting at his kitchen table having a cup of coffee, pouring out my heart to a perfect stranger. I felt—and still feel—that God had directed me to him, just as I have felt on other occasions that I have been the stranger to whom a person in need has been directed. I was still heartbroken, but the kindness of a stranger told me that I wasn't as utterly alone as I had felt a few minutes before. I felt as the psalmist did: "This poor soul cried, and was heard by the LORD, and saved from every trouble" (34:6, NRSV). (And yes, eventually Grace and I did get our problems worked out, and after thirty-one years of marriage I think it's going to last.)

Other times, it's much harder to know whether our cry for help has been heard at all, as things go from bad to worse to even worse to worse still. But imagine if, instead of naming our anxieties, needs, wounds, and disappointments, and turning them into requests to God, we let other forces take control of our inner world: self-protection instead of guidance, revenge instead of patience, panic instead of courage, retreat instead of resilience, placating instead of setting boundaries, self-hatred instead of mercy, blame instead of compassion, fantasy instead of determination, despair instead of healing, bitterness instead of peace, resignation instead of resilience. Imagine the change in our inner ecology after ten minutes, or ten days, or ten years of living without the expanding influence of petition. Where would we be, and who would we be, if we couldn't turn outside ourselves, direct our needs to the living God, and cry *help*?

Through this practice of expansion and petition, we discover something priceless: the <u>sacred connection can grow stronger through</u>, not in spite of, our <u>anxieties, wounds, disappointments, struggles, and n</u>eeds. *[handwritten: AND thru our strengths]* The Compassionate One is our gracious friend, and we don't have to earn anything, deserve anything, achieve anything, or merit anything to bring our needs to God. We can come just as we are. If it takes our weaknesses and disappointments to teach us this truth, then may our weaknesses and disappointments be blessed, just as the apostle Paul said:

If I must boast, I will boast of the things that show my
weakness. . . . [The Lord] said to me, "My grace is sufficient for
you, for power is made perfect in weakness." So I will boast all
the more gladly of my weaknesses, so that the power of Christ
may dwell in me. Therefore, I am content with weaknesses,
insults, hardships, persecutions, and calamities for the sake of
Christ; for whenever I am weak, then I am strong. (2 Cor. 11:30;
12:9–10)

So, now it's time to put this book aside again, perhaps take out a
piece of paper or open up a new page on your computer, and condense
your anxieties into a list of little requests and big requests. It's your opportunity to scan your soul for wounds, worries, and weaknesses. It's
your opportunity to ask God for help in transforming your pain, so
you don't transmit it. It's your opportunity to stand with God and see
yourself from the vantage point of a friend, speaking kindly and compassionately to God on your behalf. You are loved, so you deserve this
opportunity. You really do.

# CHAPTER 14

# Please: *At Least Two Hearts Care*

*The Practice of Compassion and Intercession:*
*Strengthening Through Empathy*
Alternate Words: *Mercy, Bless, Peace, Grace*

Our prayer is public and for all, and when we pray, we pray not
for a single person, but for the whole people, because we are all
one. The God of peace, the teacher of harmony, who taught us
unity, willed that each should pray for all, according as he carried
us all in himself alone.

ST. CYPRIAN[1]

As you know from my story about being tracked down in the
woods of Pennsylvania, one of our children is a cancer survivor. About
midway through Trevor's three-plus years of daily chemotherapy, I was
standing in the kitchen one afternoon, sorting through mail. I came to
the monthly newsletter from a support group for parents of kids with
cancer, and something happened to me as I read through it.

First, tears began streaming down my face, and soon I was so overcome by emotion that I found myself bent over the kitchen counter,
head in hands, tears now running down my forearms. But I wasn't
exactly sure why. They weren't simply tears of grief for our still pre-
carious situation that moved me that afternoon. No, by then the actual
and potential losses that go along with a cancer diagnosis had become
the new normal for us, part of our daily routine. It was something else,

something I had seldom felt at such a profound level: a rising feeling of connection with every other family with a sick child.

After months of having to hold our son while he received painful spinal infusions or bone marrow aspirations, after months of having to live with the daily danger of relapse and never knowing if we would end the day at home or in the hospital, after months of fatigue bordering on exhaustion, my heart was strangely warmed, enlarged, and invigorated with empathy and compassion. My broken heart was becoming a broken-open heart.[2]

So far, we have considered the role of five simple words in the spiritual life. First we considered three words of Simplicity: *here, thanks,* and *O* (spiritual practices through which we present ourselves to the Presence, thank God for life's innumerable gifts, and joyfully celebrate God's unfathomable wonder and goodness). Then we turned to words of Complexity, words that grapple with life's difficulties. We reflected on *sorry,* the vital connection of confession, the practice that sabotages our failures by drawing us beyond denial or despair to honesty, humility, and grace. Then we turned to *help,* the prayer that uses our own weaknesses and needs to strengthen the vital connection. Now we move beyond our weaknesses and needs to those of others, from *help* to *please.* The traditional name for this spiritual practice is *intercession,* a word whose Latin roots suggest "going between" ("inter," meaning "between," and "cede," meaning "go," as in "proceed" or "exceed"). Through intercession, we offer ourselves as a bridge between the needs of others and the love and comfort of God.

Wisdom, in whatever small ways I've experienced it, has involved learning the advantages of disadvantages and the reverse as well. As I learned that afternoon in my kitchen, when we experience the downside of pain and struggle, we can also experience the unexpected upside of increased compassion for others. It doesn't always work this way, of course; sometimes our pain overwhelms us, and we plunge into the vortex of inwardness. But if we experience some degree of sacred comfort in our own pain, we eventually find ourselves empowered to turn outward in sacred compassion toward others.[3]

When we practice *compassion* through simple words of intercession, we affirm two profound truths. First, that God cares for all who suffer and are in need, and second, that we care too. If we didn't believe God cared, we wouldn't turn to God, nor would we do so if we ourselves didn't care. When we call out *please* on behalf of someone else, we build a bridge between our compassion and the compassion of God. We say to God and ourselves, "Someone is suffering, and at least two hearts in the universe notice and refuse to turn away—God's heart and my own."

The simple intercession we utter to God on behalf of someone in pain or need—*please*—is required equipment in a complex world where all is not as it should be. Those in pain need to receive our compassion, of course, but no less do we need to extend it. To understand why, try this thought experiment. You are watching the news on TV or reading the news in print or online. You learn about another war in another troubled corner in the world, or maybe it's another ecological disaster or outbreak of bigotry, or another famine or epidemic of a terrible disease, or another species threatened with extinction. Hearing this news about your fellow creatures in some terrible predicament means that you now are also in a predicament of your own. Consider your options.

You could just change the channel or click over to a new site—there must be a game show or sitcom or something that will not be so disturbing. But what kind of person are you becoming if you routinely practice the avoidance of pain and habitually choose ignorance about the suffering of your fellow creatures?

You could keep watching and gradually become overwhelmed by all the evil and suffering in the world, slipping deeper and deeper into depression, cynicism, paralysis, and despair. If that's the case, haven't you become another casualty added to the catastrophes you have seen? Haven't you been sucked into the problem instead of becoming part of the solution to it?

You could become so accustomed to tragedies and atrocities that they no longer bother you. You could call that lack of concern realism. But wouldn't that mean that you have also become less compassionate, maybe even less humane and human?

You could find someone to blame for the suffering and feel, instead of compassion, fury and self-righteousness as you identify the villains behind the victims. But is a blaming, furious, self-righteous version of yourself a step upward?

You could rage at God for allowing these things to happen or maybe even decide to stop believing in God. But does that increase the likelihood that you will sustain sufficient faith, hope, and love to get involved in a constructive way?

Clearly, then, the suffering of others invariably puts each of us in a predicament of our own, a moment of choice. Will we, in our chosen response to the suffering of others, become more calloused, uncaring, embittered, or overwhelmed? Or will we strengthen the sacred connection with God and others, feeling compassion and desiring relief for our fellow creatures in pain? This choice screams out the reason compassion matters so much in the spiritual life. If we don't strengthen the vital connection of compassion, we will slide toward the tragic disconnections of apathy, self-distancing, and despair.

In confession, we courageously face the painful truth about our moral faults and failures and those of our nation, party, religion, tribe, or family. In petition, we courageously face the painful truth about our weaknesses, wounds, and worries. Through the practice of compassion or intercession, we courageously face the pain in the world. Through the simple word *please*—or related words like *mercy, bless, peace,* or *grace*—we choose connection over disconnection, compassion over apathy, commitment and expansion over constriction and contraction.

This choice helps explain why we are in some sense better off *not* having satisfying answers to vexing intellectual questions about why suffering, evil, and pain exist in the world (the technical word for attempted answers to these questions is *theodicy*). If we can say, "Oh, there's a clear reason for this," we can remain aloof, safe in the cool and lofty realm of impersonal logic in relation to human suffering. We can explain instead of empathize, theorize instead of pray, and answer instead of act. But in the absence of a satisfying logical explanation for human suffering, we must descend from our brains into our hearts and respond to the suffering of others with tears and action, not just words and more words.

So, we practice compassion and intercession not because we have fully satisfying answers to explain the suffering of others, but because we don't. The practice of compassion or intercession, in this light, is not just a response to the agony of another in pain; it is also the response to our own agony of not having answers about why anybody is in pain. It is a way of saying, "For a fellow creature to be in pain and without help in God's universe is simply unacceptable to both God and me. So I will go in between the two. I will grasp the hand of God with one hand and grasp the hand of my neighbor in pain with the other. I will join God in willing comfort, blessing, peace, and grace for my sister or brother in need."

Now, the word "compassion" has come up for us again and again. I think if you asked most people these days, "What is the religion of compassion?" their first answer would be Buddhism, because the *dharma* (teaching) of Siddhartha Gautama truly does emphasize compassion in an exemplary way. Meanwhile, many other religious communities—especially monotheistic ones—have been putting their least compassionate feet forward lately, distinguishing themselves as religions of stridency and violence rather than of compassion. That's why I believe all of us must help convert our religions toward compassion, following the good example of the best Buddhists.[4]

To Muslims, for example, one of the most revered ways to refer to God is as "The Compassionate, the Merciful." Similarly, Judaism associates compassion with God's deepest identity by linking it with God's name: "The LORD, the LORD, a God merciful and gracious, slow to anger, and abounding in steadfast love and faithfulness . . ." (Exod. 34:6). And for Christians, Jesus was undoubtedly a man of compassion. Compassion is, again and again in the Gospel narratives, the way Jesus sees (see, e.g., Matt. 9:36; 14:14; 15:32; Mark 6:34). When he looks over a crowd of people, he doesn't see a "damned crowd that doesn't know the law," as some of the religious leaders do (see John 7:49); he sees people who are "harassed and helpless, like sheep without a shepherd" (Matt. 9:36). He looks at a woman caught in adultery and sees not someone to be executed by her "righteous" accusers, but rather someone to be forgiven and given another chance (John 8:1–11). He sees that woman at the well with compassion, not condemning her for her long string of lovers, but offering her a taste of living water (John 4:7–30).

When a woman with a notorious reputation crashes a dinner party being held in his honor and makes a potentially embarrassing scene, he sees her not with revulsion, but with compassion (Luke 7:36–50). When he sees a physically short, socially unpopular enemy collaborator named Zacchaeus perched in a tree, he doesn't see him as a bother, but as a brother (Luke 19:2–10). When he sees a gaggle of kids looking for hugs, when he sees a blind beggar or group of despised lepers calling out beside the road, when he sees a widow who has recently lost her son to an early death, even when he sees the Roman soldiers gathered around the foot of his cross casting dice for the robe they have stripped from him, he sees with compassion (Mark 10:13–16; 10:46–52; Luke 7:12–15; 17:11–14; 23:34–35).

And if the apostles are to be believed, and I believe they are, when people saw this compassion in the eyes of Jesus, they somehow knew that God was compassionate in the same way. In word and by example, Jesus taught that *God's perfection is a compassionate perfection.* Compassion is inherent in all God is and does, extending even to people deemed antagonistic, ungrateful, and evil (cf. Matt. 5:43–48; Luke 6:32–36).

Even the way Jesus died revealed to them the degree to which God joined them in their suffering. The political "powers that be" claimed—as they almost always do—to represent God or the gods, embodying the divine bias for law and order. But in their brutal treatment of Jesus, the powers that be overreached. The cross, intended to expose its victims as weak and defeated by the superior power of the state, ended up exposing the state itself. The cross exposed Caesar and his system as brutal and heartless, quick to judge, condemn, and resort to violence to keep the oppressed in line. So in his suffering and dying Jesus embodied for his followers God's solidarity with the crucified, not the crucifiers, with the downtrodden, not the oppressors, with the meek, not the mean.[5]

And the leaders of the religious establishment were exposed just as the political leaders were. They didn't have a monopoly on God as they pretended to do. In the end, their moral bankruptcy was exposed when they rejected the leadership of Jesus and affirmed the ways of Caesar (see John 19:15). So through Jesus's life, sufferings, death, and resurrection, the early disciples came to believe that God does not stand aloof to condemn us for our weaknesses and wrongs, but rather that God compassionately enters and shares our pain and shame, taking even our failures up into God's own life, where our evil is overcome by God's goodness, our ugliness is overwhelmed by God's beauty, and our sickness and toxicity are overwhelmed by God's vitality.

Reading that newsletter in my kitchen that afternoon, and many times before and since, I've felt that I was rubbing up against the deep, deep current of compassion that flows from God's heart throughout creation. Like a nail rubbing against a magnet, I think each exposure has been changing me. Because my transformation is so far from complete, and because the needs around me are so great, I am eager to strengthen this vital connection.

# CHAPTER 15

# Please: *Bearing the Stretcher*

At its best, my prayer does not seek to manipulate God into doing my will—quite the opposite. Prayer enters the pool of God's own love and widens outward.

PHILIP YANCEY[1]

I WAS IN CAPERNAUM RECENTLY. It's a beautiful little town on the northwest shore of Lake Galilee in Israel. As I sat by the shore and watched the sun glisten on the water, as I listened to the waves lapping against smooth shoreline stones, I felt myself transported back in time to the days when this was Jesus's hometown. I could picture him looking out over the water just as I was, watching fishing boats rock on the waves, seeing a storm cross the mountains beyond the lake to the east. I could imagine him observing sheep and wildflowers on nearby hills, or listening to crows and sparrows in the scrubby bushes and trees scattered around. And I could picture one dramatic day when a large crowd gathered in a home not far from the shore to hear him teach. As Mark tells the story (2:1–12), the crowd filled the available space inside and spilled out the open door into the street.

There was a man in Capernaum who had been paralyzed, and whether he persuaded his four friends to do so or they thought of the idea, they carried him on a stretcher toward the house, hoping Jesus would heal him. But the crowd was impenetrable, and there was no way in. What could they do? I imagined one of them coming up with a crazy proposal. Climb up on the roof—whether it was thatched or tile, I don't know—and open up a hole through which they could lower the man on his stretcher so that he would bypass the crowd and land right smack in front of Jesus. It was a crazy scheme, but bold, and it just might work. There were no other options, so they gave it a try.

And when they did, Mark says that Jesus was impressed by their faith—not just the faith of the paralyzed man, but that of his friends as well. And so Jesus pronounced forgiveness and healing on the man, and *their* faith—which had already opened a hole in the roof—opened new possibilities for the man. He walked out, Mark says, carrying the stretcher on which he had been carried. I can only imagine how the awestruck crowd parted to make room for him to leave in a way they hadn't been willing to do when he arrived.

Those four friends, I think, dramatize our sixth simple word, *please,* and the spiritual practice of intercession to which it points. They literally carried their paralyzed friend; they let the weight of his condition become their burden to bear, and let his problem create problems for them. In a sense, his paralysis became their paralysis, and their ability to move became his ability to move. Whether or not the man had faith, they did, and as a result a miracle happened. When we practice compassionate intercession, we become the stretcher bearers for others in need. Whether or not they have faith and hope, we put our faith and hope to work on their behalf.

There is a Christian doctrine that is intended, I think, to embed this reality in the heart, but too often it remains only an item of doctrinal controversy: the priesthood of all believers. The doctrine was originally articulated as part of a Protestant critique of Catholicism. It affirmed that every Christian was free to approach God without a priest serving as intermediary. Others took it further, saying that the doctrine intended to obliterate the distinction between clergy and laity, so that all people could perform priestly duties in church—preaching, baptizing, administering the sacraments.

Few, though, understood the doctrine to suggest that the priesthood of all believers meant primarily that all the faithful were to function as priests for their neighbors *outside the church*—to carry their stretcher, to bear their burdens, to supply faith where faith was lacking. Seen in this light, the doctrine isn't primarily about what happens in church; it's about what happens in the neighborhood, at the workplace, along the road, on the sidewalk, at the edges of crowds. It's a call for people of faith to bear to God those without faith and simultaneously to bear God to them. It's not about esoteric controversy in the religious subculture, but rather about practical compassion in the world at large, about being the vital connection between the religious and nonreligious, the faithful and the skeptics, the spiritual and the not so spiritual.

Our neighbors lack faith for many reasons: intellectual skepticism, bad experiences with de-ligion, simple spiritual laziness, being overwhelmed by the manure that life's proverbial fans widely spread. Our job isn't to criticize or scold people for their lack of faith; it's to carry those whose faith has been paralyzed, to keep faith for them, and to see carrying them not as a burden, but as our calling.

Back in Capernaum the day of that roof incident, the religious experts had a front-row seat for the whole story, but they remained critical rather than compassionate to the end. They suffered, it seems, from their own kind of paralysis. Today, both groups—the stretcher bearers, on the one hand, and the religious experts, on the other—still beckon us to join them. Which group will we join? Will we sit comfortably inside the house with front-row seats for unbeatable religious programming, oblivious to the people who suffer on the margins of the crowd outside? Will we intellectualize about the suffering of others, theorize about how somebody should help them, criticize those who try for not doing better? Or will we join the stretcher bearers, feeling the pain of fellow human beings and making it our own, so that we carry *our pain*—their pain together with our pain for them—to the One we name the Compassionate?

The word *mercy* again serves as a good substitute for or supplement to *please,* even more so in Latin or Spanish. *Misericordia* or *conmiseración* suggests that the sufferer's misery strikes an empathic chord of solidarity in the heart of God and a compassionate neighbor. Sometimes, I find myself praying, "Lord, have mercy on us all," because in compassion, the distinctions between my pain, your pain, our pain, his pain, her pain, its pain, and their pain disappear. I find myself appealing to God's *misericordia* and *conmiseración* for the whole of humanity, the whole of creation.

It's worth adding here that sacred compassion doesn't stop with human beings. The ancient psalmists knew that God's compassion extends to every created thing (see Pss. 104:7–27; 145:9), and Jesus didn't doubt that God's concern included the sparrows and wildflowers (Matt. 6:25–30). So our compassion, if it is to join with God's, must include all the animals, all the plants, and all the ecosystems that connect them to one another—and to us. The compassionate Spirit of God, Paul claims, helps us feel the groaning of all creation, a groaning for release from evil, decay, futility, and abuse (Rom. 8:19–24). The trees groan as forests are destroyed by human greed. The seas groan as its fisheries are depleted and toxins accumulate due to careless human behavior. The forests and jungles groan as species disappear, victims of our failure to be wise stewards of God's good world. Even the winds groan as the earth warms due to human haste, waste, and greed. Creation's groaning becomes part of our groaning, and it is all taken up into the Spirit of God, who in some way brings all of our intercession into God's own heart.

I felt this with unusual intensity one summer day as I was driving along a country road beside the Potomac River in western Maryland. I came across a wood turtle. Of all turtles, the wood turtle is my favorite—intelligent and inquisitive (for a reptile), with a lot of personality (for a reptile). A brown shell on the edge of the blacktop ahead of me caught my eye, and I pulled over and walked up the hill toward it. As I came closer, I realized it had been hit by a car just a matter of minutes before I came along. On the hot black macadam, with little bubbles of tar forming on the surface, a dark red, almost purplish pool of blood now the consistency of pudding was drying in the sun. Just uphill from the pool, there was this beautiful animal—sculptured shell with yellow flecks, bright orange limbs, coal-black head, and a golden circle around the pupil of each eye. To my surprise, she was still alive.

I knew she was female by the more slender shape of her head and the flatter contour of her carapace. I counted seven broken fragments of her upper shell, and I could see the pouch of her body cavity expanding and contracting between the shards. She was alert and watched me approach, seeming neither afraid ("Oh no, what next?") nor relieved ("Help coming?"). My first thought was to rescue her, to take her home, try to glue her shell together, and give her some antibiotics and tender treatment so as to rehabilitate her. But she was gasping for breath, and I realized that since her lungs had been punctured, she could not survive.

My next thought was to finish the job, to put her out of her misery, to euthanize her. But I couldn't, not because I lack the nerve, but because of the way she looked at me with her gold-rimmed eyes. I cherish no illusions about the mental capacities of reptiles, but I imagined, if she could think and speak, she would be saying something like this:

So, here you find me in my final predicament. Those cars come so fast, and I had no idea that I was in danger until . . . Crack! . . . and now I feel my blood draining out of me. Please don't disturb me. Don't try to tip me over to see the condition of my underside. It's no use. It's too bad for that. I have just a few minutes left. Are you thinking about putting me out of my misery? Please don't—I'm not in too much pain, really. In fact, before you walked up, I was thinking that I have never felt the pleasure of life as fully as now. And neither have I noticed how green my world is, how utterly alive, how bright and strong is our sun, how warm is the ground heated by it, how privileged each creature is to be able to move even an inch, which I have tried to do once more, just to savor the feeling and freedom of movement one more time.

So please, stay here with me if you'd like, and think these thoughts on my behalf, but please do not touch me. And please do not try to help me by putting me out of what you might suppose to be my misery. Because in spite of my horrible wounds, I am not miserable. In fact, no breath of air ever felt so sweet or precious or fresh as the breath I won during that last gasp. I want to enjoy each remaining moment of this sweet life, each breath, each view of those green bushes there across the road, the movement of that butterfly there. If the only moments I ever experienced were ones I now savor, then I would have reason enough to celebrate. True, I am dying, but at this moment, I am living. That is very good.

So kneeling there with her for a few minutes, I witnessed her waning life and waxing death, living myself in a new way somehow, with that bright sunlight blazing down from above and that heat rising up from the macadam beneath. When she breathed her last, I removed her body from the roadway and buried her under some fertile forest topsoil. As I returned to my car and drove away in a kind of holy hush, I thought about the Creator, about the Spirit of Creation, who knows every sparrow that falls to the ground and every wood turtle who breathes her last. I pondered the magnitude of the heart of God, who in some way witnesses every breath of every creature, from first to last, with perfect, infinite compassion. For a few moments, I felt that I had somehow joined God in God's love for one of God's creatures.[2]

Since that afternoon, although I know some might find this laughable, I find myself whispering blessings on trees, praying for threatened wetlands, and watching birds in flight as if I were saying good-bye to friends, because in a real way I believe I am. In noticing, knowing, and loving a stream, a dolphin, a butterfly, a mountain range, a tiny salamander or songbird, I am making a vital connection with the Creator, who notices, knows, and loves each one too. God, recall the psalmist saying, has compassion an all God has made (145:9).

And if this is true regarding nonhuman creatures, how much more true it is in relation to all persons, whatever their age, race, gender, orientation, religion, status, or capacity. God's loving-kindness, another psalmist says, never runs out (Ps. 136).

Just as in the prayer of petition, sometimes the best simple word to add to *please* is the one that names the need of the other: *peace, protection, strength, hope, comfort, stamina, patience.* And sometimes the prayer whispered to God becomes a blessing spoken directly to the person in pain. So, "Please grant her peace, Lord," becomes "Peace be with you, my friend." "Please, Lord, courage," becomes, "Courage, my brother." Some of us have experienced this kind of blessing—both on the giving end, where we pronounce it, and on the receiving end, where it is pronounced upon us. We know that something powerful happens in a blessing spoken by a believer-priest.[3]

One of the highest and most powerful forms of compassion flows when we learn to pray for those who persecute us, when we dare to bless even our antagonists and enemies.[4] A white South African once told me about a time when he was on the receiving end of such a blessing. During the apartheid years, he believed what he was told by white authority figures, namely, that those working against apartheid were evil troublemakers, rabble-rousers, communists, and heretics. Chief among the troublemakers was an activist Anglican priest named Desmond Tutu. Once, walking through an airport, this large white man saw Tutu coming toward him. Overcome with rage, he moved toward Tutu and roughly, intentionally bumped him as he walked by. Tutu, much smaller in stature, fell down, landing on his backside with a thud. When Tutu opened his eyes, angry blue eyes glared down at him with a sneer of obvious disdain, only to see Tutu's shocked and dazed face gradually focus and form into a smile. "God bless you, my child," Tutu said, his brown eyes gleaming with an impossible mix of compassion and mischief.

The man stomped away, all the more infuriated because Tutu found a way to transcend his act of hatred. During the hours and days that followed, the words of blessing echoed in his memory, and gradually that big, proud white man was brought to repentance by a simple, spontaneous blessing. Tutu's nonviolence, that moment showed, wasn't simply a political strategy; it was a spiritual practice. It was rooted in this practice of intercession. The only way we will learn to respond to violent actions with nonviolent actions is by learning to respond first with nonviolent words—words of blessing, not cursing, words of prayer, not revenge, words of compassion, not retaliation.

When we are wounded by others, we're tempted to dehumanize and demonize them by labeling them with words like "communist," "imperialist," "evil," "insane," "heretic," "fundamentalist," "liberal," or "infidel." Ironically, by turning them into subhuman monsters in our own minds, we also empower them, making them larger than life and intensifying our own anxiety about them. No wonder Jesus taught that our first response should instead be to pray for them and to bless them. In so doing, we turn them back from threatening monsters into what they really are: little human beings like us, human beings with a problem—fear, rage, hate, anxiety, ignorance, misinformation, misguided values, inappropriate habits, harmful training, insecurity, or whatever.

By praying for them, by blessing them, we look beyond their faults and see their need, and we seek to help them with their need. Rather than getting caught up ourselves in the deadly cycle of violence and counter-violence, we join Desmond Tutu and many other courageous spiritual leaders on a better path, the path of peace and reconciliation.

At the heart of the prayer Jesus taught his disciples, we find a call to this path. When we pray, "Forgive us our trespasses as we forgive those who trespass against us," we transcend the normal cycles of offense and revenge that tangle and tear the sacred web of life.[5] We divest from the bankrupt economy of "eye for eye and tooth for tooth." We invest in the grace economy that returns kindness for cruelty and blessing for curse.[6] By walking this better path, we render ourselves open to better possibilities, and we make those possibilities more likely to happen.

But is that likelihood mushy and uncertain? Will praying for our enemies really make a difference? In response to our prayers, will God intervene and work miracles? Will our prayers do the trick, get the job done, flip the switch, close the deal, guarantee results, be effective? Will prayer change things? You may have already noticed that until now I've largely left these questions unasked, much less answered.

Questions like these tap into a whole range of theological assumptions that we are largely unconscious of, assumptions about God's nature and power, God's agency and desired relationship with the universe, God's ability to enforce God's will—and God's ability to limit God's will to make space for the will of other creatures. Others have written brilliantly about these questions.[7] And, less brilliantly, no doubt, so have I.[8] But oddly enough, I don't feel a book like this one is the best place to address them.

Here's why. I'm writing about the summer season of Complexity in the spiritual life as someone who has already passed through it a time or two; I've gone on to survive some autumn and winter seasons as well. These experiences have changed me. Yes, I still remember how, in my first encounters with complexity, questions about divine agency were terribly serious and important, and I demanded answers. Firm answers. Black-and-white answers. Simple yes or no answers. And I got them. But they haven't stood the test of time. As a result, back then I would have had a lot more to say than I do now about "getting answers to prayer," "praying effectively," "claiming your miracle," and so on.

But from where I am now, with some autumns and winters under my belt, I actually think a better way to deal with these questions is to say: "Yes, think about these questions, and certainly share your opinions in response to them. But don't pretend you have solved them once and for all. Because later on you'll be seeing things from a different perspective, and from that perspective much will change. What seems like a problem now won't be so problematic then. And what seems like an answer or solution now will seem like a problem then. The important thing both now and then is to keep praying, whatever answers come or don't come, whatever opinions you hold about how prayer works. Because however much or little prayer changes *things,* prayer certainly changes *you,* and you need to be changed. Remember that you still have a long way to grow, and the best way to grow is to keep praying, to keep strengthening the sacred connection."

In life's summerlike seasons of Complexity, if we do not practice confession, petition, and intercession, we will not keep growing in the sacred connection. If we do wrong, then denial, pride, or shame will cause us to disconnect. If we're in need or pain, then exhaustion, anxiety, or disappointment will cause us to disconnect. And if we're faced with the suffering of others, then we'll succumb to the temptation to disconnect through apathy, despair, self-distancing. As a result, our hearts will contract, not expand. And as a further result, the world, deprived of stronger compassion in people like us, will inevitably grow worse and suffering will increase.

But if through confession, petition, and intercession, you and I strengthen the sacred connection in the midst of life's complexities, what will happen then? Won't we become—habitually, radically, truly—more aligned with God's compassion, more empowered by it, more resonant with its holy frequency? And won't more of us who are more filled with God's compassion help make a better world?

Imagine a world filled with people who are practicing compassion for themselves and others. Hungry stomachs will be filled. War zones will be invaded by peacemakers. Abused victims will be rescued, and cruel victimizers will be confronted. Tears will be dried. And God's compassion will be behind these wonders, God's compassion alive in our hands and eyes and voices, as we bear stretchers, defy crowds, open holes in roofs, and become more part of the solution and less part of the problems in the world.

So my suspicion is that if you stop now and open your heart, you'll realize that just outside the front door of your consciousness there are some needy people. A relative or co-worker. A neighbor or friend. Someone you heard about on the radio, read about in the news, or saw on TV. If you slow down for a few minutes, there will be other neighbors—nonhuman ones—that will also come to mind: endangered species, threatened ecosystems, plundered landscapes. And now is your chance to enter into their pain.

Now is your chance to bear the stretcher by feeling its weight and carrying it to God, sharing it with God, joining God in the vital connection of compassion, generosity, and kindness.

*Christ has no body here but ours, no hands or feet here on earth*
   *but ours.*
*Ours are the eyes through which he looks on this world with kindness.*
*Ours are the hands through which he works. Ours are the feet on*
   *which he moves.*
*Ours are the voices through which he speaks to this world with kindness.*
*Through our touch, our smile, our listening ear,*
*Embodied in us, Jesus is living here.*
*So let us go now, filled with the Spirit, into this world*
*With kindness.*[9]

# PART III

# Perplexity: The Season of Spiritual Surviving

YOU ARE ALONE. EVEN God seems to have abandoned you. Here in this bitter space, answered prayers of the past seem like ironic coincidences or cruel jokes. You're like a gambler who, after a string of gambling wins, risks everything on rolling the dice for a seven. But you roll a two and a four, and now you've lost everything you previously gained. You're not just back to where you started. You're worse off, because when you started you had hope. You felt lucky. Now you feel abandoned, cursed.

In Simplicity, we reach out to God in happiness. We see the world as it should be. God is with us here, and through invocation we acknowledge God's *here-ness*. God blesses us, and through thanksgiving we pour out our gratitude to God—*thanks!* God is wonderful, and through worship we overflow in wonder that can't be contained in normal speech—*O!*

In Complexity, we <u>reach out to God in struggle</u>. We cry *sorry,* as through confession we refuse to deny, cover, or excuse our wrongs, and we instead name them, express regret, and receive mercy. We cry *help,* as through petition we turn our anxieties into requests, and we learn to share our needs and burdens with God, so we will not be preoccupied with ourselves. And we cry *please,* as through intercession we respond to the needs and pain of others by joining our compassion with God's. In each case, a spiritual practice has provided us a way of coping and surviving—and more, of <u>overcoming and thriving, of *winning*</u>. *not so much*

But sometimes, there is no winning. There are no solutions, answers, or consolations in sight. The spring of Simplicity and the summer of

Complexity slip away, and now the autumn winds of Perplexity blow in a biting cold rain. Now, what matters most to us—more than being right, more than being effective—is being honest, authentic, even brutally so. We've moved from a dualistic and pragmatic mind-set to a relativistic and critical one. Leaders we once admired as correct authority figures and confident coaches we now suspect of being frauds—pretending to know more than they do, proclaiming their opinions as facts, misleading and manipulating the naive for their own selfish purposes. Life itself is no longer the simple war or the complex game it used to be for us. On our bad days it's a joke, on our good days it's a quest, and on most days it's a bit of both.

We've grown beyond being dependent infants who look to their leaders for everything, and beyond being somewhat independent children who boast, "I can do it myself!" Now we have become counterdependent, perhaps like adolescents who find our identity among a small band of similarly alienated friends. If we acquired our faith in Simplicity or Complexity, we will probably doubt it now and may even abandon it for a while. At the very least, we will need to add a margin for mystery and unbolt some of the structural elements of our faith that have been until now tightly fitted together. Our faith becomes less the nest and more the quest at this stage, and mention of God evokes feelings of ambivalence. It's a great season for honesty and for digging deeper, but not so great for commitment, energy, or enthusiasm.

For all its angst, there's beauty in Perplexity, the autumn blaze of color between green and gone. There's the strength of ruthless honesty, the courage of dogged endurance, the companionship of the disillusioned, the determination of the long-distance runner who won't give up even though exhausted. In that act of not giving up, there is faith too, and hope, perhaps the most vibrant faith and hope of all.

There's a special catalytic moment that comes late in the season of Perplexity. Having practiced critical thinking about the thoughts and beliefs of others, at this point thinkers turn a critical eye on their own thinking. They become skeptical of their skepticism and cynical about their cynicism. And in so doing they begin to push themselves beyond Perplexity. But it's a long, hard road between here and there.

# CHAPTER 16

# When: *How Long Can I Last?*

*The Practice of Aspiration, Exasperation, and*
*Desperation: Surviving Through Delay*
Alternate Words: *How long, Where*

Whenever I get depressed by a lack of spiritual progress, I realize
that <u>my very dismay is a sign of progress</u>.
PHILIP YANCEY[1]

I BEGAN WRITING THIS CHAPTER in the days after a catastrophic earthquake devastated Haiti and continued writing as a catastrophic oil spill
devastated the Gulf of Mexico. I've heard one question again and again
over these months: How long? How long until help comes? How long
until the spill is contained? When will things be made right?

When news of the earthquake broke, death projections started at
10,000 and quickly went to 50,000. Then they rose to 100,000, and
then the estimate doubled again. When the count reached 230,000, I
read an article about all the ways God was being brought into the tragedy. One televangelist said God was punishing Haiti. Another preacher
said that it was all part of God's plan, even though we can't understand
it. Another said it was a sign of the end times. Their words felt like sand
in my mouth. Even though I am a believer in God, I felt more in sync
with a young person being interviewed on the streets of Port-au-Prince
who said he <u>no longer could believe in a God who would crush babies</u>,
children, and the elderly between slabs of concrete.

*Not caused by God*

When the death toll was still at 50,000, I received this e-mail from my friend Kent, who has lived and worked in Haiti for many years; he helped start an NGO to make a difference there, and he knows and loves Haiti in a profound way.[2] My soul finds comfort in his words, something that tastes real and right, though I'm not sure why:

> I believe in the God who multiplied fish and loaves to feed the hungry. I believe in the God who says I'm always with you. And right now, it's achingly clear—heartbreakingly, angrily clear—isn't it, that we who believe also believe in the God who is hidden sometimes, sometimes when we are most in need, to whom the Psalmist cried out, "How long, oh Lord, how long?"
>
> How long?
>
> Too long. There's no other answer right now. People are being rescued, but too many aren't, and 50,000 never will be. There will be other answers in the weeks and months ahead, but right now the only answer is too long.

"Too long." Those words often apply to things within our control— our procrastination in working for needed political reform, our delay in turning from dirty to clean energy, our slowness in curing preventable diseases and in acknowledging personal and social addictions, our failure to resolve conflicts and address the problems we love to complain about. Sometimes, those words apply to things beyond our control, like earthquakes and God.

*Never for me*

In the spiritual spring of Simplicity, life is a gentle river in which we flow merrily, and prayer is the song we sing in joy. Everything feels under control. Then, in the spiritual summer of Complexity, life becomes a stretch of rapids we must run, a game we think we can win or a challenge we think we can master, and prayer is a key element of our strategy. Through prayer we often shoot the rapids, win the game, master the challenge, regain control. Often, but not always.

Just as Simplicity once gave way to Complexity, now Complexity gives way to Perplexity. Things are out of control, and we can't get them fixed anytime soon. After an earthquake, after a phone call from the police, after a psychiatrist's or oncologist's report, after a letter from the board of directors, after an explosion or collapse or meltdown, the coping strategies that carried us thus far stop working.

For example, in confession, <u>what happens when our faults overwhelm us</u>? What happens when we have sabotaged our success and wounded others we love through our stupidity? What happens when being forgiven is simply insufficient consolation, when we need more than relief from guilt, when we need to stop doing what we're doing and change for the better? What happens when, pray as we might, vicious cycles spin and spin, gears grind, and we go nowhere?

In petition, what happens when we're praying, praying more fervently than we ever have, but the wisdom we need is not forthcoming, the self-control we seek is deteriorating, endurance has blinked out like a spent candle, and hope stopped singing hours ago? We've faced a long string of calamities, and each time we prayed, and the very opposite happened—what then?

Or in intercession, what happens when the death toll keeps doubling, and the oil spill keeps gushing, when the suffering seems so great that we begin losing our ability to sustain belief that God is compassionate or that compassion matters? What happens when the score is suffering, 142, compassion, 0, and we have despaired of compassion ever even scoring, much less catching up? What happens when we do all in our power to help those in need, yet God seems well-meaning but impotent, or distant and unwilling to help, or blankly, frankly nonexistent in the face of a rising tide of pain? What good is all this sentimental rhetoric about naked spirituality when death and evil seem to be winning by a landslide?

If the season of Simplicity is like smooth sailing and <u>Complexity is like running rapids</u>, sooner or later you smash on some rocks, you get swamped, you lose buoyancy. Your little boat of faith springs one leak, then two, then five or seven, and no matter how hard you bail through confession, petition, and intercession, you have to acknowledge that the water level is rising, your boat is going down, and the roar of more rapids awaits you downstream.

Maybe you've never experienced the kind of spiritual sinking we're going to explore in the coming chapters. Maybe you believe you never will. Maybe, in fact, you are angry with anyone who would dare doubt that God will solve all problems and keep us afloat if we simply work the confession, petition, and intercession program according to the sermons of well-meaning Stage Two preachers. Maybe you will be able to maintain this illusion until you die. But maybe you should take these chapters seriously anyway just in case, just in case you aren't as smart and invulnerable as you think you are at this moment.

I remember the first time I entered the spiritual autumn of Perplexity. I was in college. I had learned the arts of invocation, thanksgiving, and worship. I was well versed in confession, petition, and intercession. I frequently experienced dramatic answers to my prayers, and I regularly experienced powerful "touches" of the Holy Spirit—what some would call baptisms and others would call fillings and still others would call anointings or movings of the Spirit. I was working the program—praying, reading my Bible, experiencing fellowship, witnessing to my faith, and leading others to Christ—but then the <u>program stopped working</u>.

It wasn't just that I no longer felt the warm summer breezes that I had grown accustomed to. I had experienced down times, dry times, flat times before, when God's presence wasn't as present or perceptible to my soul. This time was different, because day after day, week after week, I felt the cold, damp, gray absence of God. Positive, palpable absence, not just the lack of presence, became the elephant in the room. And in the chilling bluster of that naked absence, all of my previous experiences of God seemed utterly inaccessible. Yes, I remembered they happened, but I doubted they had ever been real.

I wondered if maybe it had all been a kind of psycho-spiritual illusion, a mirage conjured by heat waves rising from a summer highway. When I prayed, I thought, "I'm just talking to myself—there's nobody really there to listen, much less answer." When I read the Bible, I thought, "This seems like a bunch of legends and mythology. And a lot of it is pretty barbaric." When I attended church, I thought, "These people are deep into a kind of social make-believe, a hyped-up group-think, a choreographed role-play. They're like little boys playing army or little girls playing house. It's just a game of pretend—pretense manipulated through the tradition and hierarchy of a priestly class that's making a good living." I didn't want to think these things, but I couldn't help it.

At first, I felt sad. I grieved my loss of feeling God's presence. But the grief was nothing compared to what came next—fear. The fear ran along these lines: What happens if the feeling of God's presence never comes back? What happens if my simple, strong, confident faith never returns? How long can I last in this wasteland? How long before I die of thirst in this scorching desert, or freeze in this cold rain that is fast changing to sleet?

How long will this dry season last? When will this cold emptiness end? When? *When?!* That is the question of the first prayer in the season of Perplexity. I want to call it the prayer of delay, fear, or frustration, but there is a slightly more hopeful term that has found a place in spiritual theology, largely thanks to the Wesley brothers, John and Charles, and their early Methodist hymnals: *aspiration*.

"Aspiration" has two meanings. More literally, it means inhalation, breathing in. More figuratively, it means any abiding hunger or thirst—the intense, persistent desire to receive something you don't have, to become something you are not yet. Put the two together, and you get close to what I'm describing here: a breathless, gasping longing, a life-and-death thirst, a deep and passionate—even desperate—desire to survive and thrive as a person of authentic faith.

John Wesley taught the early Methodists that a higher form of Christian living was possible, a state he described as "entire sanctification."[3] When people believed him—and millions did—they had to acknowledge that their actual lives of semisanctification, pseudosanctification, or faux sanctification fell far below the standard of entire sanctification, which they now believed was possible. The gap between the desired possible life with God and the possessed actual life found expression not in polite, genteel, restrained, refined classical music, but in the passionate songs and choruses of spiritual *enthusiasm,* a term that carried a sense of condescension or even derision in those days.

Here is an example:[4]

*Drooping soul, shake off thy ears,*
*Fearful soul, be strong, be bold;*
*Tarry till the Lord appears,*

*Never, never quit thy hold!*
*Murmur not at His delay,*
*Dare not set thy God a time;*
*Calmly for His coming stay,*
*Leave it, leave it all to Him.*

One feels the tension between the desire to receive all that God offers immediately and the frustration—the "drooping"—at what seems like a delay.

A similar hymn asks, "Why not now?"

*Why not now, my God, my God!*
*Ready if Thou always art,*
*Make in me Thy mean [humble] abode,*
*Take possession of my heart?*
*If Thou canst so greatly bow,*
*Friend of sinners, why not now?*

Another hymn wonders if the time of waiting for "full redemption" has ended and captures the tension of aspiration in the gap between "dying, if thou still delay" and "enter now . . . now":

*God of love, if this my day*
*For Thyself to Thee I cry;*
*Dying, if Thou still delay*
*Must I not for ever die?*
*Enter now Thy poorest home,*
*Now, my utmost Savior, come!*

Early aspiration is fervent, eager, positive—grasping for more and better. Eventually, though, unsatisfied aspiration becomes frustration and then exasperation, as the gasping soul grows impatient, oxygen-starved, parched, famished, and desperate for something—a touch of grace, a feeling of assurance—to conquer an invasion of doubt and despair—before it's too late.

As time goes on, *when* and *how long* give way to *where*. Where have you gone, God? Where are you? *When? How long? Where?* These prayers of aspiration, exasperation, and desperation groan out from our souls as we hope against hope that an answer will come before too long.

# CHAPTER 17

# When: *Survival Is Underrated*

Step 1: We admitted we were powerless over our addiction—that our lives had become unmanageable.

Step 2: Came to believe that a Power greater than ourselves could restore us to sanity.

THE TWELVE STEPS OF ALCOHOLICS ANONYMOUS

Y OU CAN FEEL ASPIRATION morphing into *exasperation* and *desperation* in a song lyric written almost three thousand years before the hymns of early Methodism. In Psalm 42, the poet moves from a tender image of thirst to the urgent question "When?"

> *As a deer longs for flowing streams,*
> *so my soul longs for you, O God.*
> *My soul thirsts for God,*
> *for the living God.*
> *When shall I come and behold*
> *the face of God? (vv. 1–2)*

The psalmist's thirst, it turns out, has been mockingly quenched—not with "flowing streams," but with his constant flow of salty tears. Just as his tears mock his thirst, so others mock him for his spiritual depression: Shouldn't his God be meeting his needs? Their words, he says later, are like a mortal wound to his body (v. 10).

> *My tears have been my food*
> *day and night,*

*while people say to me continually,*
*"Where is your God?" (v. 3)*

One senses the bitter contrast between the delayed presence of comfort and the constant presence of unfulfillment. Meanwhile, each good memory of joyful times—those bright days when he felt spiritual fulfillment together with his peers—now only darkens his long nights of alienation and pain.

*These things I remember,*
*as I pour out my soul:*
*how I went with the throng,*
*and led them in procession to the house of God,*
*with glad shouts and songs of thanksgiving,*
*a multitude keeping festival. (v. 4)*

Then comes the refrain:

*Why are you cast down, O my soul,*
*and why are you disquieted within me?*
*Hope in God; for I shall again praise him,*
*my help and my God. (vv. 5–6)*

The "why" of this refrain—addressed to his own soul—is mirrored by another even more disturbing "why" question, addressed to God: "Why have you forgotten me?" (v. 9).

All these questions go unanswered: "When?" "How long?" "Where?" "Why?" Yet above the prayer of aspiration a tattered flag of faith and hope still flies: "Hope in God; for I shall again praise him." That simple word "again"—vague and undefined, but real—seeks to answer the painful question "When?" It doesn't dare claim "soon"; instead, it more modestly claims "someday."

You ask, "When? How long?" because you know—or at least you believe—or at least you hope—that your panting, gasping, famished feelings of unfulfilled longing, abandonment, and confusion won't go on forever. A sense of peace and fullness will come *again, someday,* like spring. And so, as you wait in the meantime, in the October of loss, through chilly November, into December with its cruelly short dim days and cruelly long cold nights, you <u>talk to yourself</u>: "Why are you cast down? Hope in God." And you <u>talk to God</u>: "Why have you forgotten me? My soul longs for you!" And like a beginner repeating a mantra or like a cheerleader trying to rouse a weary team—*When? Again! When? Again! When? Again!*—you survive, one day, one moment at a time.

Many years ago I came across a sturdy old poem by Annie Johnson Flint called "What God Has Promised." It's the kind of poem one might find on a greeting card or wall plaque, but it begins with a rather surprising dose of honesty:

> *God has not promised*
> *Skies always blue,*
> *Flower-strewn pathways*
> *All our lives through.*
> *God has not promised*
> *Sun without rain,*
> *Joy without sorrow,*
> *Peace without pain.*

Then comes the affirmation:

> *But God has promised*
> *Strength for the day,*
> *Rest for the labor,*
> *Light for the way;*
> *Grace for the trials,*
> *Help from above,*
> *Unfailing sympathy,*
> *Undying love.*

Beneath the singsong rhythm and greeting-card rhymes hides a <u>poem of disillusionment</u>. The blue-sky flower-strewn illusions of false faith must be sorted from the realities of good faith—complete with rain, sorrow, pain, labor, and trials. And that process takes time. And pain. And so, through delay, through frustration, through hardships that we feel can't be endured another minute, our desire is tested and stretched almost to the breaking point. Day after day we express desire—for "full redemption," for "entire sanctification," for "a more perfect union," for an end to a season of spiritual depression and dryness, for the gap between our dreams and reality to be narrowed. In so doing, we keep our desire alive. Alive for one more day. One more step. One more moment. For this *now* we aren't giving up. And *this* now. And *this*.

"How long, O Lord?" we ask, like children wondering when they will finally arrive at their destination. "How much longer?" we ask, like a runner building up aerobic strength, fortifying our faith by pushing it to its limits, yearning for the next milestone, dreaming of the finish line, weary and breathless, but refusing to stop. That might not seem like much. But it's survival, and survival is underrated. Sometimes survival is a victory in itself.

Now my mind goes back to my friend Kent and his many friends in Haiti. How long before they receive water and food? When will medical care come? How long will they feel abandoned and vulnerable? How long until Haiti sees better days? Where was God when the earth shook? Where is God now?

And now my imagination travels down a mile below the Gulf of Mexico, where again today, sixty to a hundred thousand barrels of oil are surging into the ocean, creating catastrophic consequences that we can't imagine. When will it be stopped? How? Where was God when politicians cut deals with corporate executives, careless of their impact on dolphins, sea turtles, sea gulls, and millions of people? How long will this kind of greed-driven exploitation continue? When will answers come? When will new technologies be discovered? When will we convert from dirty to clean energy? When?

Things may be going just fine for you right now, smooth sailing, everything under control. But beneath a calm exterior, pressure may also be mounting. Unfulfilled aspiration may be fermenting into exasperation, and exasperation boiling into desperation. Counselors tell us that if we don't find healthy ways to express this rising emotional pressure, it will turn inward and become depression—sometimes manifesting in a slow burnout and sometimes in a fast flameout. As with an earthquake or an oil spill, the results can be catastrophic.

So now is the time to put this book aside and acknowledge the growing pressure hidden beneath the surface. Now is the time to listen to the impatience growing within you and to express it, not just to yourself, but to the Spirit. It might feel like a groan: *When? How long?* It might feel like an accusation: *So when, then? How much longer, then?* Its tone might be eager, frightened, fatigued, or even angry. Whatever it is, rather than letting the pressure build to unhealthy levels, how about learning to express it through this practice of aspiration, exasperation, and desperation?

Hold your *when* or *how long* or *where* before God. Make space for your disappointment, frustration, and unfulfillment to come out of hiding and present themselves in the light. Don't rush, even though you'll be tempted to see these times of spiritual dryness and aspiration as a mistake, a sign of failure you want to put behind you. Instead, slow down and hold this moment as an opportunity to express and strengthen spiritual desire. Realize that the Spirit doesn't want to shame you for groaning for fulfillment and release; the Spirit wants to join you, to empathize with you, to intensify your desire, not deny it.

So feel it; don't fear it. Just as the only way to stretch or strengthen a muscle is to bring it to the point of ache, the only way to strengthen a desire is to stretch it, to draw it out, to force it, through unfulfillment, to last longer. And that hurts. So it's okay to let it out like an "Ouch!": "This hurts! How long must it last? I don't like this! When will it end? I can't last much longer. Where are you?" If it helps, you might think of yourself as complaining to God, letting God know that you aren't satisfied and you won't just go away. You're banging on God's door and won't give God any rest until your thirst receives some satisfaction. Things will either get better or worse. If they get better, you'll appreciate the relief all the more because of the intensity and persistence of your holding your *when, how long,* or *where* before God. If they get worse, your refusal now to be satisfied will only strengthen and energize you for what's to come later on.

This space of unfulfillment is a kind of void. And since the time of the Roman philosopher Lucretius, insightful thinkers have seen in a void something more than absence.[1] A void creates, in fact, a kind of power. Without a void within it, a sponge would lose the power to absorb moisture. Air would lose the power to transmit sound or scent. In fact, nothing could move if there weren't space—a void—into which it could pass. Here's how Lucretius said it:

> But now through oceans, lands, and heights of heaven
> By divers causes and in divers modes,
> Before our eyes we mark how much may move,
> Which, finding not a void, would fail deprived
> Of stir and motion; nay, would then have been
> Nowise begot at all, since matter, then,
> Had staid at rest, its parts together crammed.
> Then too, however solid objects seem,
> They yet are formed of matter mixed with void.[2]

Through the autumnlike season of Perplexity, the void expands. Unfulfillment grows. And this is in no way pleasurable. But as Lucretius realized, the creation of empty space makes way for movement, for new potential, for new empowerment. Sadly, though, none of that is visible now.

# CHAPTER 18

# No: *The Void Expands*

*The Practice of Rage and Refusal:*
*Surviving Through Disillusionment*
No Alternate Words

If you have a false idea of God, the more religious you are, the
worse it is for you—it were better for you to be an atheist.
WILLIAM TEMPLE[1]

SOMETIMES, I THINK MOST times, the prayer of aspiration works like
a long doorless passageway. You keep trudging along, on and on, until
finally, when you are about to collapse on the floor in fatigue or boredom, you come to a door. You turn the latch, it clicks, the door opens,
and suddenly you're outside.

Or it's like a song you keep singing through the long dry season, day
after day, sweating and surviving, trying to keep the tune of faith alive
on your lips or in your mind, humming, *How long? How long?* And then
one afternoon as you're humming the tune, off in the distance you hear
thunder, you see the hump of a gray cloud rise on the horizon, and soon
on your sunburned skin you feel a breeze with a certain moist scent you
can barely remember. And then, before you know it, you are standing,
laughing, dancing in a downpour of joy. The presence of God again
baptizes you. Your season in the wilderness ends. *When* gives way to
*again.* You break through.

Usually. But sometimes it doesn't go that way. Sometimes the passageway goes on and on, and when you come to a door and open it, it's

a dark, damp closet that leads nowhere. Or the rains don't come, the crops wither in the fields, the herds start dying, and you lie down on your bed and wait to die too.

What do you do now as aspiration sours into exasperation? What word forms in your soul as you curl up in a fetal position in the closet or as you lie back on your bed as if it were a cross? The merciful parts of me hope that you never have to find this out, that you'll never need to know what I'm about to tell you. I hoped I would never need to know it. But here it is, just in case.

In these moments, you raise your fists and you rage at God. *No!* you shout. *No!* you scream. *No!* you groan. Cuss if you must, and cry if you can. But whatever you do, don't be silent. Don't let your fury and disappointment harden and die into a cold, silent block of bitter iciness in you. Keep it hot. Keep it fermenting, churning, restless, unwilling to be denied. Keep shouting, *No!*

This practice of *refusal* may sound like unbelief. It may sound like blasphemy. But don't be fooled. Those who rage at God believe there is a God who is willing to be raged at. That belief is a quivering spark that can again be fanned into flame. It's those who have stopped raging and lapsed into a frigid, rigid silence whom you should pity and for whom you should grieve. Ragers' fury and apparent unbelief signal a deeper faith that still survives—that a God worth believing and loving should not have let things go this way. The fact that things have gone this way—that things have ended up like this—may lead them to believe that God has failed. And so, they may punish God with fury and insult, blasphemy and invective, mockery and derision.

Reactive believers may try to silence them. "Don't talk that way!" they'll say. They might even threaten with damnation those who rage. But what they don't see is that the god the angry are punishing deserves to be punished. Beneath or behind that failed god is another G-d, one whose higher standard exposes the false, failed god as a fraud. The rage wouldn't exist if some vision of the true God behind the false god didn't remain. Perhaps by raging against the failed image of God, it will fall, and behind it the true G-d will appear, the true G-d to whom Meister Eckhart prayed, "God save me from god."

This is why doubters, atheists, and skeptics have an important place in the community of faith.[2] The acid of their critique flows—even though they may not realize it—from their sadness that a truer, brighter, bigger, better God isn't showing up, but only a second-rate imposter god. And their *no* is a dual rejection. First, it is a refusal to accept the second-rate imposter god's presence, and second, it is a refusal to accept the true and living G-d's absence. Can you see the remarkable faith and virtue disguised in that *no*?

It is here, in this moment of rage and refusal, that most of us have to face more directly a thousand and one thorny intellectual questions about God, prayer, and the spiritual life. We have kept these questions at bay for months, years, even decades. These simmering questions, pushed to the back burners of our mind, now begin to boil over. We wonder: If God is all-good and all-powerful, why wouldn't God have already chosen to aid a needy person apart from our intercession? Does God lack goodwill without our coaxing? Why has God allowed this person or group—or me—to suffer in the first place? How could God create a world where lovers are separated, where precious little girls are raped, where mothers send their sons off to war to be killed or to kill the sons of other mothers, where parents give birth to children with severe diseases or children nurse their parents through years of mental illness or dementia in its varied forms? Was it a lack of effective advanced universe planning? If God's goodness and compassion would never plan for suffering, and if God's wisdom and power would never allow it to go unchallenged, how can it exist—and not only in rare instances, but pervasively, horrifically, enduringly?

This rolling boil of intellectual questions leaves us with four logical options:

A. There is no suffering, and there is no God.

B. There is no suffering, and there is a God.

C. There is suffering, and there is no God,

D. There is suffering, and there is a God.

If suffering didn't exist, we wouldn't have a problem, so we know that A and B aren't true. That leaves us with C and D. If C is true, there is no intellectual problem, but neither is there a source of spiritual resources

*(margin handwriting: "to Not if you want the right that you can, to hope may not be taken from us")*

to deal with suffering. (Actually, there is an intellectual problem: Why does it bother us to accept as a fact that suffering is pervasive and meaningless?) If D is true, there is an intellectual problem, but there is also a source of spiritual resources to deal with suffering.

If we're left with a choice between C and D, D seems to be the most hopeful choice, but it leaves us in tension. We don't deny the reality of suffering, on the one hand, nor the possibility of God, on the other.

Again, this acknowledgment certainly does not constitute an answer to the intellectual problem of pain. I believe there are answers on a certain level. But even the best answers are terribly unsatisfying, and they work better in a classroom than in a hospital room, beneath a pile of earthquake rubble, or at a crime scene. They provide only cold comfort to a person in agony, and often, as they solve one intellectual quandary, they create twenty-two more. As C. S. Lewis famously and wisely stated, the best answers don't do as much good for a person in pain as a dose of courage does.[3] So to pray on in the face of outrageous suffering, it seems to me, is at heart a choice of courage and hope, even if the prayers sound like blasphemies to observers.

So we shout, "*No, no*—I will not reject God! But *no, no, no*—neither will I deny my questions either! *No,* I will not cave in to despair, but *no,* neither will I be pacified with unsatisfying answers or superficial comfort! *No!*"

Interestingly, the scriptures are less shy about raging spirituality than we typically are. Consider these agonizing opening words of Psalm 77:

> *I cry aloud to God,*
> *aloud to God, that he may hear me.*
> *In the day of my trouble I seek the Lord:*
> *in the night my hand is stretched out without wearying . . .*

And what comes next? "And God answered my prayer and comforted me"? No! The psalmist rages, " . . . and my soul refuses to be comforted." Did thoughts of God bring peace? No! The psalmist laments:

> *I think of God, and I moan;*
> *I meditate, and my spirit faints.*

"The more I think about it," he says, "the more drained I feel!" And then, as if to refuse to let us move forward to quickly seeking some relief, he adds, "Selah," which is either a call to pause and ponder, a signal for a pensive musical interlude to be played, or, more likely, both.

The psalmist, identified as Asaph, continues to feel his spiritual agony. God keeps his eyes from closing. He is speechless with pain. He wonders if God has decisively rejected him forever, if God will never be gracious again, if God's so-called unfailing love has failed, if God's promise has turned out to be a bitter lie, if God has gotten amnesia and forgotten how to be merciful and compassionate. Then he turns his thoughts to the stories of long ago—the epic stories of God's faithfulness in the past, and this seems to bring him some comfort.

But even if Asaph in Psalm 77 can come to the ledge of rage and then back away, the Korahites in Psalm 88 cannot. Their poet-protagonist begins by begging God—"God of my salvation"—to hear him, and things go downhill from there. "My soul is full of trouble," he says. "I feel like hell, my strength is gone. I'm forgotten by you and cut off from your care. You've thrown me into a deep pit of depression. Your anger batters me like a cold and bitter surf, and I'm drowning. You have turned my friends against me. They now are disgusted with me because of you. You've trapped me in a cramped cell, and I'm going blind with rage and despair" (see vv. 3–7).

Even though he calls out to God, even though every day he spreads out his hands in sincere petition, God doesn't answer. Questions besiege him, questions echoing in an empty room. God's "dread assaults" have destroyed him, he says (v. 16). A tsunami of terror has swept him off his feet, and he is now absolutely helpless, carried away by a roiling flood of despair. And, in contrast to Psalm 77, here there is not even a faint whisper of hope at the end. Feel the crushing bleakness of these final words:

> *You have caused friend and neighbor to shun me;*
> *my companions are in darkness.*

Can you dare to feel this abandonment? Can you dare to pray this kind of raging prayer and hold open this feverish void?

Can you see the faith in it? Can you see how, no less than Psalm 23 with its green pastures and still waters, this prayer of raging despair is also a prayer of faith, because the "valley of the shadow of death" is for this psalmist not just a possibility, but the actual Death Valley geography from which he prays? Can you see the primal, indestructible diamond of faith being formed under the unfathomable pressures of feeling utterly abandoned and betrayed by God?

This daring word *no* has more holiness to it than it gets credit for. Through it, we refuse to let God off the hook. We demand not to be abandoned. We reject the status quo, deny its status as acceptable. We stamp our foot in God's presence; no, more, we raise our fist and say, "I will not accept this!" And at the same time, our *no* is directed at unbelief; we obstinately refuse to let life with God degenerate into life without God. *No!*

We've come a long way from that simple word *here*. Now God appears to be *nowhere*. That doesn't seem like progress.

# CHAPTER 19

# No: *Mad with God*

The best way to pray is: stop. Let prayer pray within you, whether
you know it or not. This means a deep awareness of our true inner
identity. It implies a life of faith, but also of doubt. You can't have
faith without doubt. Give up the business of suppressing doubt.
Doubt and faith are two sides of the same thing. Faith will grow
out of doubt, the real doubt. We don't pray right because we evade
doubt.

THOMAS MERTON[1]

WHEN WE THINK OF a fist raised in rage against God, we think of
poor Job. But I must admit, I struggle with the structure of the book
of Job. I often feel that the deep middle of Job has been betrayed by
the addition of a shallow preface and dishonest epilogue. It's as if Job's
comforters, whom God silences as a bunch of pious ninnies at the end of
the middle section, sneak back and add a preface and epilogue in order
to get the last word after all. But however one reads the beginning and
end, the middle of Job rings with Job's refusal to wallpaper over the
ugly cracks in reality. For him, better to see the ugliness than to cover it
with an insipid, sentimental, flowery print of pretentious pseudopiety.[2]
And scandalously, God agrees with Job.

Consider how scandalous it is. Here is a document declared to be
part of the canon of inspired scripture. But perhaps 60 percent of it—or
whatever the exact portion uttered by Job's so-called comforters might
be—is called a gust of hot, empty air, first by Job and then by God
(16:3; 38:2)! And their puerile chatter contains—again, we have to face
it—exactly the kind of sweet, simple logic we find in Deuteronomy

and Proverbs and in the preface and epilogue of Job itself: bad things happen to bad people, and good things happen to good people. How do we reconcile this tension?

Of course, the answer is we don't reconcile it. We don't say, "There is no justice in the world." But neither do we say, "There is a simple, clear, black-and-white justice in the world." Instead, we do what Job does, and what the Bible as a whole does—we live with the tension, feel its pain, and let the discomfort churn within us. We abandon hope of an explanation that will let us happily and easily accept reality as it is. And something happens when we make this move. When we refuse all easier alternatives, we find our hearts being strangely empowered. We grow resolute, determined to throw our lives into the cause of justice, comfort, compassion, and healing, aiming our *no* at all that is hateful, unjust, false, foolish. And whenever the pain proves unbearable, we shout to God in the prayer of rage and refusal.

Things are not as they should be in our world. Nor are things as they should be in our own lives—in our emotions, in our thinking, in our behavior, in our relationships. *No* is the response to all that is unacceptable. It is a refusal to accept the unacceptable. The descendants of those who gave us Psalms 77 and 88 and the book of Job, and the rabbi Jesus know this refusal too well.[3]

In 1953, the Israeli Parliament created a solemn day of commemoration called Yom Hashoah to memorialize the Holocaust of the previous decade. The day was set aside to mourn the lives of six million killed by the Nazis between 1938 and 1945. More recently, the Conservative Jewish movement created the first formal liturgy for use on Yom Hashoah, entitled Megillat Hashoah, meaning "The Scroll of the Holocaust." It is, my wise friend Duane Shank explains,

> built largely around first-person testimonies. After an opening chapter that gives a searing overview of the victims' suffering, it offers composite sketches of a Christian journalist observing life in the Warsaw Ghetto, a Jewish woman in a work camp, and a Jewish youth who was forced to pull out the teeth from his brother's corpse and shove other dead bodies into ovens. A fifth chapter consists of a eulogy for those who died in the Holocaust;

the final chapter recounts the efforts to rebuild Jewish life after the war ended.

It is also intended to address some of the theological questions raised by the Holocaust. . . . The overriding theological message of the Megillah [Scroll] is that human beings have a right to question the divine, but they cannot expect answers—and that even without answers, the Jewish faith in God endures. The Megillah ends with the exhortation: "Do not mourn too much, but do not sink into the forgetfulness of apathy. Do not allow days of darkness to return; weep, but wipe the tears away. Do not absolve and do not exonerate, do not attempt to understand. Learn to live without an answer. Through our blood, live!"[4]

*No* isn't a rejection of God. It's a refusal to accept unsatisfying attempts to let God off the hook. And it's a parallel refusal to give up hope altogether. Perhaps you can see how the post-Holocaust cry of "Never again" is an alternative expression of the *no* of raging prayer. Perhaps, when you look into the abyss of human suffering and evil, you can see how desperately we need this painful, heroic, faithfully doubting spiritual practice. Otherwise, it's too easy to sink "into the forgetfulness of apathy."

Our outrage is addressed to God, but it isn't aimed at God, or at least not at the G-d we hope exists. We may be furious with the disappointing god who apparently exists, but our *no* faithfully calls out to the better G-d who we hope exists. We aren't mad *at* that G-d, though in our pain we may express it this way at times. Instead, we are mad with G-d—*with* G-d raging *against* the monstrous false god who appears to rule in these outrageous circumstances. We share our outrage with G-d—the real and hoped-for G-d—and we express it in the presence of G-d in confidence that this "most high" G-d will understand our disappointment with the mid-level conceptual pseudogods we inherited. G-d won't be made insecure by our honesty, we realize, and G-d can handle it. After all, we believe that G-d, of all beings, is the one most incapable of accepting the unacceptable or being apathetic in the presence of evil and injustice and pain. *No,* then, is actually a *yes* to a deep and pure belief—that G-d, if G-d exists, would rather that we be honest doubters than hypocritical believers, and that G-d, if G-d exists, is even more implacably opposed to and heartbroken about the status quo than we are.

But the practice of refusal doesn't feel like a *yes* most of the time. It feels like death.[5] And then it gets worse.

The most powerful dramatic moment possible in Greek theater, according to Aristotle, is called *peripeteia*. The agony of *peripeteia* brings a complete reversal in a person's understanding of his or her life. Think of the moment in Sophocles's *Oedipus Rex* when the protagonist discovers that he has killed his own father and married his own mother. Everything that seemed true about his life is shown to be false, and what seemed false and impossible is shown to be true. Such a moment of breakdown might be called a personal paradigm crash, and it plunges one into the deepest kind of pain imaginable. In the face of *peripeteia,* one can only cry, groan, shout, rage, and cry some more: *no!*

*Oedipus Rex* ends with Oedipus being led away into exile beyond the borders of his beloved Thebes. He has blinded himself as a kind of self-punishment for failing to see the truth. His daughters, born of his unintentional incest, have been brought to say a tearful good-bye. He begs that they be allowed to accompany him, since they have nothing to look forward to in Thebes except shame and rejection. But his pathetic plea receives this stern answer, the tragedy's penultimate lines: "Crave not mastery in all, for the mastery that raised you was your bane and wrought your fall."

Job reaches a similar tragic moment in his story. Job's wife, you may recall, offers Job a way out of his pain. "Curse God, and die," she says (2:9). Her words may be a euphemism for suicide, or they may imagine Job so angering God that a lightning bolt will come and put him out of his misery. Whatever her words intend, they suggest an end to the rage and refusal. "Get it over with," they say. But Job, like the Megillat Hashoah, refuses to get it over with. He refuses both the false comfort of his friends and the false escape of his wife. Through his refusal he chooses to live, but to do so loudly, shouting his fury to the end.

After Job vents his fury, Elihu, a young man filled with the arrogant, angry piety of a stupid, self-assured zealot, explodes "like new wine-skins . . . ready to burst," because he is "full of words" (32:18–19). Full indeed, full of something, for he blusters on for six long chapters. As he does, apparently a storm approaches, which he describes in great detail, and it is out of that storm that the voice of the Lord finally comes. And the voice of the Lord comes not with answers, but with a tornado of questions.[6] And in the face of those questions, Job feebly replies, "What shall I answer you? I lay my hand on my mouth" (40:4). Another torrent of questions deluges him, and he replies similarly, in resignation, "Therefore I have uttered what I did not understand, things too wonderful for me, which I did not know" (42:3).

And here, it seems, we come to the end of refusal, to the point where we simply say, "I don't know. I don't understand." And after that, we are silent. That silence is painful. And golden.

Could it be that here the Greeks and the Jews agree—that a tragic thread runs through every life, and it unravels in the end in an agonizing *peripeteia*? That life conspires to bring us to the realization that, contrary to everything we have known or hoped, we actually have no control, no mastery, no explanation, no argument, no understanding? That we stand, as songwriter Bruce Cockburn says, "in front of all this beauty"—and agony—"understanding nothing"?[7]

Perhaps there hides in our shout of *no* a defiant denial, a remaining shred of mastery and control, a lingering refusal to accept the truth of our smallness. Perhaps we refuse to the very last moment to accept the truth—that we are not in fact kings and masters of our destiny, that we are not good men and women who have things figured out, but rather that we all, even King Oedipus and righteous Job, are small, frail, contingent creatures. Could this be the tragic moment toward which our lives inevitably run like water toward the lowest point—the moment when our *no* sheds that last shred of self-delusion? Can there be, beyond the *no* of rage with all its ambivalence and tension, a *no* of recognition? Could our rage and refusal exhaust itself so that our *no* changes in tone from fury to lament?

We will never know if we try to rush the process, if we try to avoid *peripeteia,* if we refuse refusal. And so we must let this horrible moment crash upon us like a merciless wave, wash over us in all its grinding power, pull us down, push us down, hold us down, and threaten to drown us.

If you are in the zone of *peripeteia,* you'll face any number of temptations: to distract yourself from the pain by thrashing about in mindless activity, to numb yourself with routine, to anesthetize the pain with drugs or alcohol, to seek to return (in bad faith) to an earlier zone when life was simpler and easier, to turn the pain into anger and vent that anger at yourself or others. You can cause a lot of damage to yourself and others in the process. The only sane alternative is to hold the pain, to feel it, to in a sense stretch yourself out on the cross of it, to lie down in front of it and let it crash upon you, and, as you do, to voice your protest, disappointment, rage, and refusal with *no*—shouted, screamed, groaned, whispered, whatever.

You may find it helpful to translate that single word into many words, write your own poetry of lament and fury. Or, if that feels too demanding, you could simply begin to list, memo-style, your grievances against reality, spirituality, and the Almighty. What is it that you refuse to accept? What is it that enrages your heart? What in you stands up and will not sit down, speaks up and will not be silent, acts up and will not behave? Can you see how important it is to let what is trying to rise up within you be allowed to do so?

If you aren't there in that raging void, you can't really practice this posture. But you can, perhaps, recall encounters with it in the past, and you may be able to acknowledge the prelabor contractions that are with you even now. Where are you still seizing control, claiming mastery? What are you most afraid to lose? Where are you demanding an answer that empowers you with explanations? Can you dare imagine the rage if you had to lay those explanations on the altar?

It's okay if your answer is *no, no.* In fact, that's exactly the point. It's only by refusing until you can refuse no more that you will ever come to that quiet, naked, tender moment beyond refusal. Your *no* exhausts itself. Your furious exclamation breaks open, and from it emerges a tender question.

# CHAPTER 20

# Why: *When You Have Come to Zero*

*The Practice of Lament and Agony:*
*Surviving Through Abandonment*
No Alternate Words

*I say: It takes more*
*Faith to question than*
*to affirm.*

And the waves of pain did wash over me with a rhythmic quality. Ebbing and flowing. Coming and going. I felt I needed to
lie completely still so as not to be swept away. . . . There was no
escape, no way out except to go all the way through it. In time—a
couple hours I think—the waves of grief subsided. It's hard to
describe what happened after that. . . . I felt empty and spent, but
I also felt comforted by God's loving presence. . . . Nothing was
fixed, but I was okay. I had not been swept away.

RUTH HALEY BARTON[1]

O NE OF MY MENTORS once told me that in the school of faith, we
first take the test and then we learn the lesson. He could just as easily
have said that we first *fail* the test and then learn the lesson, because in
my experience failure is what makes me more ready to learn than anything else. In fact, failure is itself the lesson. Once you admit that you
are a failure, you are, strangely, free. Once you admit that you don't
know, that you can't know, you know something you previously re-
fused to know. Everything is possible again when you have fought and
struggled and been defeated, when you have come to zero.

*those who would*
*leave who would*
*lose it would*

If faith shoots up in the springtime of Simplicity, and if it branches
out and grows robust in the summer of Complexity, it appears to fade
and fall like leaves in the autumn of Perplexity. It falters in the impa-

tient *when* of aspiration, and then it falls to pieces in the *no* of rage. The furious *no* of raging prayer leaves one spent, exhausted, feeling blind and exiled like tragic Oedipus, feeling stupid and ashamed like honest Job, and strangely quiet. And in that quiet, in that hush and stillness of exhaustion, a subtle turning occurs, a turn from *no* to something beyond it. It's the beginning of a kind of surrender, in a way. We say, "Okay. Life hasn't gone my way. My expectations are shattered. I have no mastery, no control. Why must it be this way?"

Do you see the subtle but real shift? One minute, you are yelling, "No! It can't be this way!" and then you are whispering, "Why? Why must it be this way?"

That *why*—the prayer of *lament*—is the kind of prayer you offer on the longest night of the year, the night autumn ends and winter begins. Long ago, your *when, how long* turned into a raging *no*. Aspiration gave way to exasperation, desperation, and then a raging refusal because *how long* had become *too long*. Having spent your rage, having lost your hope, you now sink into a kind of resignation, a release of all mastery, an acceptance that life is beyond your control. Now, with a feeble voice, you turn toward God, whispering, *Why?*

The prayer is profoundly ironic, isn't it? It acknowledges, "I don't have answers," but it still dares to hope that there is an answer, so it asks. This is seasoned faith at work, chastened faith, faith humbled by a season of Perplexity. You are hunched over, holding your head in your hands, as the *peripeteia* does its disorienting work.

We should beware of theologies formed in times of prosperity and comfort, theologies formed on college campuses among undergraduates who are living on their parents' dime and their professors' patience, theologies defended by seminarians who are young Elihus, reading and theorizing about other people's *agony,* but not yet knowing their own. We should be politely aloof in the presence of theologies created and debated by scholars with secure tenure, safe in their bubbles of ease and isolation, lecturing on like Job's friends, as they keep their neat theories sequestered from their messy, grubby real lives. We should beware of springtime theologies and even summertime theologies that haven't felt the burn of numbing cold winds and the sting of icy rains that soak and chill to the bone. Those who haven't felt the pain of loss or the agony of disappointment can only teach us so much. But those who have come to this point, who have groaned or shouted or spat out the prayer of *no* and have spent themselves to nothing in the process, only they can teach us about a faith that endures when faith has failed, a hope that endures when hope has died.

And yes, you have every right to wonder if I know what I am talking about, if I've walked this road myself. And of course, if I haven't, it would be fruitless to try to convince you that I have, just as it would be unnecessary if I have.

The Bible looks different once you've survived the autumn. It's no longer a repository for theological abstractions that can be organized into a tidy fortress called a "Christian worldview" or "orthodoxy."[2] It's no longer a wallet full of credit cards that you can slap on the table to pay every bill. It's no longer a weapon by which you vanquish those who don't have the good fortune of sharing your approved opinions. No, for an autumn-humbled seeker, the Bible is the living legacy of people who have lived in the real world, a diary of complexities and perplexities survived and reflected upon. It's the family album that carries the memories of ancestors who managed to keep their faith, hope, and love alive in a world that shocked them, rocked them, and mocked them. When you're in springtime, you love the Bible for the affirmation of the goodness of life that it offers. When you're in summertime, you love the Bible for the motivation to stay in the fray that it offers. But in autumn, you love the Bible more than ever, now for the honesty it offers—honesty about the death of naiveté, the falling of all green leaves.

With this perspective, it's no wonder that one of my favorite theologians is Walter Brueggemann. In his lectures and books you encounter a weather-beaten soul who knows what it means to survive "in hope against hope," which means "through disappointment after disappointment." When he reads the Bible—and in particular the Psalms—he sees three kinds of prayers.[3]

First are *prayers of orientation*. These are the spring- and summertime prayers of people who have never asked *why*, because God and the world make sense to them. Take Psalm 1, for example. In the simple summer world of Psalm 1, the good guys are blessed with good, and the bad guys get what they deserve:

> Happy are those
> who do not follow the advice of the wicked,
> or take the path that sinners tread,
> or sit in the seat of scoffers;
> but their delight is in the law of the LORD,
> and on his law they meditate day and night.
> They are like trees
> planted by streams of water,
> which yield their fruit in its season,
> and their leaves do not wither.
> In all that they do they prosper.
>
> The wicked are not so,
> but are like chaff that the wind drives away.
> Therefore the wicked will not stand in the judgment,
> nor sinners in the congregation of the righteous;
> For the LORD watches over the way of the righteous,
> but the way of the wicked will perish. (1:1–6)

The good prosper. The wicked wither. Prayers are answered. Disasters are averted. So all's right with the world.

I remember reading someone's story in the days after the September 2001 attacks in New York City. On his way to work that day, he had prayed in the train and felt extra close to God. He was high in the World Trade Center when the planes hit. Somehow, he was able to break through a wall that trapped him in rubble and escape. He and his family rejoiced, and I rejoiced with them. But then I thought about the woman in the next office, and the guy in the one after that. Did God love them less? Was their demise their own fault, because they didn't pray as much as this man did on the train that morning? Ask those kinds of questions, and your spring and summer world starts to unravel, and you move to Brueggemann's second kind of prayer, *prayers of disorientation.*

If Psalm 1 conveys orientation, the lament that begins in Lamentations 3 conveys disorientation. "I am one who has seen affliction," the poet begins, because he has been stricken by God's angry rod. God has brought him "into darkness without any light." He complains, "Against me alone God turns his hand, again and again, all day long."

The poet describes in painstaking—and painful—detail how he feels because of God's displeasure: old, besieged, surrounded "with bitterness and tribulation," walled in, trapped, weighed down, shut out, barred from progress, lost in a maze. God has become, he feels, like a vicious predator: "He is a bear lying in wait for me, a lion in hiding; he led me off my way and tore me to pieces." (This is in the Bible!) If that's not bad enough, God is like a sniper, and has done target practice on his heart. His litany of grievances against God ends like this:

> He has filled me with bitterness,
> he has sated me with wormwood.
> He has made my teeth grind on gravel;
> and made me cower in ashes;
> my soul is bereft of peace;
> I have forgotten what happiness is;
> so I say, "Gone is my glory,
> and all that I had hoped for from the LORD." *(3:15–18)*

Is the Bible telling the truth about God and life here? Has God indeed done all of these things to him? Is this the way we should truly feel about our hardships—that they are evidence of the unkindness of God? After all, this is in the Bible.

Here's how I would respond. The poet is not telling the truth about God and life, but he is telling the truth about how he feels about God and life, and we should feel free to tell the truth about how we feel as well. But as we do, we need to remember that our current feelings about God and life, as painfully true as they are to us right now, may not be the ultimate explanation of reality. They're the truth as we see it, but not the truth, the whole truth, and nothing but the truth.

The prayer of lament takes a brief hopeful turn as the poet tries to encourage himself, but again descends into grief and finally ends in a question, repeated twice:

*Why have you forgotten us completely?*
*Why have you forsaken us these many days? (5:20)*

*Why* is the final prayer of disorientation, the prayer beyond aspiration and exasperation, the prayer beyond refusal and rage. The world doesn't make sense any more. Our old answers don't satisfy. God seems to be our enemy, not our friend. We have raged about how utterly unacceptable this is. We have faced the option of walking away and saying, "Case closed. I am now an atheist," or "&#$$% God! I'm on my own now!" But we have refused even that refusal. After all, where else could we go, once we acknowledge that we don't understand, if we foreclose on the possibility of help beyond our understanding? So we choose to keep the question open: *Why?*

Think of the autumn of Perplexity as a tunnel with two ends. At the front end of the tunnel, we are quite sure that our easy answers will start working again after this brief delay is over. It's just a matter of time, we say, praying, with intensifying anxiety, *When? How long?* As we wait, we extract promises from the Bible and rub them like magic lamps. We focus on Proverbs, Joshua, and Matthew—places in the Bible where life makes sense and chaos is contained; we avoid Ecclesiastes, Job, Judges, Psalm 88, and Lamentations, because they scare us. We build theologies of forced naiveté, celebrating the passages that comfort us and explaining away or ignoring the ones that bother us. We package these reassuring theologies in books and sermons. These books sell amazingly well in bookstores, and they elicit generous donations in religious broadcasting, because we want to believe them. Paying for them, we hope, will demonstrate our investment in them. But the farther we go into the tunnel, the less we can believe them. We feel we're being dishonest unless we let out our rage and tell the truth about how insane life feels, how cruel and uncaring God seems to be.

So in the middle of the tunnel, where it's the darkest, we assume the worst, and we rage about the unacceptability of our lightless plight, shouting, *No, no, no!* But then, if we keep groping in the darkness, stumbling one foot after the other, still unable to see anything, we begin to reopen the question. Maybe there's a reason or purpose after all, maybe there's hope after all, maybe God hasn't disappeared or failed us after all—it's just our illusions and partial beliefs about God that have failed us.

So we ask *why*. And as we do, a glimmering pinpoint appears off in the distance. At first, we rub our eyes, sure we're imagining it. But we move toward it anyway. Where else can we go? As we stumble forward, we experience what Brueggemann calls *prayers of reorientation*. Lamentation now moves to this new space:

> *But this I call to mind,*
> *and therefore I have hope:*
> *The steadfast love of the* LORD *never ceases,*
> *his mercies never come to an end;*
> *they are new every morning;*
> *great is your faithfulness.*
> *"The* LORD *is my portion," says my soul,*
> *"therefore I will hope in him."*
>
> *The* LORD *is good to those who wait for him,*
> *to the soul that seeks him.*
> *It is good that one should wait quietly*
> *for the salvation of the* LORD.
> *It is good for one to bear*
> *the yoke in youth,*
> *To sit alone in silence,*
> *when the* LORD *has imposed it,*
> *to put one's mouth to the dust*
> *(there may yet be hope),*
> *to give one's cheek to the smiter,*
> *and be filled with insults.*
>
> *For the* LORD *will not*
> *reject forever.*
> *Although he causes grief, he will have compassion,*

*according to the abundance of his steadfast love;*
*for he does not willingly afflict*
*or grieve anyone. (3:21–33)*

At this far end of the tunnel, we add to our honesty about our pain a new honesty about our hope. But this is not the naive hope of a fresh-faced child. This is the tested hope of a leathery elder, whose eyes have seen disappointment, whose heart has been broken by tragedy, and whose faith, hope, and love have endured the test.

I think of such an elder, an old man who knew a lot of pain. He had been misunderstood by those he respected. He became the object of threats and plots to kill him. Still he kept on serving God, trusting God, loving God. He kept taking risks, knowing they would lead him to suffer still more: betrayal by friends, rumors from competitors, false accusations, long periods of imprisonment, beatings, and the daily pressure of concern for those he loved. He wrote: "I consider that the sufferings of this present time are not worth comparing with the glory about to be revealed in us" (Rom. 8:18).

These words would sound trite and cheap if someone who had suffered less said them. But this scarred man dared to believe that from every anguish, glory could be born, that each pain could become a labor pain, giving birth to glory: "We know that the whole creation has been groaning in labor pains until now" (8:22). Then he sees even deeper into the heart of things, that our groanings, our *when*s and *no*s and *why*s, are actually a sharing in the groanings of the Spirit herself, for she is the mother giving birth. Similarly, Jesus said, in the unique pain of a rebellious runaway's father we can see the love that groans in the heart of God (Luke 15:11–24). Jesus himself imaged that pain as he wept in a garden, as he bled on a cross, as he prayed forgiveness for those who mocked and crucified him. And so the cry of God becomes our own. Can this mean that the practice of lament is not simply humans crying to God, but God crying through humans? Could it be that through our compounding, agonizing autumnal tragedies, we in our own small way connect and tap into the pain that lies in the heart of the Creator?

As we've seen, there are many ways we can back away from this mystery. We can try to turn our pain into anger by blaming someone, even

God. We can take the drug of retaliation by scapegoating, by finding someone or something on whom to vent our pent-up anger.[4] We can construct elaborate theodocies—theories that explain and justify how evil has a right to exist, how it is in fact right for evil to exist. These approaches retrieve us from the void; they're attempts to return from autumn to Indian summer.

But if we don't turn back, if we allow ourselves to go naked into the void, we render ourselves vulnerable to a strange discovery: that we exist, that God has given us space to exist—even when God does not seem to exist. To be abandoned is to find out how real you are. God has made you so real that you exist even when alone. Yes, this can be terrifying; something in us is still very infantlike, terrified of being alone. But along with terrifying, this realization can be electrifying, an awakening, an enlightenment, a kind of shock therapy that makes a new state of being possible. It is the terror and wonder of realizing more fully the significance of the gift we have always had—the gift of being, of existing, of standing out of the void, of being alive.

If we dare to persevere, if we dare to keep holding our *why* of lament through the longest, darkest night of the year, morning will come. And when it comes, we will carry a new gravitas, a new substance, a new reality worthy of that word "glory." We will find the new day is a moment longer, and the next night a moment shorter. And the turning of a season will have begun, even though the cold of winter hasn't yet begun to show its full force.

# CHAPTER 21

# Why: *Holding the Question Open*

All that I'm now going through
Will make me better or bitter,
Break down or break through.
Learning this patience—it takes so much patience.
It's a great education,
But why is the tuition so high?
Why God, why?[1]

W HEN I WAS A pastor, many people in my congregation worried about me (just as some of my readers do now). Why wasn't my theology as plain and simple as that of the famous preachers on religious radio and TV? For those notables, everything was clear. There was an easy formula for everything, a simple black-and-white explanation or equation, a "biblical" solution, and no *when, no,* or *why.* I would try to explain to them that life on this side of the microphone where we live isn't that simple. Even though "orthodox" faith formulas might bring in donations, sell lots of books, and give a certain kind of comfort to people at a distance, I would say, such a formulaic faith doesn't work so well at close range, where life is lumpy, messy, ragged, chipped, and torn.

In fact, the same formulaic, easy-answer faith that fills some people with confidence fills others with dread and despair. It turns *why* into a weapon. It isolates the person crying in the hospice or grieving at the graveside. "*Why* didn't you have enough faith?" It heaps more guilt on the person in the psychiatric ward. "*Why* don't you just pull yourself together?" It blames the parent at the PFLAG (Parents, Families, and

Friends of Lesbians and Gays) meeting, not to mention what it does to the son or daughter in question. "*Why* can't you see what's black and white and conform to what's right?" It mocks the person sitting in the back row of the empty church who is experiencing *peripeteia* or the person who won't even dare come that far inside. "*Why* don't you just believe?" Honest pastors who live on the same side of the microphone as their people can't wield *why* as a weapon. They can't simply broadcast the springtime and summertime faith of integration 24/7. No, on this side of the microphone, we must all go through disorientation together, so together we can discover reorientation on the other side.

And that's what we find in one of our most cherished psalms, Psalm 23—not a formulaic faith, but a faith that has walked through the dark valley and come through on the other side:

> The LORD is my shepherd, I shall not want.
> He makes me lie down in green pastures;
> he leads me beside quiet waters;
> he restores my soul.
> He leads me in right paths
> for his name's sake.
>
> Even though I walk through the valley of the shadow of death,
> I fear no evil;
> for you are with me;
> your rod and your staff—
> they comfort me.
>
> You prepare a table before me
> in the presence of my enemies;
> you anoint my head with oil;
> my cup overflows.
> Surely goodness and mercy shall follow me
> all the days of my life,
> and I shall dwell in the house of the LORD
> my whole life long.

Yes, thank God, in this life there are green pastures, still waters, overflowing cups, and laden banquet tables. But there are also valleys of the shadow of death in which evil lurks and enemies wait for a misstep or mistake upon which to pounce. To sustain us through those dark valleys, we are given simple words of aspiration, refusal, and lament: *when, no,* and *why.*

The most powerful dark-valley prayer in the Bible, I believe, is also the shortest, uttered by Jesus as he hung on a cross: "My God, my God," he cried, expressing the tattered remains of faith. Doesn't that simple word "my" express some hold on God, some claim, some relationship? But then comes, "Why have you forsaken me?" Could there be a more naked expression of doubt than those words? The forsaking is in the present perfect tense, meaning that it has already happened, is a done deal, and is at this moment ongoing. Abandonment is the splintered, brutal reality to which Jesus is nailed as he says these words. He is suspended and stretched spiritually just as he is physically, crucified between the "my" of faith and the *why* of abandonment. This is his *peripeteia,* if you will, the moment at which everything he has trusted has collapsed under him. But even in that moment of total darkness, could the word *why* still hold open a crack in the door, a hope against hope that there is some reason for this madness?

Now that word I just used, "reason," is problematic. If by it I mean "explanation," I don't think it's helpful, because, as we've seen, offering an explanation for evil, abandonment, or suffering creates as many problems as it solves. If "reason" means "plan," we're equally in trouble. Do we really want to say that God happily engineers earthquakes, rapes, crashes, murders, and childhood diseases all as part of a preordained plan? ("Yes, I know this rape is unpleasant now, and yes, this genocide is quite frightening now, and yes, that fire is quite hot, and that collapsing ceiling is quite heavy, and starvation is a tough way to die. But don't worry. It's all part of a plan.") Is it possible to save that kind of God from being a heartless puppet master?

Both explanations and plans put us in a determined universe, a mechanistic universe, a universe without real freedom, an engineered, rat-in-a-maze universe. Explanations do so by telling us something about the present. They say in the nature of things this is inevitable; it must happen, must be this way, because this is just how the gears turn, and this is how the engines fire. Plans reach back into the past, telling us that the present explanation isn't a design flaw, but was actually preengineered intentionally. They say all this was preordained, written into the script by God, designed in every detail, so that every nerve ending would burn with exactly this excruciation at this moment. Not to worry.

But there's another possible meaning for that word "reason," a meaning that together with the word *why* can liberate us from a determined, mechanistic universe. Instead of saying, "What plan in the past predetermined this suffering and therefore explains it in the present?" we could ask a very different question: "What possible good in the future can be brought out of this tragic suffering in the present?" This question makes no assumption that the present moment is inevitable or intentional. But it also makes no assumption that the present moment is meaningless. It holds open the possibility that some future meaning, some future value, some future good could be wrested from this present tragedy and loss. Ultimately, this is what we all need when we suffer— not explanations or reasons, but meaning.

The *why* that seeks an explanation or a plan looks backward; the *why* that seeks meaning by bringing some future good out of this agony looks forward. The former invites passivity and resignation. The latter seeks a new creative possibility, even at the nadir of hope, at midnight on the longest night of the year. It says, "Well, the worst has happened. There it is. It's all in ruins, all a loss, a complete failure and disaster." But instead of saying, "I'll just curse God and die," it dares ask, "What good can we pull from this mess? What meaning can we make of this madness?"

It's dangerous to try to psychologize Jesus, I know, but let's go back once again to the night before his crucifixion. Jesus has a sense of where things are going, and so he goes to pray in an olive grove called Gethsemane. Matthew and Mark speak of his feeling "agitated" and "deeply grieved," even "to the point of death," so much so that he doesn't want to be left alone (26:38; 14:34). At this moment, if Jesus lived in an explanation-driven, plan-driven universe, we would expect him to pray, "I know this can't be avoided. I know it's part of your plan. So give me the strength to go through with it." But that's far different from what he says: "If it is possible, let this cup pass from me . . ." That word "if" tells us something terrifyingly significant: at this moment, Jesus doesn't have clarity about a predetermined, set-in-concrete plan. At this moment, he wonders if there can be some other way. But if not, he says, "Yet not what I want but what you want."[2]

To go through with a plan is one thing. But to step into the abyss of *if* is another thing. And I sense a powerful resonance between this *if* in Gethsemane and that *why* on Golgotha. Jesus isn't trusting a plan; he is trusting God. He believes that, whatever happens, God can turn it for good. I have tried, but I have never succeeded in imagining a trust more naked and pure than this.

In uttering that question *why,* Jesus validated that pain, abandonment, doubt, and despair are indeed part of the human condition, and they are even part of a life well lived. But they are not the last word. They can be questioned. Jesus thus comes out in solidarity not only with faithful people, but also with doubters, questioners, and skeptics everywhere. He sustained both *my God* and *why God,* naked faith and naked honesty.

Do you see what this means for us? When we are in the middle of the tunnel, at the low point of the valley, on the longest, darkest night of the year crying *why, why, why* in the void, we are both alone and not alone. Jesus is with us, and through him God is with us, even as we declare our doubt and faith in the same agonizing cry. Now here I am being transparently trinitarian, and some may not be able to go here with me. But for me, as I seek to enter that moment and ponder it from the inside, here's what I see.

God isn't above all this, looking down with the divine clipboard on which sits the divine checklist, checking off achieved divine objectives on the divine plan as they occur. Whipping, check. First nail, check. Second nail, check. First pint of blood, check. And so on. Neither is God apart from this, somehow at a distance, uninvolved. No, G-d is a part of this, in it, fully crucified in the agony of this personal, histori-cal, political, social, spiritual, finite, infinite moment. In Christ, G-d is godforsaken. In Christ, G-d hangs without a script or skyhook, without an escape clause written into the contract, without an explanation or plan, without a reason in that sense, and without a prayer, except that simple word *why*.[3]

And in that simple, painful word is found all the hope that exists in the universe, not a hope that reaches backwards for an explanatory plan, but a hope that reaches forward, into the darkness, saying, "Can we work any good from this?" And whatever resurrection means, however we conceive of it, it must mean that yes, even in this, even in the worst, even in the end, even in *peripeteia,* good can be willed or sought or hoped for. Good can be worked. Good can rise again.

So even now you can dare to hold the simple word *why* before God. As you hold it, first imagine yourself alone. Alone, feel your own pain, your own unanswered prayers, your own exhaustion and disappointment. Don't rush away from it. Let *why* be a container, and let it fill with all the pain you've kept at bay. If tears come, let them. If they don't, it's okay.

Still alone, now you expand your circle of empathy, thinking of others you know, bringing their agony into your own *why*. Alone you feel the suffering that nobody is doing anything about, and you cry *why*. Alone you feel the utter unacceptability of an unjust past and an unjust present, and you hold your *why* in your soul before G-d and the universe, on behalf of everyone whose hopes have been mocked by bitterness. Remember, you are not seeking an easy explanation that will make injustice acceptable; rather, you are refusing all such explanations. As they present themselves, you dismiss each one with another *why*. If no one else in the universe raised the question, you would raise your *why* alone.

Now imagine yourself being joined by others, or rather imagine yourself joining them, because millions were in this place of agony and lament long before you knew it existed. So imagine yourself now joining the countless people whose company you have tried all your life to avoid: the forgotten and the despairing, the suffering heroes and the uncelebrated martyrs, the losers and the failures, the mystified and the bewildered, the wannabes and the has-beens. You've always sought a place among the successful elite, in the winner's circle, the inner circle, but you now find yourself nowhere, in darkness, with so many others. Their lot is yours now; you are identified with them in the "we" who suffer. And with them you cry *why*.

After this identification has settled in, it's time to let your *why* lean forward. You have questioned an unacceptable and unjust past and present; now you must tilt your question toward the future. Perhaps now your *why* becomes a *why not*. Why not a better future? Why not more compassion, more justice, more harmony, more connection, more vitality, more beauty, more truth, more grace? Why not? Let your *why* and your *why not* hold open the possibility of a future where things are not perfect, but are at least moving in the direction of hope, of light, of life. In this way, your *why* gradually can become an expression of will. You choose to will future good in the midst of present evil, to will future light in the midst of present darkness, to will future resurrection in the midst of present death. Hold that *why* as an act of will.

If this is difficult for you, it may help you to turn your *why* against something. *Why* should I *not* give up hope? *Why* should I *not* become cynical, jaded, despairing? *Why* should I *not* lose faith? *Why* should I *not* just seek to save my own skin and say to hell with everyone else? Implicit in your question will be the answer, "So that some good may come."

Here in this willing, I believe, you will sense G-d is present already, forever willing goodness, truth, and beauty and waiting for others to will it too. If you sense that Presence, simply will with it, letting that will say, in essence, *here's why*.

When you practice lament, when you are stretched and suspended on the cross of abandonment, you do not feel heroic. You do not feel like a runner about to cross the finish line. You do not feel that a hopeful Sunday is coming after a nightmarish Friday and a blank, lifeless Saturday. You feel exhausted and finished. You feel as though you're fading, dying, letting go. And so you do. Having kept the question open as long as you can, you let go.

Dare you do so now? Dare you drop, crying *why*, falling not from the God above you, but into the G-d below you?

PART IV

# Harmony: The Season of Spiritual Deepening

Y OU NEVER KNEW YOU were capable of feeling, much less surviving, such pain. You felt that you were about to break open, that all your blood and all your insides would explode out of you if the pressure lasted for one more second. It couldn't get any worse, you thought. But then it did. Contraction after contraction. Worse, and worse, and worse still. And then, grunting, panting, sweating, screaming, you took a deep breath and pushed once more, feeling it was futile to do so, but doing so anyway. Suddenly—it was hard to believe—suddenly there was this gush and the feeling of something slipping between your thighs, and the midwife picked up your daughter and lifted her to your breast. A gasp, a cry, a beautiful cry. Tears—yours, your husband's, even the midwife's. Clean towels, warm blankets, a camera flash, and there in your arms is your little girl, and it's happening without your trying, without her trying; you are bonding to one another, sweaty maternal skin to slippery infant skin, in a bond that can never be broken.

Harmony. It comes through pain, after pain. The artist agonizes, and finally, no not yet, no not yet, yes, yes, at the finally after finally, beauty comes. The team struggles, defeat, defeat, defeat, and then victory. The struggle for liberation faces setbacks, betrayal, duplicity, more betrayal, hope, disappointment, more setbacks, vicious lies, humiliation, defection, despair, and then, almost as an afterthought because it has come so much harder and later than expected, breakthrough.

There are joys in Simplicity. There are victories. There are joys in

Complexity too, and even certain satisfactions in Perplexity. But there is a quiet fullness of joy that comes after Perplexity. We might call it humility, even maturity, or better, Harmony, because it not only transcends the previous stages, but includes them. It integrates Simplicity, Complexity, and Perplexity into a rich, dynamic four-part Harmony. It's a clear and open space, a quiet time and place that makes room for new melodies to take shape and find voice. There is nothing like the life that is born through the hard labor of becoming, enduring, never giving up, never letting go, and then, paradoxically, letting go, and then receiving all you had hoped for and more.[1]

When Stage Three, Perplexity, gives way to Stage Four, Harmony, there is a quiet transcendence—a transcendence that brings along or includes the previous stages rather than leaving them behind. So the right-versus-wrong dualism of Simplicity, the effective-versus-ineffective pragmatism of Complexity, and the honest-versus-dishonest relativism of Perplexity are taken up and expanded into something bigger in the Harmony of Stage Four.

The first black-and-white simplicity now fills out into a second simplicity that is full-color and alive. If first-simplicity truths were bold, judging, and exclusive, second-simplicity truths are no less bold, but they harmonize, integrate, and reconcile. You can feel this grand second simplicity glowing in elegant, harmonizing words like these:

"I desire compassion and not sacrifice" (Matt. 12:7).

"Seek first God's reign and God's justice, and everything else you need will come to you in time" (Matt. 6:33).

"Love God with all your being, and love your neighbors as yourself" (Matt. 22:36–39).

"Faith, hope, and love abide, these three, but the greatest of these is love" (1 Cor. 13:13).

If in Stage One we knew that everything was knowable, in Stage Two we knew that everything was doable, and in Stage Three we knew that everything was relative, now we in some way come to know with the old sage that "everything is suitable for its time" (Eccl. 3:11). We can finally begin to accept that all our knowing, past and present, is partial (1 Cor. 13:12). Harmony requires this posture of humility, which allows us to finally see authority figures neither as godlike (as in Stages One and Two) nor as demonic (as in Stage Three), but rather as human beings like us, often doing the best they can and even then making plenty of mistakes along the way. This newfound humility also allows us to find our identity in a new way in relation to others: not in Stage One dependence, not in Stage Two independence, and not in Stage Three counterdependence, but in the more mature interdependence of mutuality.

And what happens to our view of God in Stage Four? In some ways, this is the stage when faith takes off its dualistic, pragmatic, and relativistic clothing and seeks to encounter God nakedly. Of course, in Stage Four we know we must use words, just as we have in previous stages, but we also know that our words conceal as they reveal. Similarly, we must celebrate the rich heritage of our religious traditions, but those traditions are now the foundation on which we build, not the ceiling under which we are trapped. Stage One orthodoxy now morphs into what some have called paradoxy—the realization that every true statement about God (including this one) cannot fully contain the true majesty and wonder of God. This humility before God helps create harmony among all of us who believe in God, making it harder for us to maintain the old us-versus-them dualisms that have so often animated religious conservatives and liberals alike. (For this reason, Stage Four people will often react against this four-stage framework itself, feeling that it separates them from others to whom they want to be connected and with whom they want to be identified.)

And where from here? Is this the pinnacle? Have we now arrived? As you might expect, this season of Harmony eventually opens into a new Simplicity. This new second Simplicity eventually matures into a new season of higher Complexity, and so on, in an ascending spiral of growth and discovery that continues as long as life itself. Far from feeling we have finally arrived, in Stage Four we finally begin to understand that arrival has never been the point.

# CHAPTER 22

# Behold: *The Emergence of the Meditative Mind*

*The Practice of Meditation and Wonder:
Deepening by Seeing*
Alternate Words: *Indeed, Amen, See, Eureka, Maybe, Ah*

Wonder is the alpha and the omega of the human mind. It stands at the beginning and end of our quest to understand ourselves and the world. Aristotle said philosophy begins in wonder. It is the most primal of emotions, at once ordinary and disturbing. As the sixth sense, the natural religious sense, wonder is the royal road that leads us to the other elemental emotions, and thus to a renewed sense of the sacred.

SAM KEEN[1]

IT WAS EASTER SEVERAL years ago. I had just survived a decade that had basically kicked the stuffing out of me. I was thinking about the meaning of resurrection in my life, and in the stories of Lazarus and Jesus. This song took shape over a couple of weeks:

*When we think back on our journey over many years,
Nights of joys and laughter, and days of trials and tears,
With piercing, draining sorrows that broke us on our knees,
While deep inside hide our regrets that no one ever sees . . .
How can comfort find us locked up in our darkest room?
How can we leave the past behind and escape it like a tomb?*

*Sometimes we feel like Lazarus, buried in our shame,*
*But the risen Christ is on the move, and we faintly hear our name.*
*From deep fatigue and heartache, we come back full and strong . . .*
*From guilty isolation, to a place where we belong.*
*We wonder every springtime when birds are on the wing,*
*When the forests show a mist of green and the brooks and marshes sing,*
*How can tender life endure the winter's vicious storms?*
*How can fragile breath survive the freeze till April warms?*
*Life keeps resurrecting. How, we don't understand.*
*But when the risen Christ comes near, spring breaks across the land.*

I had lost a lot during those years of spiritual deconstruction and struggle, mostly things I've since been better off without. But the loss was acutely painful nonetheless. It was especially tough, because I was never sure that anything would replace the spiritual "baby teeth" that were loosening and falling out one after another. As I wrote that song, I remember feeling that at least one new substantial realization had come, that God truly is the God of resurrection. God truly is the one who brings you through the valley of the shadow of death. In the dead of winter, God is the source of a new springtime hope. It was a moment of *Eureka! Voilà! Indeed! Behold!*

In Maryland, where I've lived most of my fifty-four years, the birds start singing in late January and early February. Even though it's technically winter, the days are already growing longer. The official beginning of spring on March 21 is still weeks away, but somehow the birds know. And so do the plants, as sap silently surges up the trunks of trees and bulbs bulge in the soil. It's not obvious yet; the ponds may still be covered with ice, and the tree buds are still small, clenched tight. But quietly, life is staging an insurrection against the cold, preparing to emerge again based on a hint and hunch of coming warmth. One morning, there it is, a crocus popping through the snow. A few days later, you hear a V-shaped flock of geese moving north above you. One rainy afternoon, you smell the soil as it unfreezes and releases its subtle, moist scent. *Behold!*

*Behold* is our simple word for the practice of *meditation*. It's a call to notice, not just to glance. It's an invitation to open your eyes, blink, linger, and see in a new way. It is to normal seeing what listening is to normal hearing or what concentrating is to normal thinking. *Behold* evokes focused attention, a holding of what is seen so it can be slowly savored. *Behold* is, in this sense, a word uttered first to our own souls: "Look and see," we say to ourselves. "Notice. Be aware. Watch. Appreciate. Maybe—just maybe there's more going on here than you've ever seen before."

But *behold* is more than talking to ourselves. As we summon ourselves to attention, we acknowledge to God that what God has been trying to show us is finally coming into focus. So *behold* is a prayer indeed. "Ah, Lord, now I see! It was there all along, but I didn't get it! Wow! Amazing! Beautiful! Wonderful! Behold!"

All of these words arise from what Christian mystics call nondual seeing, nondual thinking, or the contemplative mind.[2] By practicing this new way of seeing, we turn the calendar page, as it were, to begin a new year.

In the spring season of Simplicity, we see in a dualistic way. Everything we see is immediately categorized in relation to the ego. It is evaluated in relation to self-interest: good/evil; us/them; advantageous/disadvantageous; superior/inferior; benefit/cost; right/wrong; in/out; pleasurable/painful; safe/dangerous; acceptable/unacceptable; winner/loser; ally/enemy; and so on. These comparisons and contrasts are absolute judgments, *punto final,* period, end of story, case closed.

In the summer season of Complexity, we see in a multiplex way. Our dualism begins to break down. We move from black and white to shades of gray. We go from seeing the world in terms of twos to seeing the world in threes, fours, fives, dozens. We go from fixed categories to gradations, spectra, and ranges, from bounded sets to centered sets. We move from binary categorization to sophisticated classification, and so judgment and analysis become complexified. In this stage we begin to be able to see some good in what we had previously categorized as evil, and some evil in what we had previously categorized as good.

In the autumn season of Perplexity, we see in a relativistic way. We take the scrutiny we have developed to dissect the opinions, perspectives, and beliefs of others, and we turn that scrutiny on our own opinions, perspectives, and beliefs. We self-distance enough to self-examine, self-critique, and self-deconstruct. We give everything a second thought; in other words, we repent. Like leaves falling off trees, our previous certainties and judgments fall to the ground, until the only absolute left is that there are no absolutes. That paradox is chilling, and to hold it feels like dying.

So now, the winter season beyond Perplexity begins with a kind of nakedness. Naked trees. Frozen ponds. Hibernation. Starkness. Long, dark, silent nights, and cold days blanketed in snow. Autumn exhaustion leads now to winter's rest. That chattering, hypervigilant consciousness—that first judged in Stage One, and then analyzed in Stage Two, and then deconstructed in Stage Three—now goes silent. It takes a breath. When we open our eyes in this space, we begin to see and know with the meditative mind.

What you look for determines what you see. What you focus on determines what you miss. The way you see determines what you are blind to and what you render invisible. So this meditative kind of seeing accepts the limitations of earlier and noisier ways of seeing, and it practices, in their place, a new vision, a new beholding. When we behold in this new way, we enter a second naiveté. We begin to remember what was forgotten when we ate of the tree of knowledge of good and evil in the Garden of Eden story. We learn to behold the goodness in everything, the goodness that the Creator beheld in the freshly made world: _behold_—"it was very good" (Gen. 1:31).[3]

It's not that everything is good. Far from it. Nobody who has practiced _when, no,_ and _why_ would ever say that. It's that there is good in everything or there is potential to bring good out of anything. It's not that everything is the same. Far from it. It's that everything both differs and belongs, everything can be redeemed, everything can be forgiven. It's not that everything is relative, with no firm or fixed identity, but that everything is related, so its identity is bound up somehow with the identity of everything else.

We used to look for evil to judge, evil to name, shame, and blame. But that was an easy thing, so easy that we now find the whole exercise rather boring, childish, and small-minded. It was also an ego-flattering and prideful thing, placing us in a godlike position. We now wish to see without that arrogance, without that air of superiority or supremacy.

Now as we learn to behold the good, the world is bathed in a gentle luminosity of compassion instead of a harsh light of analysis, inspection, and judgment. Before we looked for flaws, which gave us an excuse to reject, but now we look for goodness, which gives us reason to respect. Instead of looking for dangers to flee and fear, we look for possibilities to pursue and encourage. We turn from evaluating to valuing. We grow from faultfinding to something far bigger and better: beauty-finding, beholding, seeing in love, seeing with God.[4]

This new seeing, of course, includes the way we view other human beings. The apostle Paul had to learn this. Like many of us, he worked hard to become an angry religious man. He had made a big investment in judging, exposing, imprisoning, and even killing those whom he labeled inferior and wrong. Notice how he describes the transformation he has experienced "in Christ"—it is a transformation in seeing or encountering:

> The love of Christ is pressing us toward this realization: if one died for all people, then all people have died. And if one died for all people, then all people should no longer live for themselves, but for him who died and rose from the dead on their behalf. So now we encounter all persons in a new way. No longer do we encounter them from within a self-centered mind-set; that was the flawed, egotistical way in which we once encountered Christ himself. Now, having encountered Christ in a new way, we encounter others: for all who are in Christ, all creation is new! The old things have passed away. Behold! All has become new! (2 Cor. 5:14–17, author's translation)[5]

Last year's sight—the sight of spring, summer, and autumn—was the sight of a scorekeeper or faultfinder. We stood with the Pharisees, stones in hand, staring at a woman caught in adultery. All we could see was a sinner needing punishment. Now, in the early light of a new year, we stand with Christ, in Christ, beholding a daughter needing love. Last spring, summer, and fall, we stood with the disciples, disgusted by a Gentile woman, an outsider who had the nerve to ask *our* Messiah for help. Now, in the clear cool light of winter, we stand in Christ and behold through his eyes a woman of great faith and great love. Once we stood with Peter, seeing Cornelius and his friends as "unclean," because they were different from us; now, in the light of a new day, we behold people "in Christ," beyond the old categories of us and them, clean and unclean (John 8:1–11; Matt. 15:21–28; Acts 10:1–48). This new way of seeing is so different from our old way of seeing that we now say, "Though I was blind, now I see" (John 9:25).

Behold, a new creation! A new reality! A new universe! In the old, flawed, egotistical mind-set, I used to see some people as my friends and others as my enemies, some as superior and others as inferior, some as clean and others as unclean, some as worthy and others as unworthy, some as "us" and others as "them." I judged their value in relation to me and my safety, my interests, my opinions, my pride, my profit, my lust, my affiliations, my fear. *Behold!* Now I am able to escape the black-hole gravity of my old egocentric perspective, aptly described by novelist Walker Percy as "the great suck of self." Instead, we rise to see with the living God, seeing others with the living, loving, holy God's compassionate eyes.[6]

But my renewed vision doesn't stop with the faces of others; it continues when I look in the mirror. Up until now I have seen myself as a mix of good and bad, good I am proud of and bad I am ashamed of—again, seeing myself in relation to my own interests in being popular, powerful, approved, successful. If I'm tempted to self-worship, I live with one kind of blindness about myself: failing to acknowledge my character defects. If I'm tempted to self-loathing, it's another kind of blindness: failing to see my worth as God's beloved creature made in God's image.

But now I disconnect from those old viewpoints of myself, and I join God, who sees me in the true light of compassion, and knows me better than I know myself. My faults aren't excused, but they are swallowed up in love and forgiveness. My weaknesses aren't covered up, but they are not the point. My dark side isn't denied, but neither is it thrown in my face as an accusation. My strengths are neither exaggerated nor minimized; they simply are. And so I join God in seeing me. *Behold!*

But there's still more. My new way of seeing leads me to see all creation differently. I used to look at a forested hillside, and all I saw was how many profitable board feet of lumber it could produce for me or how many tons of coal I could blast out of it to sell. I looked at an empty field and called it "undeveloped," oblivious to the beautiful ecosystem that had developed there over millennia. I imagined the profit I could make by "developing" it with bulldozers and blacktop into a strip mall. But that was seeing in the old way.

Now, with Moses in the desert, I see a common bush aglow with a holy nonconsuming flame. Now, with Isaiah standing before a forest, I see the leaves in the windswept branches shimmering, and for me they are applauding God. Now, with the psalmists, I see wild creatures thriving in God's care. Now, the waves roar and lightning pierces the sky in dramatic celebration of God's glorious majesty and splendor. Now, with Jesus, I see the flowers of the field and the birds of the air as God's beloved creatures, each and every thing possessing true and intrinsic value apart from any price put on it in the meat markets of human economy. No wonder Martin Luther could say, "If you could understand a single grain of wheat, you would die for wonder."[7]

Most wonderful of all, if we dare venture into the new creation, you and I will behold God in a new way. We used to encounter God from our self-serving vantage point—for what God could do for us, advancing our agenda, coddling our insecurities, fulfilling our desires, reinforcing our prejudices. But now, even God shines in a new light. God has been transformed for us—not that G-d has changed in essence or character, but that our concept or image of G-d has changed, adjusted, expanded, been corrected, slightly at least, in the direction of who G-d truly is. *Behold!*

Something happens at this stage that is very difficult to describe: we learn as never before to separate G-d from our God concepts. We learn that it is one thing to trust our beliefs, believe in our theology, or have confidence in our doctrines and creeds about God. But it is a very different thing to trust God directly, desperately, helplessly, nakedly. We believe in G-d-beyond-beliefs as distinguished from the-god-of-my-beliefs. I think this is the distinction people in various twelve-step recovery movements are making—albeit inarticulately at times—when they refer to "God as we understand him" in steps 3 and 11.[8] The "Power greater than ourselves" of step 2 obliquely refers to the One we have identified as G-d in these pages. So by referring to G-d as "God as we understand him," we acknowledge that our best understanding of God is just that—our current best attempt to understand One who by definition, excels, overflows, and transcends anything and everything we will ever think or say. When we acknowledge that no word, concept, name, image, temple, system, creed, or religion can ever contain G-d, we climb a high mountain with the prophet Isaiah and shout to the valley below, "Behold your God!"[9] We are reduced to saying, "I can't tell you in words alone; you have to see for yourself."

And so we come to this practice of simply beholding, in humble stillness, in wide-eyed awe. And we realize, perhaps with some dismay as well as wonder, not only that the God we now behold is bigger than our previous understandings, but also that this will always be the case. Language fails us at these moments. Our pronouns falter, because God is more than we understand when we say "he," "she," "it," or even "you." Our nouns stumble—even revered nouns like "power," "father," "rock," "spirit," "creator," "being," "Lord," "God," and even "G-d." Even our most paradoxical and mysterious nouns break open—like "Trinity," "the Divine," "the Sacred One," or "the Holy One"—because even they can't fully contain or define the mystery to which they point and ascribe honor. Our verbs point, but even they can't contain, and our best statements stutter, as true as they are. Yes, to say "God is great" speaks the truth, but it might simultaneously obscure the equal truth that God is gentle and kind or that God dwells with the lowly. At a moment like this, when we feel that the reality of our Subject oversaturates and bursts every attempt to contain it, we may be tempted just to be silent, to say nothing. But how can we? How can we not speak of a God so wonderful to behold?[10]

I first began to bump up against this paradox in the middle of the difficult years that I described at the beginning of this chapter. I was doubting my beliefs about God, deconstructing my theological system, and questioning my concepts of God. The experience was terrifying. It was terrifying in large part because I was a human being who had become as accustomed to living in my belief system as I was to living in my house, my marriage, my skin. It felt as if my faith-home was caving in with me inside of it. It felt as though my faith-marriage was collapsing. I no longer felt comfortable in my own faith-skin.

Beyond that, I had the added practical stress of making my living as a teacher of the theological system in which I was at home and to which I was wedded in deep commitment. So it was as if my home, marriage, and career were all simultaneously collapsing. My entire life was being sucked into the vortex of some terrible whirlpool, hurricane, or tornado.

To whom do you turn in such a circumstance? All I can say is that I had no one to turn to, no one other than God, the G-d, that is, who transcended and therefore could be separated from my beliefs, systems, and concepts. I can't explain how the transfer of trust from God to G-d happened, only that it was messy, slow, reiterative, and terrifying. And wonderful. The process remains unfinished, of course. As it unfolds, there are moments when I find myself in the eye of the storm, and there I can breathe. And *behold*.

# CHAPTER 23

# Behold: *Faith Beyond Belief*

A mystery is a problem that encroaches upon itself because the questioner becomes the object of the question. Getting to Mars is a problem. Falling in love is a mystery.

GABRIEL MARCEL

THERE IS A KIND of slow-motion quality to finding yourself in this eye of the storm, and the slowness can only be described as reverent or holy. Beholding is a slow and reverent seeing with God, a slow and reverent knowing with God, a slow and reverent holding of everyone and everything in the light of God—others, ourselves, all creation, even God. In that suspended moment, we breathe in *wonder,* and we breathe out *behold.* There are many ways we might try to express this beholding: "Ah, now I see. How did I miss it for so long?" Or "So that's what was really going on when I used to think I understood." Or "Ouch. I can't believe I was so wrongheaded and ignorant before!" Or "Wow. Maybe there's still more I haven't seen and understood." Or "Before I had the words but not the meaning; now I have the meaning—but I can't find the words to do it justice." Or "Beautiful. Indescribable."[1]

Whatever words best capture the experience, meditation becomes a practice of returning to and holding the wide-eyed wonder of childhood. We don't waste a lot of time upbraiding ourselves for how wrong we've been about so many things. No, we simply let our mistakes fade into the past, and we focus instead on seeing anew, seeing whole, beholding the beauty we missed for so long.

This seeing-with-God is especially precious, because we have just passed through the season of *when, no,* and *why.* The pain, the dissatisfaction, and disorientation of that declining season have created the void into which surprise and wonder now silently burst. The aspiration, exasperation, fury, rage, doubt, and abandonment now give way to wonder, joy, and peace. Sometimes that peace comes to us all at once, in a moment of ecstasy and revelation. But more often, I think, it's like a gradual dawning, as when Joseph looked back over his life with all its betrayal, delay, unfairness, and mistreatment and gradually began to see that, although others intended him harm, God intended his well-being all along; others did evil, but even from their evil, God created good (Gen. 50:20).

And to the degree we can maintain the prayerful seeing and insightful prayer of meditation, when new troubles come our way, new threats, we can maintain a kind of peace, a peace beyond understanding, which means that we remain free of turmoil without having figured out what's going on. We can rest in God in the eye of the storm, seeing our difficulties neither as punishment for some past offense nor as evidence that God's protection has gone off-line, but as an opportunity for God to speak expanding good into an expanding void. This is why this kind of seeing is often associated with the word "wait" in scripture. "Wait on the Lord," we are told. Don't slide back into anxiety and anger. Don't rush ahead in a rush to judgment. Don't demand a quick solution (as you may have done when you were praying *when*). Don't assume the worst (as you may have done when you were praying *no*). Don't presume that an answer is forthcoming (as you may have done when you prayed *why*). No, just wait. Relax. Rest. Don't feel the situation has to be fixed. Hold on, and keep yours eyes open, and you will eventually behold what you do not see now.

The waiting, the slowing down, applies to our pleasures too. Don't rush through this pleasure, but savor it as a gift from God. Taste it. Enjoy it. Linger here. Join God in seeing what a wonderful thing, what a wonderful moment, what a wonderful gift this is. Often, the gift is an insight. You're reading a book, perhaps even this one, or, even better, scripture itself, and you see something. *Behold!* you say. But rather than rushing on to the next thought, you put the book down; you close your eyes, and you hold the thought in your mind as you might hold a spoonful of delicious ice cream or a sip of extraordinary wine on your tongue. "Ah," you say. "Mmmm," you say. "Delicious," you say. You are speaking the language of meditation. This is what Gregory of Nyssa meant when he said, "Only wonder understands." Just to hold an insight in a shared, wondrous *behold* with God—perhaps we need to invent a new word to describe it: *wonderstanding.*

This ability to behold is especially essential when we encounter paradox and mystery. We see things we can't understand, and we are tempted to shrink them to fit into our existing constructs, paradigms, worldviews, or thought systems. We want to explain what we see, to capture it in words, to resolve its tensions, but if we do, we will shrink, flatten, or reduce our vision. If we resist that reflex even for a few moments, we can simply stand in silence, in awe, and see—see both sides of the paradox and not need to explain one side away.

Many experiences come to mind when I think of this practice of meditation in my own life, but I'll only recount one. It occurred during that tough season of doubt and deconstruction; it was one of those eye-of-the-storm moments. I was preparing a sermon, a sermon about which, by the way, I don't remember anything. I had my Bible open on my desk, and another book too. I may have just read a quote from St. Augustine, but I don't remember the details. I do remember that it was in the afternoon, and as I was reading, thinking, and pondering, I began to sense that something was waiting for me if I didn't rush on to the next thought.

Then, it was as if I broke through to a deeper level, or fell through the floor—that might be a better image for it. I stopped reading. I stopped writing and working on my outline. I just sat there in my chair and closed my eyes. If you had seen me, you would have said, "Poor guy. He's fallen asleep, he's taking a nap." And in a sense I was. I was resting, resting in God's presence. My thoughts were like a flock of birds flying overhead. They floated by, floated by, and then they were gone. All I could feel was a joyful stillness surrounding me, a clarity cooling me, a peace breathing into me.

As I sat there, a question formed itself in my mind. I didn't feel as though I had created the question or had to go after it or reach for it.

I just felt that it opened up in me, having formed by surprise in my mind. The question seemed to spill from God's mind to my own: "Is there any thought you can have of God that is too good?" And for some moments, I just sat with that question, and as I did, I received something: a deep and powerful realization of the goodness of God. I was suspended in that realization for some time. Other questions slowly presented themselves: Can you accept that you will never, ever, ever contain God? That you will never, ever capture God in words—even though you are a preacher and writer, working with words? Can you just behold, in silent wonder and reverent awe?[2]

Since that afternoon, meditative seeing—seeing with God, seeing in God—has become a more and more important part of my spiritual life. Every day provides constant opportunities to experiment. Consider these three scenarios that you could try right now.

First, you could go to a public place and practice beholding people with God. You'll no doubt hear your chattering, analyzing, critical mind assessing each one in accordance with its own agendas, desires, drives, and neuroses: fat, thin, rich, poor, stylish, frumpish, sexually attractive, sexually unattractive, my kind of person, not my kind of person, Christian, non-Christian, and so on. Instead of living within this cramped space of judgment, observe it—behold it from a distance. "There it goes again," you might say with amusement. "My limited human mind is acting as if I were God and I were qualified to judge these people." Consciously separate yourself from that small mental courtroom; step outside it and above it into God's larger, more gracious space. Allow the Spirit to help you see these people in God's light—each one precious, each one in need, each one at once beautiful and broken and dangerous and dignified. Whenever you find yourself shrinking back into the dualist, courtroom mind, simply observe it, name it, and step outside it as you return to a more generous, gracious beholding with God.

Second, you could go to a natural place—anywhere, really, where there's a patch of sky or a blade of grass or some grains of sand—and behold God's creative work. Let your senses wake up—sight, of course, but also smell, hearing, and touch—and imagine yourself in an art gallery where every single thing is a work of art, and each work has been placed in relation to others. Again, you'll probably hear your well-exercised critical faculties at work: mosquito (bad), flower (good), weed (bad), lawn (good), and so on. Simply observe your critical observations, and don't allow yourself to be limited by them. You may be drawn to one specific thing—a single leaf, a branch, a stone, a patch of sky reflected on water. Pause with it and simply let it show itself to you, with a sense of openness to see God's fingerprints, God's signature, God's glory shining through it. It may help to quietly say *behold* to yourself, and as you do, to invite yourself to see with God. Don't be surprised if you feel a tenderness, a love arising in you. That love is inherent to the way God sees everything God has made.

Finally, you could find yourself in an uncomfortable place—in a dentist's chair, on a crowded bus, in the room next to a couple arguing, in a hospital bed or waiting room. Here again, you will no doubt hear the buzz of anxieties, complaints, arguments, and judgments bothering your soul. But again, if you observe your reactions, you can release them rather than being bound by them, and you can allow yourself to live and breathe, even for a few brief moments at first, outside them. You can open your heart to God (holding the word *here* will help you, as will holding *help, please,* and *when*) and gradually allow yourself to see with God, to see the situation in a larger frame of reference, to see the people who may be annoying you, even to see yourself within the scene. You can let the whole scenario be bathed in God's gentle, gracious light, and in that light, even for a few stolen moments, you can *behold*.

More and more of our lives can be taken up into this kind of beholding—eating slowly, savoring each mouthful; walking slowly, treasuring each step; reading slowly (as you may have been doing at this moment without realizing it), holding each fragment of meaning that accumulates into a larger and larger meaning, a wonder to behold.

This profound and joyful beholding defies all explanations. Like a fragile butterfly, to capture it would be to damage or kill it. And that's how I feel at this moment. After having written all these words, I feel

that I have failed to capture it. A few words written by St. Augustine—
maybe the ones I was reading that day?—seem to honor beholding far
better than my many words can:

> *All shall be amen and alleluia.*
> *We shall rest and we shall see,*
> *We shall see and we shall know,*
> *We shall know and we shall love,*
> *We shall love and we shall praise.*
> *Behold our end which is no end.*

# CHAPTER 24

# Yes: *A Universal Spiritual Vocation*

*The Practice of Consecration and
Surrender: Deepening by Joining*
No Alternate Words

At Plum Village, I teach the young people a simple verse to practice while walking: "*Oui, Oui, Oui,*" as they breathe in, and,
"*Merci, merci, merci,*" as they breathe out. "Yes, yes, yes. Thanks,
thanks, thanks." I want them to respond to life, to society, and to
the Earth in a positive way. They enjoy it very much.

THICH NHAT HANH[1]

WHEN WE SPEAK OF joining God in seeing, it is as if, having
climbed a long path up a mountain, we reach the summit and gain a
view so vast that it takes our breath away. What could be more majestic and inspiring than transcending our normal frame of reference and
mounting up with eagle's wings to see from a loftier viewpoint? That's
why we must linger here and let the *behold* ring and echo in our hearts,
sharing our vision with God. But our journey is not yet finished. We
cannot stay on the mountain; rather, we must descend back to the valley
again.

It would be tempting to stay forever on the high ridge of meditation,
except that when we see with God, we see with compassion. And just as
compassion brings God down to earth to share in our pain and struggle,
compassion leads us into downward mobility too. Going down again,
down into the valley, will mean distractions, temptations, regressions,

misadventures, conflict, struggle. Compassion motivates us to accept these challenges for the sake of others. But it's not just for the sake of others that we must leave the mountain of meditation; it's for our own continuing growth too. God isn't finished with us yet. And so the Spirit of God says, "Come on. Let's go. Follow me. Follow me down, deeper down and deeper in. For the sake of others. And for your own well-being too." And when our heart says *yes,* we are entering the next spiritual practice, the practice of consecration and commitment, surrender and submission.

It surprises many people to hear God call them down. We think God is up. We're trained by the ladder of success to think it's for climbing, not descending. But God's mobility is opposite to our own. I'm writing these words at the beginning of Advent, when we Christians celebrate God's downward movement to us, God-in-Christ coming down to a poor and humble woman, down into her womb, down into a stable, down into hay. And that's just the beginning. When Jesus comes of age, he doesn't climb a mountain and live above the fray in a contemplative cave or commune. No, after a brief period in the wilderness (much of which, in that part of the world, is very mountainous and prime territory for lofty, expansive views), he moves continually down into the mess of human history. He moves down into the struggles of human politics and economics, down into the ugliness of human ignorance and misunderstanding, down into the horror of human injustice and bigotry, down even into the tragedy of human violence and murder.

That is the substance of one of the first Christian hymns, Philippians 2:6–11, and it tells us not only that Jesus was humble and downwardly mobile, but more—that God is humble and downwardly mobile.[2] The final vision of the Apocalypse (Rev. 21–22) dares proclaim this same truth, that God's presence, symbolized by a cubical city (evoking, no doubt, the Holy of Holies in the Temple), moves downward to be among humanity. So, when we join God on the mountain and see from within a new creation, we shouldn't be surprised that God's next call is to come on down. Will we surrender, yield, commit, submit to that downward call with our *yes?*

In the beginning of our venture with God, we heard our name being called and we said, "Here I am." That was the call to communion. But now we have the call of commission. First came the call to transformation—to yield ourselves to God's transforming work in our lives. Now comes the vocation to transforming mission—to join with God in God's work in the world. Having joined God in being together and seeing together, now we agree to join God in serving together—and, yes, in suffering and dying together. The call to service is offensive to those who seek fame, comfort, advantage, safety, and status. But it is joyful and good to those who seek to put compassion into action.

In my early years as a Christian, this consecrated life of surrender was known as "total commitment," and I sought it as wholeheartedly as I could (and still do). As we saw earlier, John Wesley called it "entire sanctification," and his critics derided it as "enthusiasm," as if someone should be ashamed of being completely "into God" (which is what *en-theos-asm* actually means). Pentecostals at their best know this is what "being filled with the Spirit" is all about. It's not just speaking in tongues or jumping and shouting (or planting "seed gifts," hoping for a big return on investment). Rather, to be Spirit-filled is to be surrendered to the Spirit, so the fruit of the Spirit, the power of the Spirit, and the gifts of the Spirit will flow from our lives. Some Roman Catholics tended to isolate this kind of life for "the religious" and exempted "the secular" or "laypeople" from it. But countermovements throughout Catholic history emphasized that all dimensions of all our lives may be taken up into God's sacred creative project. This integration later became a hallmark of much of the Reformed tradition in Protestantism. So faithful people from all sectors of the religious world have known in their bones that all of us are called to a consecrated life. All have a divine vocation—whether they are farmers, teachers, lawyers, scientists, homemakers, or shopkeepers. The invitation and vocation are there—we just need to say *yes*, to pray and practice *yes*.

Evangelicals have long understood the need to call people to commitment. For Evangelicals, you're not automatically born into a spiritual life, like being born Polish or blonde or left-handed. Rather, the spiritual life is like a marriage, and you must say yes to it. That's why Evangelicals often emphasize that first yes through something called an altar call or "gospel invitation."[3] But just as one "I do" is necessary but not sufficient for a marriage, so that first yes is essential, but still requires the follow-up of more yeses. Baptism can serve as a second yes. (For denominations that baptize infants, Confirmation serves as a first yes.) Participating in the Eucharist is yet another yes, as is volunteering for a ministry or attending church regularly. But even those yeses eventually become routine and automatic, habits rather than conscious choices. So what's after that? Revival services, with their special "anointings," "movings," or "blessings" of the Spirit, which periodically challenge people to revive their yes again and again.

Whatever our tradition, however, we eventually realize that our *yes* must become not simply an event, but a practice. Each of us must learn to hold open our *yes* to the Spirit on a moment-by-moment basis. Jesus used an image for this practice that was both powerful and—to his hearers, anyway—familiar: a branch abiding in a grapevine. The branch can't bear fruit on its own, he said. But if it abides in the vine, it will naturally bear fruit season after season. Yes, pruning will come, and pruning may be painful, but again, if the branch just abides, just stays, just says *yes* season after season, that pruning will result in ever more fruitfulness as the years go by (John 15:1–11).

Ideally, public gatherings for worship create opportunities for people to reaffirm their *yes* at least weekly. And special holy seasons—Advent, Lent, and Pentecost for Christians; Ramadan for Muslims; Passover for Jews; and so on—also build reaffirmation and rededication into the annual calendar. But often the reaffirmations that count the most come up unexpectedly. A friend in need on a busy day, a stranger in need alongside the road, an enemy or antagonist in need in the middle of conflict—these "inconveniences" become opportunities to put our own agendas and comfort aside and say *yes* to abiding in the vine, *yes* to joining God in compassion, *yes* to being God's hands and feet, eyes and ears.

Our *yes* counts most when we receive mistreatment rather than praise for our effort. That's why the theme of suffering for doing good is so central to all our spiritual traditions. To say *yes* to doing good and then be ignored, to say *yes* to doing right and then be misunderstood and criticized, to say *yes* to being loving and then to be vilified and even crucified—this is the territory into which we will all someday be invited. This is the *yes* of "not my will, but your will be done."

Why is
this inevitable?
Because of
random consequences?    or

Because, you see,
it disrupts power systems!

# CHAPTER 25

# Yes: *Do You Love Me?*

God be in my head, and in my understanding;
God be in my eyes, and in my looking;
God be in my mouth, and in my speaking;
God be in my heart, and in my thinking;
God be at my end, and in my departing.

FROM A FIFTEENTH-CENTURY
FRENCH BOOK OF HOURS[1]

Richard Rohr says this about prayer:

Prayer is not primarily saying words or thinking thoughts. It is, rather, a stance, a way of being present. It's a way of living *in* the Presence, living in *awareness* of the Presence, and even of enjoying the Presence. Presence knows Presence.

The full contemplative is not just aware of the Presence,

but trusts,

allows,

and delights in it.

All spiritual disciplines have one purpose: to get rid of illusions so we can *be present*. These disciplines exist so that we can

see what is,

see all that is,

see who we are,

and see what is really happening right now.[2]

The spiritual life Richard describes is a *yes* life. In the quiet of winter, it whispers yes to what has been, to what is, and to what is to come. This *yes* of consecration provides the counterpart to the *no* of refusal; it isn't a mere contradiction, but rather a continuation and completion.

We see exactly this yoking of refusal and consecration in the story of Peter in the Gospels, especially the Fourth Gospel. It's hard to impose traditional storytelling categories on any of the four Gospels. Each has its own unique terrain and structure, reflecting different rhetorical purposes and spiritual insights.[3] There are, it seems, new conflicts and miniclimaxes on every page, and although the resurrection should be a happy ending, it also seems more like a "to be continued," marking a new beginning.

The last chapter of the Fourth Gospel takes place on a shoreline along the Sea of Galilee, far north of Jerusalem. The feel is open and expansive in contrast to the tight, constricted feel of the not so holy city. Some days earlier, back in the city, Peter had boasted of his great loyalty to Jesus, and Jesus warned Peter that he would deny him three times before the rooster signaled dawn the next day. Determined to live up to his boast, when a group came to take Jesus into custody, Peter demonstrated his loyalty—by pulling out a sword and striking a member of the arrest party. (He thus inaugurated two long-standing Christian traditions: first, religious violence, and second, behaving in a manner completely inconsistent with Jesus himself.)

Jesus rebuked Peter and healed the victim and then was taken in ropes or chains to the courtyard of Annas, the high priest. Peter and another disciple followed at some distance and eventually managed to gain entry to the courtyard. Seeking to remain inconspicuous, they huddled with others in the evening chill around a charcoal fire (an important detail). In the light of that fire, Peter saw Jesus being interrogated and roughed up by a member of the high priest's staff.

During that long night, whenever Peter was suspected of being affiliated with the man in custody, he denied their connection. As morning dawned, a rooster crowed, and Peter realized he had fallen into exactly the kind of denial Jesus had predicted. He went out, another Gospel writer tells us, and wept bitterly. (Those tears, I suspect, represented his moment of lament, just as Jesus's tears had done the night before.)

As morning dawned, Jesus was convicted of religious blasphemy (claiming to be one with God) and civil treason (claiming to be a king). He was taken by the Romans and tortured, executed by crucifixion, and buried. But two days later, Jesus began appearing again to a growing circle of disciples—including Peter. Jesus's hands and feet were scarred, but to the disciples' unimaginable joy Jesus was in some real way truly, truly, truly alive.

We aren't told how many more days pass, but (in John's Gospel) Peter and friends go back to Galilee.[4] Peter invites a handful of fellow disciples to join him fishing. Did this represent a sense of closure, the fact that the adventure was over now, and they were back to their old way of making a living? Did Peter make the assumption that, because of his humiliating denial, he was no longer fit to be a "fisher of people," so he was demoted back to fisher of fish? Or was it simply the comforting rhythm of the waves, of casting the net and retrieving it, that drew Peter out on the water again? We aren't told his inner motives. But we are told that Peter and friends spend a sleepless night fishing and catching nothing, reminiscent of that recent sleepless night when Jesus had been arrested.

At dawn—recalling both the dawn when the rooster crowed and the dawn when Jesus was rumored to be alive again—a voice from the shore tells the disciples to cast their nets on the starboard side of the boat, which they do, only to have a huge school of fish fill their nets. Peter quickly jumps in the water and swims ashore. There he discovers that Jesus has made a fire, and not just any fire, but a *charcoal* fire. The flickering light, the hiss and crackle, and the acrid smell of that charcoal fire, of course, together evoke the bitter memories of that recent chilly predawn darkness when Peter had denied Jesus.

Jesus asks the disciples to bring some of their fresh fish for breakfast, and he provides bread—again evoking that night when, over broken bread, Peter had made his now humiliating boast. After breakfast, still within range of the light, sounds, and smell of the charcoal fire on the beach, Jesus invites Peter for a walk. Some steps away from the fire, he asks a question: "Peter, do you love me?" Three times, perhaps once for each of his recent refusals, he asks him. Peter's reply epitomizes this simple practice of surrender: *yes*.

This would be a happy ending of sorts, a heartwarming moment. But the curtain doesn't fall, and the plot takes an unexpected twist. Now Jesus tells Peter that a time is coming when he will be taken forcibly against his will and will in fact die. He will face the boast he made and the test he failed back in Jerusalem, and this time, Jesus says, he will pass it; he will be faithful to the point of death. Then Jesus says, "Follow me." Will Peter follow Jesus, knowing that it will mean confronting his greatest failure, his greatest fear?

It would be yet another happy ending if Peter simply said yes. The violins could swell, Jesus and Peter could embrace and face the sunrise, the other disciples could huddle in a group hug of tears and laughter, and the credits could roll. But the opposite happens. The ending remains shockingly open, the question stunningly unanswered, the command—"Follow me"—blatantly left hanging. Instead—could there be a more anticlimactic move than this?—Peter points to one of the other disciples and does something so unheroic, so petty, so backward, so untransformed, so cowardly that it is hard to imagine. He evades the question entirely. "What about him?" he asks.

So as the Gospel ends, Peter's future hangs in the balance. Will he say, "Yes, I will follow you, Lord, even to death?" We turn the page, not knowing. The evangelist's rhetorical strategy isn't hard to guess: the open ending puts each of us in Peter's place. We each know our own false starts, our own foolish boasts, our own abysmal failures, our own pathetic relapses. Will we supply the *yes* that Peter dares not give?

A pious, devotional *yes* is easy to say. But Jesus has pressed the matter further with Peter. He has defined very specifically the terms of reengagement. First comes the call to love the one he denied. Then Jesus links Peter's *yes* with a repeated call to join him in mission: "If you love me, feed my sheep." And finally Jesus pushes further still: "If you love me, follow me into suffering, even to death." The *yes* that is requested of us can only be requested, never forced, because a forced yes is no yes at all. Will you say *yes* to love, *yes* to service, *yes* to risk, suffering, and even death?

You'll notice this essential pattern in the spiritual life. The purpose of the spiritual life is not simply to connect us more deeply to God; it also must connect us more deeply to our neighbor—reflected in Jesus's words, "Feed my sheep." The *formation* we have experienced through our first ten practices prepares us *for mission* in this eleventh simple word. Through the great joy of springtime practice to the great work of summer practice through the great pain of autumn practice, we now come to the great love evoked in the word *yes,* a love that cannot separate God and others, but rather, that loves God in others and loves others in God, saying to both a single *yes,* even to the point of sacrifice, suffering, and death.

Most of us, of course, won't die as martyrs. But all of us will die. And as we approach our death, we will have our walk on the beach, our opportunity to say *yes* to God even in death. We will see that life itself is a gift that we are in the end asked to let go of for the sake of others. We will relinquish our space here so someone else may fill it; we will vacate our room so someone else may have a place to stay. We do this in love for future generations, just as past generations did for us, trusting that we will receive an even greater gift of an even more wonderful life for having relinquished this one. Will we say *yes?*

As a child, the thought of death terrified me. It seemed like a nightmare, an eternal falling into a bottomless abyss of the unknown. I remember pushing the thought away, hoping it would become less terrifying as I grew up. And it has. Of course, I don't know how it will be when my time comes, but I wonder if it will come to me as three questions not unlike the questions posed to Peter that morning.

"Brian, do you love me?"

"*Yes,* Lord, you know I love you."

"Brian, do you love me even more than life itself?"

"*Yes,* Lord, for life is the gift and you are the giver. Without the giver, there is no gift, but with the giver, there is the gift as well."

"Brian, will you let go of the life you have known so far, and will you follow me through the doorway of death into a new dimension of life?"

"*Yes,* Lord. *Yes.*"

And my *yes* of surrender and trust will allow me to let go of this life, and fall not into a bottomless pit of darkness, but into love, into light, into God, into the company of all our ancestors who are upheld in God's love, into a fullness of life that I cannot even imagine now. That falling will be a rising.

And in a sense, that *yes* will simply be the fulfillment of the *yes* that I began practicing in my youth that night under the stars, that I have prayed morning by morning and day by day ever since, and that I hold even now at this moment, each breath in a *yes* of grateful receptivity and each breath out a *yes* of release, surrender, consecration.

The other Gospels begin with Jesus saying "Follow me," but the Fourth Gospel, fascinatingly, ends with this invitation. When my heart is healthy and awake, when I listen into the silence like a child listening into a seashell, I hear God's voice calling me into adventure and life: "Follow me, imitate me, learn from me, dance with me, work with me, join me." And I realize that this is what life is: joining the Life in being alive. This is what holiness and love are: joining the Holy and joining Love in being holy and loving. This is what joy and sorrow and hope and regret are: joining the living God in response to life's diverse experiences. And this is what death will also be, which removes the sting from death and makes death disappear into life: joining God in a reality we have not yet seen or even imagined.

Episcopal priest Robert Farrar Capon has said that the biblical story starts with a breakup and ends with a wedding, and so the history in between is most truly a romance. Yes, the romance is filled with tragedy and comedy, but it always and at every moment remains at heart a love story, and every moment is a proposal. The gift of every moment is the Holy Spirit's holy seduction, the tender proposal of God: "I love you. Do you love me? Will you join me in at-one-ment, unity, reconciliation, reunion, belonging, membership, love? Will you accept my proposal and enter into the vital communion of theosis—union with God?" *Yes, yes, yes, yes, yes.*

In death, with our final *yes,* we turn out the light in our little room and a greater love envelopes us. May this moment of consecration be a practice and rehearsal for that one.

Perhaps now, before turning the page, you will pause to feel the proposal the Spirit is making to you. Whether for the first time or the ten thousandth, you can reach out your *yes* to the yes that extends to you:

"Yes, I love you. Yes, I want you in my mission. Yes, I forgive you. Yes, I accept you as you are. Do you love me? Do you want to follow me, to join me in my work of healing, feeding, caring, and self-giving? Are you with me, as I am always with you?"

Perhaps you can put this book down in a moment, adjusting the rhythm of your response to the rhythm of your breath. God offers you life, grace, love, hope, purpose, mission, mercy, and meaning, and you receive them as you inhale your next breath: *yes.* And as you exhale, you reciprocate, offering your life to God, joining God in God's compassionate mission, joining your full presence with God's presence in this world: Yes . . . *yes.* Yes . . . *yes.* Yes . . . *yes.*

CHAPTER 26 *Holy Listening*

# [ . . . ]: *Naked, Clothed in Silence*

*The Practice of Contemplation and Rest:*
*Deepening by Being With*

Silence is the language of God, and the only language deep
enough to absorb all the contradictions and failures that we are
holding against ourselves. God loves us silently because God has
no case to make against us. The silent communion absorbs our
self-hatred, as every lover knows.

RICHARD ROHR[1]

We put words between ourselves and things. Even God has
become another conceptual unreality in a no-man's-land of language that no longer serves as a means of communion with reality. The solitary life, being silent, clears away the smokescreen of
words that we have laid down between our mind and things. In
solitude we remain face to face with the naked being of things.
And yet we find that the nakedness of reality which we have
feared is neither a matter of terror nor of shame. It is clothed in the
friendly communion of silence, and this silence is related to love.

THOMAS MERTON[2]

MATURE MUSICIANS DON'T RUSH through each note of a song,
so they can say, "Good! Another song completed! Check that one off
the list!" No, the best musicians enter into the mystery of music with
a sense of wonder and leisure mixed with intensity, the opposite of
hurry. They feel, just as experienced listeners to great music do, that

*(handwritten margin notes: "Do we are basically of self-hatred?", "People", "Two views of silence.")*

music ushers them into a kind of transcendence over time, where past, present, and future are taken up into something bigger, deeper, and wider—the song itself. They realize that each isolated note, like a word, has meaning within the musical phrase in which it is found. And the full meaning and beauty of that phrase only take shape in relation to the phrases before it and after it, and those combined phrases constitute a movement or verse that similarly becomes meaningful through interaction with the other movements or verses that constitute the song.

And even the song isn't an island unto itself; its meaning arises within its genre—the blues, techno, folk music, classical music, tribal music, Irish jig, Latin jazz, whatever. And those genres have meaning and identity in relation to one another. And the whole body of music today—you can anticipate this—has meaning in relation to the music of the past, and even in relation to the as yet uncreated music of the future.

So the master musician brings to each note, to each song, to each genre, and to the whole body of music some degree of awareness of this infinite regression and infinite expansion of meaning and connection—an awareness that goes beyond conscious thought, but is nonetheless real. Something similar, I think, could be said about painters with color and shape, or poets with letter and word, or storytellers with character and incident, or dancers and actors with gesture and posture.

And spiritual people with spiritual practices. The resonating meaning of the simplest practice—*here, thanks, O, sorry, help, please, when, no, why, behold, yes*—transcends itself and expands to connect with everything, always. There is another even grander dimension to this resonating, expanding field of meaning, but it's hard to convey.

As musicians draw the bow across the strings, blow across the reed, or press their fingers upon the keys, at some level they know that silence is the field in which music happens. Without the space, or field, of silence, there can be no music. Under or around or above or before or after each note or song there is silence, a silence so necessary that we might call it holy. Painters know something similar about negative space, as do dancers and actors about the empty space of the stage, as do landscapers, farmers, and gardeners about the space between plants. Empty space and silence are, we might say, good. We might say they are as precious as—perhaps even more precious than?—the colors, actions, words, objects, or sounds with which we fill them, because they create the possibility for not only the actuality of this song, this painting, this poem, but the possibility for uncounted other actualities as well.

And so imagine the musician who loves music intensely, but also loves silence, the field of absence that makes the presence of all music possible. And imagine the painter who loves color and shape and line, but also loves the void of negative space for the possibilities it holds. And imagine the dancer who loves movement and also stillness. And now imagine the person who loves God and who therefore loves spiritual practices, but who also loves—can I say it this way?—*not* practicing. Being in silence. Being at *rest* with God with no words at all. This is not the passive silence of emptiness, complacency, or negation, but rather the living silence that is pregnant with infinite possibilities.

And so the last of our simple words is no word at all. The withheld word. The unspoken word. The word that doesn't need to be said. The breath without a sound. If you want to give it a descriptive word, perhaps *be* would suffice, as in, "Be still and know that I am God. Don't think. Don't speak. Just *be*." Better still would be the sound of a breath, a sigh of relaxation, an *ahhh* of rest, and the silence that ensues.

I don't know if this story about Mother Teresa is true or not, but it tells the truth whether or not it happened. Mother Teresa was asked by a reporter what she said to God when she prayed. She replied, "Mostly I just listen." The reporter then asked what God said to her. "Mostly he just listens," she replied. Could it be that the loving, attentive, mutual listening of the soul and the Spirit constitute the greatest expression of spirituality? Lovers know that this is true; they know there is a kind of attention, a kind of "just listening," that is one of the highest imaginable expressions of love. Holy listening holds space open between beloved and Beloved, the soul and God, and that space, like the silence in which all music happens, holds infinite possibilities.[3] Although all three of our Stage Four practices could be called *contemplation,* I am reserving the word for this kind of silent attentiveness, this holy receptivity to possibility, this beautiful, sacred, restful, naked silence.

Part of me hated contemplation in my younger years. I didn't get it, and when others tried to introduce me to it, something inside me rebelled, even if I complied out of a sense of duty. There were tasks to be checked off my to-do list; there were souls to be saved, sermons to be preached, problems to be solved, goals to be achieved, and (how arrogant and naive was this?) the world to be changed or *transformed* in my lifetime. Contemplative prayer felt too much like doing nothing in the midst of such frantic urgency. Frankly, it seemed like wasting time.

Which, of course, was the point. In resting, in quietness, in nothingness, I would have been practicing a kind of trust to which I assented mentally, but struggled to actually internalize, trust expressed in biblical passages like these:

> Unless the LORD builds the house, those who build it labor in vain. Unless the LORD guards the city, the guard keeps watch in vain. It is in vain that you rise up early and go late to rest, eating the bread of anxious toil; for he gives sleep to his beloved. (Ps. 127:1–2)

> For thus said the Lord GOD, the Holy One of Israel: In returning and rest you shall be saved; in quietness and in trust shall be your strength. But you refused and said, "No! We will flee upon horses"—therefore you shall flee! and, "We will ride upon swift steeds"—therefore your pursuers shall be swift! (Isa. 30:15–16)

> I am the vine, you are the branches. Those who abide in me and I in them bear much fruit, because apart from me you can do nothing. (John 15:5)

Perhaps it was seeing how little fruit my fretful activity produced. Perhaps it was simply wisdom gained through experience. But eventually I began to realize that to be an activist—to get good things done, and done well—meant that I must see contemplation not as a burden, duty, or distraction, but as a gift, as an opportunity, as a joy. This explains why my friends at the Center for Action and Contemplation say that the most important word in the name is "and." Similarly, Jim Wallis, in my favorite of his many good books, says:

To be a contemplative means to find a motivation deeper than the hope of results. You have to be sustained by more important things. . . . It is a paradox: to be successful you must finally give up the demand for success and do what you do from the deeper motivations of what you believe is right.[4]

When I first read those words many years ago, I sensed they were right, but I also knew they were beyond me. I could only place "versus" between action and contemplation, and it took a long time to really settle into the wisdom of "and." For so many years, I was desperate for results—big ones, and fast. I was caught up in words, ideas, slogans, and myths, striving to build an identity of importance to prove myself and my worth. All in God's name, of course. The result was a cycle of elation and depression, hope and disappointment, furious activity and deflated cynicism. I saw the same progression in my life that Thomas Merton once described in a letter to his friend Jim Forest—from working for results, to working because of the value of the work itself, to working for specific people whom I love, to allowing myself "to be used by God's love," to being open to God's power working through me, and finally, simply living, which Merton calls "the great thing."[5] The progression involves a shift in hope from what I can do to what God is doing. It's a shift from self-consciousness—"How am I doing? Am I doing enough?"—to consciousness of God—"What is God doing? How can I fit in, support, participate?" And at the core of that consciousness of God is a quiet attentiveness, an active receptivity, a blaze of listening.

My friend Steve Bell gets this. He is a gifted songwriter and musician. He's done thousands of concerts through the years, but one moment at one concert stands out among them. Here's how he described it for me in an e-mail:

It was toward the end of a concert I was performing in Virden, Manitoba. I had my band with me and we were backed by the Winnipeg Symphony Orchestra for the last of what was an eight-concert tour of rural Manitoba. This final concert was in a tiny community theater that seated a little more than twice the number of people in the orchestra, who were comically cramped onto the stage behind me.

At one point, Mike, my piano player, was taking a solo; he seemed particularly inspired, as the whole evening had a great, almost magical energy to it. I was intrigued by some of the rhythmical ideas he was playing with in his solo, and we locked eyes as I dialed into what he was doing by doing everything I could with my guitar to support and accent his ideas. Not always, but often enough, you can get so absorbed by what another player is doing on stage that you almost lose consciousness of yourself as you become absorbed toward the other.

Suddenly, and surprisingly, it dawned on me that as much as I was absorbed in supporting Mike's playing, he was doing the exact thing toward me. I was playing off him, and he was playing off me—neither was leading. We were both "othering" at the same time. And almost as suddenly as I realized this, the whole scene stopped like a freeze frame, like someone hit pause on the DVD player. And there was a brief suspension in which the voice of God spoke to me and said, "Pay attention to this, Steve. This is Who I am." And just as quickly, the whole scene was back in full motion, Mike was burning up the piano, and I was so overcome with a sense of psychic vertigo that I thought I might faint.

For weeks afterward I was a bit of a mess. I was weepy, unable to concentrate, totally overwhelmed by what had happened and equally as desperate to understand. Somewhere in there I came across a book by Rowan Williams called *The Wound of Beauty* and immediately resonated with that title as though I knew exactly, experientially, what that meant.

The phrase that has come to me since is "mutual othering." That the highest moments of human experience and fullness occur when we lose ourselves (or finally find ourselves) in flourishing the other . . . mutually. And this because it is in each rare moment of mutual othering (interbeing, perichoresis) that we most resemble the One whose image we bear; God, whose oneness is not a numerical oneness, like a tree is one, but a relational oneness—like a forest is one. From here I think I can know that God does not merely endorse, recommend or prefer Love, but rather, God *is* Love.

When Steve's selfless attention met Mike's selfless attention, time disappeared. Everything froze and fell away. The song continued, the exceptional playing continued, but he and the pianist were lost in what a musician might call the infinite groove, what we might call the vital connection.[6] If you've experienced a moment like that—in music, in sport, in conversation, in lovemaking, or in prayer—you know that this is what it's all about. This is it. And you can say no more, but simply feel the transcending of time in the abundance of holy "otherly" attention.[7]

This sense of attentiveness is essential to naked spirituality. This is the spirituality of the postreligious and the postatheist. Literary theorist Mikhail Epstein compares it to a blade of grass daring to rise from a crack in a sidewalk. In that hostile environment, quiet is better than loud. Minimal is better than ornate. The simplicity of poverty is better than the excess of affluence. And silence is better than words—not the barren silence of boredom, but the pregnant silence of listening. Epstein explains:

It is not the Word which is holy now, but rather Listening and Hearing. . . . In the post-atheist era, we have begun to understand that God's silence is a way of His listening to us, His attention to our words. Such active silence is necessary for the continuation of dialogue where one speaker alternatively gives the floor to another. After God had uttered His word in the Old and New Testaments, in Scripture and in Flesh, what else could He say? It is time for human beings to reply to God, to respond to His word.[8]

What we seek, he says, is to be "in the presence of Divine Listening." Prophets and religions proclaiming the Word of the Lord have their value, Epstein says, but "hearing is the last realm that cannot be colonized by the reifying force of atheism. God's word, no matter how inspirational and mysterious, can still be reified, retold, reinterpreted, ridiculed, rejected. But . . . God's hearing is unsurpassable, it surrounds and encloses our voices like the horizon." He explains:

> Thus, post-atheist spirituality is neither the religion of God's *voice,* as it was and continues to be in traditional churches and denominations; neither is it agnostic indifference, existential despair or atheistic challenge in the face of God's *silence.* Rather, it is a feeling of responsibility arising from the belief that God is silent because He is *listening* to us.[9]

Could it be that the joy we pursue in life—whether the joy of playing an instrument or a sport, of chipping a sculpture from stone or building a business from the ground up—is the joy of knowing that there is a silence, a void, a space that waits for us to fill it? And could it be that God, the creator of both us and that void, is the witness, the audience, the Listener for whom we are always performing? And could it be that contemplation is the pause button that freezes time, so that we listen to the Listening and witness the Witness?

# CHAPTER 27

# [ . . . ]: *Full Circle*

[The words'] intent is to create space, to open up the possibility, to make available the moment—the now—for the in-breaking of the Holy. When our worship moves into this space, words and silence merge. Then, style, method, language, and format become inconsequential, and prayer dissolves into what the mystics so often experienced: a simple "Ah!" before the mystery of it all.

BARBARA FIAND[1]

To BE EFFECTIVE OVER the long haul, to make a real and lasting difference, you need to have a secret life rooted in a secret silence and calm stillness. In that stillness, you know there is a Listener, a Witness, holding you in loving attention. You know that what you are doing has value even if there are no visible results, because the Witness has witnessed it. This is the unseen ice that buoys up the visible iceberg; this is the silence into and from which the music comes. This is the dark void into which creativity bursts like light.

A friend once described a dream to me that he felt God had given him on my behalf. He had been watching a television show about a huge dam being built in China. The reservoir was taking many years to fill up, but once full, it would provide electricity for millions of people for centuries. In the dream, he watched the water level slowly, slowly, slowly rising. This, he felt, was to be a picture for me of my life. During the long delays in which nothing seems to be happening, when nothing seems to be working, when no power is being generated, in those silent times of waiting, potential energy is accumulating from which lasting power will flow in due time.

Which brings me back to the previous chapter, reflecting on music and musicians. Where does my impatience come from—my desire to get this and that done as soon as possible, my irrational desire to "get finished" fast? I love the music and enjoy the making of each note, but yet I seem to want to get the song over with as soon as possible. Why? When I finish this song, what then? Hurry on to the next, to finish it as soon as possible? I feel like one of those contestants in an eating contest, jamming hot dogs in my mouth with one eye on the clock. My default mode of hurry tells me that I have so much more to learn from silence, from being still, from simply being, letting the reservoir slowly fill, storing up a deep but quiet power.

Many of us first experience this contemplative silence in the aftermath of tragedy. You've been rushed to the hospital with chest pains, put through a million hurried tests, then sped on a stretcher to your room and transferred to your bed. Another flurry of activity—monitors attached, blankets and bed adjusted—and then suddenly the nurses are gone and you're alone. You look down at your left hand lying palm up on the sheet, and suddenly you notice it. You move your fingers. You reach your right hand over and stroke the skin, notice the different sensations on palm, fingers, forehand. This hand has been yours for your whole life, but you have never really noticed it as you do now.

And then, as if by magic, the awareness of being alive spreads, as it were, up your hand and arm and across your chest, down your arm to your opposite fingertips, and then down your torso and legs to your toes, and up your neck to the top of your head. And for a few golden moments you are not only alive; you are aware you are alive. And whether or not you've been religious up to this moment, you suddenly know the meaning of the words "glory" and "holy."

Or you're cutting the lawn and over the mower's growl you hear, behind you, the screeching of brakes out front. You remember your daughter was riding her tricycle in the driveway, and your heart jumps a beat. You turn around and see her trike lying in the middle of the street, and a few yards away you see a pickup truck with the front door open; by the front bumper you see a teenage boy on his knees, leaning over something. And in that slow-motion moment as you break into a sprint across the front lawn toward the scene of the accident, you realize the full dimensions of your love for your little girl, who is scratched and bruised but okay, and you feel as never before the meaning of the word "love."

You've been a half day's drive away from home for a holiday with your family, but you get news that there's been a tornado, earthquake, landslide, or wildfire in your town. Your heart is pounding as you rush back into your neighborhood. You see devastation on all sides and neighbors picking through rubble. You turn the corner, and where your house should be there's a void. But rather than feeling loss, you realize that the people who matter most to you are alive and with you and that everything else can be replaced, and you feel, as never before, "blessed."

The practice of contemplation puts us in a similar frame of mind, minus the triggering tragedy. It integrates awareness, aliveness, holiness, love, appreciation, and blessedness, all in the presence of God, in whom we live, move, and have our being, all in the present timeless moment. We value or deem things more as God values and deems them, so for us they become re-deemed, which is why the contemplative dimension of the spiritual life could also be called the redemptive dimension. It brings together all that we have learned, lost, gained, and become through the previous seasons and practices of the spiritual life and helps us simply *be* in holiness, love, and blessedness, a state of being that, once you've experienced it, gives meaning to the word "heaven."

How do we practice contemplation? Of course, like many of life's best things, it's better shown than told, better experienced through practice than explained in words. If you were to meet with a spiritual director and ask to be introduced to contemplative practice, he or she might give the following directions.

First, get comfortable in your body. Sit or kneel in a comfortable position. Breathe deeply several times, so your body feels at rest. Now for the harder part. Bring your inner aliveness to a place of attentive quietness and rest in God's presence. Gradually put yourself in the posture of listening, of receptivity, waiting to hear rather than waiting to speak. Now realize that you are listening to God's perpetual listening; your openness and receptivity mirror God's openness and receptivity to you.

If unfinished business demands attention, you can attend to it, using the practices you have already learned—invocation, gratitude, and worship; confession, petition, and intercession; aspiration, refusal, and lament; meditation and consecration. But there will always be unfinished business of some sort, so at some point, you'll simply need to let the unfinished business go. How to do that? Try imagining each worry, concern, or distraction that comes to mind as a pebble that forms in your hand. Name it, and then imagine letting the pebble fall. Or imagine it as a leaf floating toward you on a stream. Simply acknowledge it and let it pass. If you try to fight it, you'll increase its "sticking power." Just let it come and go. Let the internal narrative chatter, the whirring of the internal computer, be suspended, and then return to a posture of quiet receptivity to God, in God's presence.

It's not important that you feel anything, although you may. It's not important that you have a vision or feel you receive some message from God, although you may. It's not important that you receive some flash of insight or whisper of guidance, although you may. What is important is that you pull back from activity, from being driven by this or that need, impulse, or compulsion that distracts you from who you already are and who God always is. Let the dust settle. Let the water clear. Let God be God to you, with you, in you. Just breathe. Just be. Listening, being listened to. Resting, in a greater Rest.

The spiritual director might help you see that this is the meaning of grace—the realization that you are already loved, already accepted, already enough, without doing anything. You are loved nakedly, and grace is the warm blanket that enfolds you. You are loved not because you are good or because you do good, but because God is good, not because you must achieve and sustain being lovable, but because God is love. The surplus of God's loving goodness fills to overflowing every lack or vacuum you bring to the equation.

After this instruction, the spiritual director might read a psalm, perhaps like Psalm 131, ascribed to David as "A Song of Ascents"—the kind of psalm one would sing on the final stages of a pilgrimage to Jerusalem:

> O LORD, my heart is not lifted up,
> my eyes are not raised too high;
> I do not occupy myself with things

*too great and too marvelous for me.*
*But I have calmed and quieted my soul,*
*like a weaned child with its mother;*
*my soul is like the weaned child that is with me.*
*O Israel, hope in the* LORD
*from this time on and forevermore.*

The spiritual director chooses such a psalm because it offers a wordless image: a child at rest in mother's arms, not desiring milk but content to hear mother's heartbeat. With that image, the spiritual director would leave you—not to think about the image, but to enter it and pass through it, and to be with God in the peaceful, intimate way it describes.

You may begin to learn contemplative prayer in a private session like this with a spiritual director or perhaps on a retreat or in a special gathering with a church group. But these special times of practice are intended to make contemplation a regular and natural part of your daily life. You will gradually learn to take a little vacation spontaneously when needed, a few moments of Sabbath, times when you stop working, thinking, trying, striving, stressing. These miniretreats can happen as you sit in a chair, take a slow walk, lie in bed in the middle of the night, ride on a crowded airplane or subway or bus, wait in a doctor's office, lie down in a field, or rest beside a stream. Nobody around you needs to know, but you are checking out of the mad rush and checking in with the living God.

Two streams in the Christian faith are converging, I think, to teach us about contemplation. First, there is the Pentecostal stream. Pentecostalism is, with little doubt, one of the most significant movements in Christian history, growing in a single century from a handful of people to six hundred million, constituting a quarter of the Christians in the world. What accounts for this phenomenal expansion? Many things, no doubt, but a renewed focus on the direct experience of the living God would be central to anyone's accounting, along with the expectation that the experience of God will ultimately bring neither fear, dread, and self-loathing nor a crushing weight of ceremonial propriety and tense reverence, but rather joy and liberation, effusive well-being and wholeness.

Pentecostalism has also provided means—practices—for experiencing God in this way: exuberant singing, passionate preaching, shouting, raising hands, even dancing. All of these practices both create and express a kind of breakthrough that allows participants to get beyond normal inhibitions and preoccupations, and there, on the far side of our normal mode of semiconsciousness, we find God waiting for us or, as it is often expressed, we experience Spirit coming to us or upon us, visiting us, or baptizing us in renewing joy, reviving peace, and transforming power.

We might say that Pentecostalism teaches us to experience God on the far side of normalcy. If it's normal to sit and listen, then you stand and sing. If it's normal to stand and sing, then you raise your hands and shout. If it's normal to raise your hands and shout, then you jump for joy and dance. Like Peter, you step out of the familiar boat and find God as you walk on strange water, here and now.

At the opposite end of the spectrum, we might say, is the contemplative stream. It shares the same confidence that the living God can be joyfully experienced, and it too offers practices for experiencing God. But we might say it finds those practices in the opposite direction.[2] Instead of creating space for experiencing God through loud preaching and shouting and singing, it creates space in quietness and restful silence. Instead of preferring a huge crowd, it tends toward solitude. Instead of venturing boldly beyond realm of normalcy, it dares acknowledge God at the very center of normalcy. Instead of praying, "Come to us, God. Visit us, God," it says, "Let me realize, God, that you are already here, always here, here, now."

Perhaps you see, in those words *here* and *now,* that we have come full circle. The last day of winter has become the first day of spring. We have arrived where we began, at a moment of invocation, awakening to the presence of God. Like a hawk or eagle soaring up on a thermal column of air, we have spiraled up in a widening arc. We have come full circle, but at a higher altitude, from the first springtime of Simplicity to a second and bigger Simplicity. Soon we will also enter a second and deeper summer of Complexity, and so on. We will experience all

the seasons and their practices again, but at a higher altitude and with
a loftier view and deeper vision, from invocation to thanksgiving to
worship; from confession to petition to intercession; from aspiration to
refusal to lamentation; from meditation to consecration and contemplation.

We have ascended into the experience described by another psalm,
Psalm 46:

> *God is our refuge and strength,*
> *a very present help in trouble.*
> *Therefore we will not fear, though the earth should change,*
> *though the mountains shake in the heart of the sea;*
> *though its waters roar and foam,*
> *though the mountains tremble with its tumult. Selah. (vv. 1–3)*

Whether in the Pentecostal way or the contemplative way, we have
found a refuge, a safe and secure space where the terror of crumbling
mountains and foaming waters can't touch us. As we've seen, that word
"Selah" probably signaled a musical interlude in the original public
performance of this psalm or perhaps a period of silence—either way,
a time to practice contemplation, to experience what the poetry has
pointed toward. In contrast to the shaking earth and raging sea, we now
have the image of a powerful, peaceful river of joy:

> *There is a river whose streams make glad the city of God,*
> *the holy habitation of the Most High.*
> *God is in the midst of the city; it shall not be moved;*
> *God will help it when the morning dawns. (vv. 4–5)*

Jerusalem, of course, has no such river. This is a mystical river,
the flow or current of the Spirit's presence in the center of our lives.
Through the night it ran while we slept, and now, at daybreak, we see
it, we feel it, running strong and clear and silent again today. And we
are glad. That invisible river flows with unimaginable power:

*The nations are in an uproar, the kingdoms totter;*
*he utters his voice, the earth melts.*
*The LORD of hosts is with us;*
*the God of Jacob is our refuge. Selah. (vv. 6–7)*

Suddenly, the tinny uproar and tottering chaos of the "morning news" seem trivial and old; the real headline isn't the latest coup d'etat or petty political scandal. The real news, the good news, according to the psalm, is the "with us" presence of the living God, a presence in which we learn to dwell as a refuge, a place of security and safety. That realization becomes the refrain to which we return in the last lines of the song:

*Come, behold the works of the LORD;*
*see what desolations he has brought on the earth:*
*He makes wars cease to the end of the earth;*
*he breaks the bow, and shatters the spear;*
*he burns the shields with fire.*
*"Be still, and know that I am God!*
*I am exalted among the nations,*
*I am exalted in the earth."*
*The LORD of hosts is with us;*
*the God of Jacob is our refuge. Selah. (vv. 8–11)*

The inner peace of the river of God doesn't bring personal calm to our individual lives alone. The psalmist sees its ultimate effect and invites us to behold it as well: violent empires are reduced to ruins (desolations), bringing an end to war, a destruction not *by* weapons but *of* weapons. In that postwar peace and eu-topian stillness we find God's self-revelation and God's true exaltation: "I am," God says. "I am exalted." It is a new day for all humanity, a new creation, everything made new. The ultimate cause of activism—the end of war—is intimately related to the personal practice of contemplation. The world changes as we are changed; peace comes to the world as peace flows in our innermost being and out through us to others. "Let justice roll down like waters!" the prophet Amos said. "And righteousness like an ever-flowing stream!" (5:24).

There is nothing more radically activist than a truly spiritual life, and there is nothing more truly spiritual than a radically activist life. If you fight for peace with an unpeaceful spirit, you guarantee that unintended consequences will trump your intended ones. If you struggle for a sustainable economy with unsustainable effort, you guarantee your own failure. The earth's outer ecology will, inevitably, mirror our inner ecology. So there can be no lasting poverty reduction in society unless we grapple with greed reduction in the soul. If we want loving relationships, joyful communities, and peaceful nations in society, we must cultivate an inner fecundity of Spirit. That, of course, is no argument for passive pietism and quietism; it is, rather, a call to the most costly, radical activism, the one that calls us to be the change we want to see in the world. It is the call to *be* the light of the world—not merely to complain that the world is too dark. It is the call to *be* the salt of the earth—not merely to protest the world's rottenness. It's fruitless to argue being versus doing: you can't do what you won't be.

Do we dream of a more peaceful world? Then we nourish the vital connection with the Spirit of peace, and we live from that deep well. Do we thirst for a more verdant, flourishing world? Then we nourish the vital connection with the Spirit of life, the breath of life, the living God of life, and we become seed sowers and garden growers at every turn. Do we burn for a message of justice to penetrate the hard hearts of the powerful and complacent? Then we nourish the vital connection with the Spirit of truth, and justice will flow from us like water, always seeking the lowest place where it is needed most.

There is a river that runs like a song through this world, a river of sacredness, a river of beauty, a river of reverence and justice and goodness. I know that some people have only rarely seen or barely sensed it. But I also know that you and I are learning to live like green trees along its shore, drawing its vitality into us, and passing it on for the healing of our world. Its waters are clear, refreshingly cool, and clean, and if you dare, you can strip naked, dive in, and swim.

*Selah.*

[ . . . ]

# The Sea Toward Which
# All Rivers Run

> When the soul is plunged into the fire of divine love, like iron, it
> first loses its [coldness and dullness], and then growing to white
> heat, it becomes like unto fire itself. And lastly it grows liquid,
> and, losing its nature, is transmuted into an utterly different qual-
> ity of being. . . . As the difference between iron that is cold, and
> iron that is hot, so is the difference between . . . the tepid soul and
> the soul made incandescent by divine love.
>
> RICHARD OF ST. VICTOR[1]

TWELVE SIMPLE WORDS, FORMATIVE words that can help us grow an
incandescent life with God, a life of vital connection with the whole
regenerative community of creation.[2] You have probably anticipated
where these twelve simple words must lead—to one word that enfolds
them all, the final word, love.

Jesus was right. Paul was right. John was right. The Buddha was
right. Even the Beatles were right.[3] It all comes down to love, or call
it compassion, if you prefer. Love is the vital connection. A life with
God is a life of love.[4] You know God by loving God. You know God
by loving others. You know your neighbor, a stranger, or an enemy
by loving him or her. You know a tree, a bird, an ecosystem, or a
planet by loving it. Even yourself—you only know yourself by properly loving yourself. We are trained to see the universe as working by
means of fundamental forces—gravity, electromagnetism, weak and
strong atomic forces, and so on. But might these physical forces serve

as metaphors for the one ultimate fundamental force in the universe, love? Could love be the gravity that brings us together, the magnetism that attracts us, the electricity that makes us shine, the force that holds us strongly together in community—but not so strongly as to fuse us?

Love begins with presence (*here*). It appreciates (*thanks*). It adores (*O*). It regrets all that wounds or obstructs love (*sorry*). It interprets need—in oneself or in the other—as an occasion for loving connection (*help, please*). It sees delay or distance (*when, no*) as opportunities for intensifying desire. It dares hope in the beloved when all hope is gone (*why*). In the end, it sees without judgment (*behold*), surrenders to tender proposals of the beloved (*yes*), and finally finds no greater joy than simply being together in silence. *Love* is the last word.

Through love, all is re-ligamented, reread, reinterpreted, rejoined, reconnected. Through love, at-one-ment triumphs, not in simple oneness where many beings are conquered by or assimilated into one being, but in the joyful one-anotherness of interbeing—the joyful relation that the language of the Trinity soars to celebrate. In that loving community of creation there is both unity and diversity, both melody and harmony, difference without division.

And so it is that the last simple word is the best and the biggest, comprising and fulfilling all others. Spirituality is *love*. To hold nothing but naked *love* in your naked heart—not just the word, but the reality—always, for all, that is the sea toward which all rivers run.

## Appendix A

# Group Practice

ALL GROUPS THAT GATHER regularly develop a liturgy, a protocol for meetings that embeds certain patterns and practices into the group's life. Liturgy is often defined as the work of the people, but I like to define it as the workout of the people.[1] The group's shared practices enable its members to bond with the meanings and values deemed important. In so doing, they build the group's inner strength much as a physical exercise strengthens muscles. The twelve simple practices in this book are already being used in thousands of creative ways in faith communities around the world, as they have been for centuries. But even so, I believe we stand in great need of liturgical renewal. So many new possibilities await invention, rediscovery, and development, and so many of our gatherings are criminally lackluster and comatose.[2]

Too many gatherings run on a checklist mentality: "Here are the things we have to do again this week, so let's get them done." That mentality involves people in a series of practices without reference to the meanings or values they are intended to celebrate or strengthen. One could argue that this kind of mindless practice is worse than no practice at all in that it alienates and bores participants, turning them against the very practices they need. That's one reason so many people have turned away from organized religion. The religious community they were a part of maintained this well-organized checklist mentality, but forgot the purpose, mission, and meaning of its practices.

Whether you're working in a traditional church or in an emergent faith community of some sort, you can help pioneer the kind of liturgical renewal we need, and I hope these twelve simple practices will assist you in that process.

William Temple (1881–1944), Anglican priest, Bishop of York, and

Archbishop of Canterbury, famously defined public worship like this: "To worship is to quicken the conscience by the holiness of God, to feed the mind with the truth of God, to purge the imagination by the beauty of God, to open the heart to the love of God, to devote the will to the purpose of God." For those of us who want to explore, claim, and expand the unfulfilled formative potential of public worship, Temple's definition is particularly useful, because it links practices to specific faculties or powers of the human soul. We could easily expand Temple's five elements to include all twelve of the practices we have considered:

- Opening the heart to the presence and love of God through invocation (*here*)

- Awakening our attention to the generosity of God through gratitude (*thanks*)

- Purging the imagination by the beauty of God through worship (*O*)

- Quickening (or invigorating) the conscience to the holiness of God through confession (*sorry*)

- Transforming our anxieties by the peace of God through petition (*help*)

- Nurturing our empathy through the compassion of God through intercession (*please*)

- Sustaining our endurance through the faithfulness of God through aspiration (*when*)

- Acknowledging our disappointments within the mercy of God through refusal (*no*)

- Exposing our wounds to the healing of God through lament (*why*)

- Expanding our vision in the wisdom of God through meditation (*behold*)

- Devoting our will to the purpose (or mission) of God through consecration (*yes*)

• Resting our souls in the attention of God through
    contemplation (. . .)

How could these practices be integrated into a group experience?
Here are some initial suggestions:

1. If your group reads this book together, you can naturally gather
   to converse about some chapters and then experiment with the
   practices they introduce. Participants could keep a prayer journal
   during the week, focusing on the week's simple word. Then when
   you gather, each could choose one or more entries to share. Nothing could be simpler than starting a page with one simple word and
   then letting a prayer flow from that word.

2. The Twelve Simple Prayers (Appendix C) could be used in whole
   or in part during gathered worship.

3. I will host on my website (brianmclaren.net) some space for sharing resources that can supplement "holding the moment"—songs,
   litanies (interactive prayers), common prayers (written and read
   in unison), visual resources (clips from movies, great art, videos),
   sermon ideas, and so on. Drawing upon our God-given creativity,
   we can unleash a wave of needed liturgical renewal.

4. You could build a weekend retreat around the twelve practices,
   scheduling half-hour sessions for each practice, with time in between for quiet reflection, reading, sharing of experiences, and
   fellowship. One person could lead all twelve practices, or twelve
   people could each practice—in private—with one and then lead in
   public from their own experience.

5. You could plan a series of four sermons or teachings introducing
   each trio of practices and then lead people in experiencing them,
   taking just two or three minutes per practice.

6. Each practice could be integrated with a body prayer, perhaps introducing one per week. (See Appendix B.)

## Appendix B

# Body Prayers

THERE ARE ENDLESS WAYS gesture and posture can be used to augment these simple practices. Here are a few possibilities.[1]

*Here:* Hold your palms open and facing down, saying, "I am here in this place, now." Then turn them upward, saying, "I am here in this place, open to you, God."

*Thanks:* Raise your fists in defiance (against greed and the "never-enough" system) and then open them as a gesture of thanksgiving to God, appreciating the abundance you already possess.

*O:* Turn your open eyes toward the sky and open your hands upward, gradually bringing your hands to your heart, lowering your head, and closing your eyes, mirroring a glance toward the greatness of God leading to a humble, heartfelt response.

*Sorry:* Cup your hands over your face as you name your wrongs, then open them as cups to receive God's mercy, finally splashing your face with mercy as with cold, clean water.

*Help:* Imagine your anxieties as a cloud above you and clench your fists to express your anxiety. Then imagine the cloud condensing into a request and capture the request in cupped hands. Raise the request to God in open hands.

*Please:* Place your hands on your heart and call to mind the name of a person in need. As you lift that person into God's compassion, lift your hands to God as if you were lifting a baby into God's arms.

*When:* Stand at attention with your head raised upward and hands at your side, as you name your aspirations and exasperations. Let your erect posture say, "I am waiting."

*No:* Cross your arms in an X, with your hands in fists, as you tell God what you will not do, accept, believe, or settle for.

*Why:* Kneel with your hands open at your side, or lie prostrate with your hands open at your side, in an expression of not knowing and not understanding.

*Behold:* Hold your hands outward as if welcoming or beckoning, as if to say, "Let it come, let it be, let it be seen."

*Yes:* Interlace your fingers or lightly press your hands palm to palm, as if balancing God's *yes* to you and your *yes* to God.

*[. . .]:* Rest your hands in your lap, one cradled in another or fingers interlaced, expressing your rest in God's loving gaze.

# Twelve Simple Prayers

ONE SIMPLE WORD ISN'T intended to preclude other words. Rather, by using the one word, you create space for other words to arise. So you can create and tend soul space with one word, but then let others flow as well. On my website (www.brianmclaren.net), I've posted twelve prayers associated with the twelve practices that have emerged from my own experience. But more important and helpful to you than reading my words will be to compose some of your own. The following prompts can serve that purpose. My suspicion is that if you were to use these prompts again a month, a year, or a decade from now, very different responses would come, and you could trace the themes of your own spiritual story through subsequent responses to the same prompts.

## Here

Here I am, Lord.
(Where are you? Physically? Emotionally? Personally? Socially?
    Spiritually?)
And here you are, Lord.
(Describe your experience of or feelings about God at this moment.
    How would you name God today?)
Here we are together.
(How would you describe your togetherness with God?)

## Thanks

Thank you, Lord, for . . .
(Name gifts as they come to mind.)

*If I stopped being grateful . . .*
*(Tell God what would happen to you if you didn't give thanks.)*
*Thank you!*
*(Describe how you feel to be so blessed.)*

## O

*O, how _____ you are!*
*(Fill in the blank with a general quality that you associate with*
  *God, such as "creative," "mysterious," etc.)*
*You . . .*
*(Complete the sentence with specific examples of the general quality*
  *you just named: "You made the cricket singing outside my*
  *window.")*
*O, how I _____ you!*
*(Fill in the blank with an appropriate verb, such as "love,"*
  *"honor," "appreciate," etc.)*

## Sorry

*I'm sorry, Lord. I . . .*
*(Confess what causes you regret—an action, an attitude, a flaw, a*
  *failure.)*
*I feel . . .*
*(Describe how you feel about what you have confessed.)*
*Have mercy on me, gracious God, so that . . .*
*(Describe what you want to do or how you want to live as you*
  *move forward.)*

## Help

*Today I am anxious about these little things: . . .*
*(Name your minor concerns or anxieties.)*
*And I am concerned about these big things: . . .*
*(Name your major concerns or anxieties.)*
*Help me, Lord. To face these challenges, I need . . .*
*(Name what you need from God.)*

## Please

*I carry a burden today for _____.*
*(Name a person or group for whom you feel compassion.)*
*Please supply what they need, Lord: . . .*
*(Name what they need.)*
*I join you in your great compassion so that . . .*
*(Describe the outcome you desire.)*

## When

*How long, Lord, until . . . ?*
*(Describe what you are longing for.)*
*I'm waiting, Lord, for you to . . .*
*(Describe what you need God to do or supply for you.)*
*Until then, I trust you and reach out to you for . . .*
*(Describe the virtue or personal quality that you need to be*
  *sustained this day, this moment.)*

## No

*I refuse to believe that . . .*
*(Describe the doubt that you are struggling against.)*
*This is unacceptable to me because . . .*
*(Name the beliefs and hopes that you are holding on to.)*
*No, Lord! May it never be that . . .*
*(Describe the outcome you feel must be avoided.)*

## Why

*Why must it be that . . . ?*
*(Describe what has happened.)*
*I had hoped . . .*
*(Articulate the hope that has been dashed or disappointed.)*
*In the middle of this pain, I affirm . . .*
*(What good can you will with God?)*

## Behold

*Behold! Now I see . . .*
*(What previously resisted truth or insight do you now see in a new*
  *light?)*
*Behold! Now I feel . . .*
*(Describe how you feel and how it differs from what you felt*
  *before.)*
*Spirit of God, now I know . . .*
*(What new confidence has arisen within you?)*

## Yes

*Living God, I feel you are offering me . . .*
*(What do you feel God wants to give you? To what do you want*
  *to be receptive?)*
*I say yes. Living God, I believe you are asking me . . .*
*(What requests, invitations, or promptings do you feel arising in*
  *your soul?)*
*I say yes. Living God, I offer myself to you.*
*(Describe what it means for you to surrender yourself to God.)*

## [ . . . ]

*I am with you, Lord. As a . . .*
*(In what ways are you with God?)*
*We are together, living God, as one.*
*(Silence.)*
*We. Amen.*
*(Silence.)*

For additional resources related to this book, you are invited to
www.brianmclaren.net.

# NOTES

## INTRODUCTION

1. In my previous book, *A New Kind of Christianity: Ten Questions That Are Transforming the Faith* (San Francisco: HarperOne, 2010), I addressed the danger of focusing so much on the head that we forget the heart. "In the end," I said, "if this quest leads only to a reformation in our thinking and talking, it is not a new kind of Christianity at all, but just a variation on an old kind. . . . So our quest calls us first and foremost to nurture a robust spiritual life . . . a deep desire to know and love God" (p. 226). Those sentences provide the bridge between that book and this.

2. The quote continues: "As you know, the act of lovemaking requires some degree of nakedness, and perhaps sacred silence to absorb the communion that is happening. The same is true in loving and being loved by God. We have to let go of our false self (as superior or as inferior) to be ready for real unity with God" (Richard Rohr, *Simplicity: The Freedom of Letting Go* [New York: Crossroad, 2004], p. 97).

3. This life characterized by naked encounter with God is what another Catholic thinker, Karl Rahner, meant by being a mystic in his famous quote: "The Christian of the future will be a mystic or he [or she] will not exist at all."

## CHAPTER 1: SPIRITUAL EXPERIENCES AND SPIRITUAL EXPERIENCE

1. Quoted in Jane Redmont, *When in Doubt, Sing* (Notre Dame, IN: Sorin, 2008), p. 312.

2. Nobody captures the embarrassments of growing up fundamentalist better than Frank Schaeffer in his sparkling fiction, including *Portofino, Saving Grandma,* and *Zermatt* (Cambridge, MA: Da Capo, 2004), and his disarmingly vulnerable nonfiction like *Crazy for God* (Cambridge, MA: Da Capo, 2008).

3. Barbara Bradley Hagerty exemplifies a nonreductive, multiperspective exploration of spiritual experience in *Fingerprints of God: The Search for the Science of Spirituality* (New York: Riverhead, 2009).

4. The hope was that they would eventually become Republicans too.

CHAPTER 2: "BUT I'M SPIRITUAL"

1. Kenneth Leech, *True Prayer* (Harrisburg, PA: Morehouse, 1995), p. 39.

2. The adjective "organized" deserves additional attention. Obviously, what people are looking for isn't "disorganized" religion. But they sense that as religion becomes captive to an organization or institution, something vital can easily be lost. That "something vital" includes many things: a mission of social transformation (as opposed to a regime of social control), a sense of dynamic community or fellowship (as opposed to static institutional membership), and the experience of vital spiritual *connection* that we're exploring in these pages (as opposed to ritual or conceptual conformity).

3. I'm using the word "communion" here as an alternative to the union of fusion on the one hand and the division of separation on the other. The two remain two, but are intimately joined in love; there is difference without division.

4. According to Cicero (first century BCE), the Latin root of the word was *re-legere* (the root of our words "lectionary" and "lecture," meaning "to read"). So religion involved reading ancient texts again and again for new meaning. This meaning is related to reinterpreting—giving things a second thought. These two etymologies can be seen as mutually supportive. See Timothy Beal, *The Rise and Fall of the Bible* (Boston: Houghton Mifflin Harcourt, 2011), p. 184.

5. It's interesting that two of the key metaphors in the New Testament seek to capture this connection. Jesus's term "kingdom of God" (which I explore at length in my book *The Secret Message of Jesus* [Nashville, TN: Thomas Nelson, 2006]) portrays a connection or community that includes God and creation. This beautiful whole is, in this way, bigger than either God alone or creation alone and comprises both. Similarly, Paul's term "body of Christ" connects God-in-Christ and humanity-in-creation, bringing them into a larger communion—again not a simple union or fusion where one is absorbed in or reduced to the other, but where one and the other experience an "at-one-ment," a "one-anotherness," in which otherness remains, but doesn't divide.

6. We might say that there are forms of deadly connection that contrast with vital connection. Colonialism, domination, assimilation, hostile takeover, conquest, and lust, for example, all seek a deadly connection that degrades the identity of "the other" into "the one." Vital connection, however, enhances, dignifies, celebrates, and preserves "otherness" in the sacred communion of "one-anotherness."

7. I'm leaving unaddressed the issue of clothing as an expression of personality, flair, style, class, and so on, although such a discussion would produce useful insights about religious life.

8. Because this is a book about spirituality rather than scholarship, I'm putting aside questions of authorship, source criticism, historicity, and so on, and taking the Gospel stories at face value, seeking meaning, guidance, and insight for our lives today.

9. Although powerful impersonal images are used to describe the Spirit—fire, wind, water, and so on—we don't relate to the Spirit as an impersonal force or an "it," but rather as a "You." That "You" is not smaller or less than a force, but greater and more. The impersonal images help us avoid reducing the Spirit to a projection of human personhood, but the You-ness of the Spirit helps us avoid reducing the Spirit to an impersonal force. In this dynamic tension, we encounter both You-ness and mystery, and that tension deserves to be preserved and celebrated rather than resolved one way or the other.

10. Some readers will say that Jesus too created an in-group that rendered others into an out-group. No doubt, his followers were quick to do so (see, for example, Luke 9:54). But Jesus consistently rebukes his disciples when they use their affiliation with him as an exclusive barrier; he intends their identity as his disciples and apostles to be a bridge to others, not a barrier that excludes them.

11. For example, in healing a blind man (9:1–12), he moves from physical blindness to the deeper reality of spiritual blindness. In providing bread to a hungry crowd (6:1–14), he points to the deeper reality of spiritual nourishment. And in raising Lazarus from the dead (11:38–44), he points to a higher kind of life that transcends physical death.

CHAPTER 3: TWELVE SIMPLE WORDS

1. Quoted in Kenneth Leech, *True Prayer* (Harrisburg, PA: Morehouse, 1995), p. 39.

2. Thanks to the work of Dallas Willard and Richard Foster for this approach to spiritual disciplines or practices. See especially Willard, *Spirit of the Disciplines* (San Francisco: Harper & Row, 1988), and Foster, *Celebration of Discipline,* rev. ed. (San Francisco: HarperSanFrancisco, 1988).

3. Some, like pragmatist philosopher William James, emphasize the personal dimension. Others, like sociologist Emile Durkheim, emphasize the social dimension (which he calls the "cult"). Similarly, some religious traditions—like Evangelicalism—emphasize the personal, while others, like Roman Catholicism, emphasize the social. But in the end all agree both dimensions matter. See Jack Barbalet, "Classical Pragmatism, Classical Sociology: William James, Religion and Emotion," in Patrick Baert and Bryan Turner, eds., *Pragmatism and European Social Theory* (Oxford: Bardwell, 2007), pp. 17–45. Also available at http://www.jackbarbalet.com/uploads/CLASSICAL_PRAGMATISM.pdf.

4. A book like this one, in this light, has value in introducing you as an individual reader to personal practice. It can have greater value when a reading group uses it as a basis for social practice. Its greatest value comes, I think, when a group of practitioners finds and maintains a relationship to an ongoing faith community or tradition where spiritual practices have been embodied over many generations. For more on this subject, see Michael

Polanyi, *Personal Knowledge: Towards a Post-Critical Philosophy* (Chicago: Univ. of Chicago Press, 1974).

5. One of the most heartbreaking stories I hear from my spiritual-but-not-religious friends again and again runs like this: "When I tried to find a community where I could deepen my spirituality, *I was judged and turned away because I wasn't spiritual enough.*" These inhospitable communities are like banks that won't give you a loan unless you prove you don't need it or health insurers that won't insure you unless you prove you're already healthy, and they help give religion a bad name. Much of my life's work, first as a pastor and now as an author, is aimed at rectifying the sad reality that welcoming and transformative spiritual communities remain too few and too hard to find.

6. Those thinkers included William Blake (innocence, experience, higher innocence), Søren Kierkegaard (aesthetic, ethical, religious), William Perry (dualism, multiplicity, relativism, commitment), William Fowler (primal, mythical-literal, synthetic-conventional, individual-reflective, conjunctive, universalizing), and Clare Graves, Don Beck, and Ken Wilber (archaic/instinctive, animist/tribal, egocentric/exploitive, absolutist/authoritarian, scientific/strategic, relativistic/communitarian, systemic-integral, holistic), along with Sigmund Freud, Erik Erikson, and Abraham Maslow.

7. Of course I don't intend these twelve to be an exhaustive list. Rather, they are a primer—a good start.

8. I've included traditional religious words like "invocation" and "intercession," but I've tried to pair them with less explicitly religious words like "presentation" and "compassion." This pairing will be of benefit to both religious and spiritual-but-not-religious people, providing a mixture of familiarity, freshness, and accessibility.

9. In other words, harmony warms into a new simplicity, which leads to a new complexity, and so on. If, following the work of Alexander Shaia in *The Hidden Power of the Gospels* (San Francisco: HarperOne, 2010), you wanted to link one of the four Gospels to each season, I would suggest Mark/Simplicity, Matthew/Complexity, Luke/Perplexity, and John/Harmony.

10. See "Two Giant Fat People," in *The Gift: Poems by Hafiz, the Great Sufi Master,* trans. Daniel Ladinsky (New York: Penguin Compass, 1999).

## PART 1: SIMPLICITY: THE SEASON OF SPIRITUAL AWAKENING

1. The phrase "first love" evokes both the romantic experience of being "in love" and the spiritual experience of lost love of Rev. 2:4.

2. My thinking here is especially indebted to William Perry Jr., *Forms of Intellectual and Ethical Development in the College Years: A Scheme* (New York: Holt, Rinehart, and Winston, 1970); and "Cognitive and Ethical Growth: The Making of Meaning," in Arthur W. Chickering et al., *The Modern American College* (San Francisco: Jossey-Bass, 1981), pp. 76–116.

3. It also may give us a few secret moments of great anxiety about the danger of being wrong—or, just as bad, being *considered* wrong by our in-group, with its strict standards.

## CHAPTER 4: *HERE:* STARTING RIGHT NOW

1. Quoted in Esther de Waal, *Seeking God* (Collegeville, MN: Liturgical, 2001), p. 65.

2. I realize that Lewis himself would recoil from the implication that could be drawn from this line from the poem—that God is a "thing."

3. The Hebrew prophet Elijah mocked this idea that God requires a wake-up call (1 Kings 18:27). When he confronted the prophets of Baal and witnessed their extravagant attempts to get God to do their bidding, he taunted them along these lines: "Shout louder! Maybe your god is deep in thought, or maybe he's busy, or away on a trip. Maybe he fell asleep!"

4. The refrain of an old hymn, the standard of Baptist altar calls, captures this here-ness beautifully: "Just as I am, I come, I come."

5. Isms have been humorously defined as conceptual systems that try to convince us they contain all there is(m).

6. Richard Rohr, *The Naked Now: Learning to See as the Mystics See* (New York: Crossroad, 2009).

## CHAPTER 5: *HERE:* NAMING THE MYSTERY

1. Sam Keen, *In the Absence of God* (New York: Harmony, 2010), p. 74.

2. Many readers will wonder if I believe these stories to be historically reliable. For some, Bible stories seem like fairy tales or silly legends because they contain supernatural elements, and so should be treated with suspicion, even condescension or mockery. For others, because the stories are in the Bible, they must be taken as factually, historically accurate in every detail. I'm not bothered by supernatural elements (although I am bothered by the modernist assumptions behind the watertight categories of natural and supernatural). Nor do I concern myself much with the historical accuracy of all these stories. Instead, whether these stories are journalistically accurate or literarily and imaginatively enhanced, I seek to plumb the profound, inspired meaning and wisdom they are intended to convey. If there was a man named Moses who saw a bush burning one day and said exactly the things we find in Exodus, that's wonderful. If the story, instead, is meant to convey through an artistic account a crucial realization that has arisen in human culture more generally about the God-human relationship, that's fine too. Either way, whether the story is historical or imaginative, I am free to receive it and savor it in all its revelatory fullness. I hope you feel the same freedom.

3. Ardent Bible readers may see a tension between this depiction of God as a nonconsuming fire and the opposite depiction in Deut. 4:24, echoed in Heb. 12:29. I might suggest that the only thing God can "consume" or

destroy is evil. In that light, "God is a devouring fire" would be better rendered, "God is a purifying fire." The bush, being a good element of God's good creation, has nothing evil to be purified of. Thanks to Shane Claiborne for this insight, via personal conversation.

4. The reference to Moses's father is fascinating, since Moses was separated from his true father and raised as an adopted son in Pharaoh's family as a consequence of Pharaoh's paranoid attempt at population control. So God could be saying, "I am the God of your actual father, the slave, not your adoptive father, the slave driver." In other words, "I am the God who names you with your true and original identity."

5. This occurs, for example, when the patriarch Abraham argues and bargains with God in Gen. 18:22–32. Similarly, when the word of the Lord comes to Jeremiah, Jeremiah responds with an excuse: "I do not know how to speak for I am only a boy" (1:6). And when Mary receives an angelic visitor, she asks a question: "How can this be?" (Luke 1:34).

6. The name "Israel" means "striver/wrestler with God."

7. Here is St. Francis's actual prayer: *Dio mio e mio tutto! Il Signor Iddio, io sono niente, ma tutto e la Vostra* ("My God and my all! Lord God, I am nothing, but all is yours").

8. Cynthia Bourgeault describes this idea of home beautifully in her book *The Wisdom Way of Knowing: Reclaiming an Ancient Tradition to Awaken the Heart* (San Francisco: Jossey-Bass, 2003), especially in the poem on pp. 38–40.

## CHAPTER 6: *THANKS:* THE HAPPINESS OF APPRECIATION

1. Quoted in Sam Keen, *In the Absence of God* (New York: Harmony, 2010), p. 92.

2. Thanks to Josef Pieper for this insight, in *Happiness and Contemplation* (South Bend, IN: St. Augustine's, 1998).

3. This is an important theme in my book *Everything Must Change* (Nashville, TN: Thomas Nelson, 2007).

## CHAPTER 7: *THANKS: DAYENU*—ENOUGH AND MORE, AND MORE

1. Evelyn Underhill, *Life as Prayer and Other Writings,* ed. Lucy Menzies (Harrisburg, PA: Morehouse, 1991), p. 186.

2. Sadly, under King Solomon, they did just that. Today's victims too easily become tomorrow's victimizers—a pattern repeated again and again in history.

## CHAPTER 8: *O:* PRACTICING JUBILATION

1. John Muir, selected and adapted. See http://hummingbirdworld.com /spiritnature/Muir.htm.

2. Like all good things, authentic Pentecostal worship is in many, if not most, places under assault by a kind of hyped-up bastardization, useful in priming people for making big offerings to clever purveyors of the so-called prosperity gospel, which seldom helps anyone achieve prosperity except the preacher.

3. Barbara Ehrenreich, *Dancing in the Streets: A History of Collective Joy* (New York: Holt, 2007). Thanks to Ken Medema for recommending this book.

4. Kester Brewin, *Other: Loving Self, God and Neighbour in a World of Fractures* (London: Hodder & Stoughton, 2010).

5. Read again, in this light, the story of the sacred convocation in Neh. 8. Holiness demanded not grim solemnity, but joy.

6. William Temple (1881–1944), Anglican priest, Bishop of York, and Archbishop of Canterbury, defined worship in terms that comprise our spiritual practices of confession (quickening the conscience), meditation (feeding the mind), invocation (opening the heart), and surrender (devoting the will). Worship as explored in this chapter would correspond most specifically to his "purging of the imagination by the beauty of God." See Appendix A for more on Temple.

7. For more on this unitive way of seeing, see Richard Rohr's *The Naked Now: Learning to See as the Mystics See* (New York: Crossroad, 2009), and "Jill Bolte Taylor's Stroke of Insight," available at http://www.ted.com /talks/jill_bolte_taylor_s_powerful_stroke_of_insight.html.

8. Andrew Newberg and Mark Robert Waldman, *How God Changes Your Brain* (New York: Ballantine, 2010). Michael Gerson's review can be found at http://www.washingtonpost.com/wp-dyn/content/article /2009/04/14/AR2009041401879.html.

## CHAPTER 9: *O: NOT JUST A WORD—A WAY OF LIFE*

1. Jane Redmont, *When in Doubt, Sing* (Notre Dame, IN: Sorin, 2008), pp. xvii, 207–8. The original prayer in Hebrew: *Baruch ata Adonai, Elohenu, melech ha-olam shecheheyanu, v'ke-y'manu, v'higi'anu, la-z'man hazeh.*

2. For a brief reading of Romans, see my *A New Kind of Christianity* (San Francisco: HarperOne, 2010), chap. 15.

3. Here I am echoing an insight from Dallas Willard in *The Divine Conspiracy* (San Francisco: HarperSanFrancisco, 1998).

4. For more on fixed-hour prayer and related ancient practices, see the Ancient Practices Series, for which Phyllis Tickle serves as general editor, which I had the privilege of introducing with *Finding Our Way Again: The Return of the Ancient Practices* (Nashville, TN: Thomas Nelson, 2008).

## CHAPTER 10: *SORRY: HOLIER THAN MYSELF?*

1. Richard Rohr, *Falling Upward: A Spirituality for the Two Halves of Life* (San Francisco: Jossey-Bass, 2011), p. 8.

2. Gareth Higgins wrote *How Movies Helped Save My Soul* (Lake Mary, FL: Relevant, 2003).

3. The Greek word for "confession" in the New Testament captures this idea beautifully. *Homologeo* literally means "to say the same thing." In confession, I try to say the same thing God would say about my behavior.

4. Nobody I know has written more insightfully about the relationship between personage and person than Paul Tournier, beginning with *The Meaning of Persons* (San Francisco: Harper & Row, 1982).

5. Of course, to modern ears animal sacrifice sounds brutal as well. But in context, slaughter was the first stage in cooking a meal—as much a part of life as visiting the grocery store and opening the refrigerator are for us today.

6. By the use of the word "possessed" in the previous sentence, I am echoing insights about the demonic in scripture for which I am indebted to Walter Wink. See, for starters, *The Powers That Be* (New York: Doubleday, 1998).

CHAPTER 11: *SORRY:* UNLEASHING OUR OWN BECOMING

1. Quoted in Jane Redmont, *When in Doubt, Sing* (Notre Dame, IN: Sorin, 2008), p. 100.

2. This environment of grace, by the way, differs greatly from an imposter environment often labeled "accountability." In groups built around a misguided sense of accountability, people often reinforce the sin-avoidance mind-set. They share their secrets and failings at a weekly meeting under the assumption that they'll do better next week in order to avoid the shame of being exposed as a failure. In other words, accountability stops being about the grace of radical acceptance and becomes instead about the fear of shameful rejection.

3. You can imagine parallel dynamics being set in motion when we define ourselves in the opposite state, saying, "I'm a bad person."

4. We will deal further with the experience of being wronged in the practice of compassion and intercession.

5. The early church had a fascinating practice that has been lost in all but some Eastern Orthodox churches. At baptism, new converts would spit toward the west. The land of the setting sun was seen as the home of the devil, and new converts were in this way spitting in the face of the devil. At the beginning of their Christian life, they were switching sides and renouncing evil, ritually expressing that they were now members of a community that took evil seriously and positively despised it. Confession, seen in this light, allows us to maintain our hatred for evil, while simultaneously avoiding the temptation to pretend we are free from it. It allows us to simultaneously hold a high standard of behavior while acknowledging that we fall far below it—all the while aspiring to elevate our behavior rather than depress our high ideal.

6. *The Big Kahuna* (1999), Franchise Pictures. For more information, see www.imdb.com/title/tt0189584/.

7. In the Eastern Orthodox tradition, various versions of the "Jesus prayer" have proven themselves deeply valuable to millions of people, including me. The version I have employed for years, "Lord Jesus Christ, son of the living God, have mercy on me, a sinner," can hold open space in the soul for confession, especially when the word "sinner" is emphasized. It serves as a sentence-long expression of *sorry*. The prayer can also be used less as a practice of confession/regret and more as a practice of invocation/awakening, functioning as a sentence-length expression of our first spiritual word, *here*.

8. This perfect integration explains why we humans are commanded not to judge. We aren't so good at shining a light on one another that is both just and merciful. Only God's light gets that integration right.

## CHAPTER 12: *HELP:* SPIRITUAL JUJITSU

1. In his autobiography, Bob Dylan tells about being asked, "You a prayin' man, huh? What do you pray for? You pray for the world?" He replied, "I never thought about praying for the world. . . . I pray that I can be a kinder person" (*Chronicles, Volume One* [New York: Simon & Schuster, Pocket, 2004], p. 206).

2. Thanks to John Haught for this insight, in *God After Darwin: A Theology of Evolution* (Boulder, CO: Westview, 2007).

3. Some people's theology won't allow them to speak of Jesus growing. The New Testament has no such hesitancy, as Luke 2:52 and Heb. 5:7–8 make clear.

## CHAPTER 13: *HELP:* TAPPING INTO THE CURRENT OF POWER

1. Ken Wilson, *Mystically Wired* (Nashville, TN: Thomas Nelson, 2009), p. 6.

2. Bruce Wilkinson, *The Prayer of Jabez* (Sisters, OR: Multnomah, 2000).

3. Sometimes a fourth *f* is added to the reptilian response repertoire: to fight, flee, freeze, or . . . copulate, which may explain why powerful and stress-ridden people so often self-destruct through sexual misconduct.

4. Other reasons include the following: (1) I can reread old prayer journals to get perspective on my spiritual journey. (2) The discipline of journaling my prayers helps me keep track of whether I have actually been praying or not. (3) Journaling helps me focus specific attention on each of the twelve different practices we're exploring in this book. (4) In a small group or with a spiritual director, I can share various parts of my journal as a window into my spiritual life. (5) The act of writing prayers helps me slow down and go deeper, accessing deeper parts of me than I would if I were praying without writing. (6) Sometimes, written prayers become

works of art—poems, songs, or stories. For others with appropriate talent, they might also inspire drawings or paintings.

5. I originally learned this simple but helpful idea from John Maxwell. He is also the speaker who quoted Abraham Lincoln in the story shared in the previous chapter. For more on John's work, see www.johnmaxwell.com.

## CHAPTER 14: *PLEASE*: AT LEAST TWO HEARTS CARE

1. Quoted in Kenneth Leech, *True Prayer* (Harrisburg, PA: Morehouse, 1995), p. 22.

2. Thanks to Parker Palmer for this beautiful image, from "The Broken-Open Heart: Living with Faith and Hope in the Tragic Gap," available at http://www.upperroom.org/weavings/pdf/PalmerReprint.Weavings.pdf.

3. This is described poignantly by the apostle Paul (2 Cor. 1:3–11), who confesses to a spell of near-suicidal depression when he was "so utterly, unbearably crushed that [he] despaired of life itself" (v. 8). Eventually, he experienced God's comfort and was able to pass it on to others.

4. A team led by Karen Armstrong has helped us move in this direction by drafting the Charter for Compassion (http://charterforcompassion.org), which reads as follows:

> *The principle of compassion* lies at the heart of all religious, ethical and spiritual traditions, calling us always to treat all others as we wish to be treated ourselves. Compassion impels us to work tirelessly to alleviate the suffering of our fellow creatures, to dethrone ourselves from the centre of our world and put another there, and to honour the inviolable sanctity of every single human being, treating everybody, without exception, with absolute justice, equity and respect.
>
> *It is also necessary* in both public and private life to refrain consistently and empathically from inflicting pain. To act or speak violently out of spite, chauvinism, or self-interest, to impoverish, exploit or deny basic rights to anybody, and to incite hatred by denigrating others—even our enemies—is a denial of our common humanity. We acknowledge that we have failed to live compassionately and that some have even increased the sum of human misery in the name of religion.
>
> *We therefore call upon all men and women* to restore compassion to the centre of morality and religion, to return to the ancient principle that any interpretation of scripture that breeds violence, hatred or disdain is illegitimate, to ensure that youth are given accurate and respectful information about other traditions, religions and cultures, to encourage a positive appreciation of cultural and religious diversity, and to cultivate an informed empathy with the suffering of all human beings—even those regarded as enemies.
>
> *We urgently need* to make compassion a clear, luminous and dynamic force in our polarized world. Rooted in a principled determination to transcend selfishness, compassion can break down political, dogmatic, ideological and religious boundaries. Born of our deep interdependence, compassion is essential to human relationships and to a fulfilled humanity. It is the path to enlightenment, and indispensable to the creation of a just economy and a peaceful global community.

5. Since this is a primary theme of the paradigmatic biblical story of the Exodus, you might think such a point would not need to be made. But history—including contemporary religious history—proves otherwise.

## CHAPTER 15: *PLEASE:* BEARING THE STRETCHER

1. Philip Yancey, *Prayer: Does It Make Any Difference?* (Grand Rapids, MI: Zondervan, 2006), p. 308.

2. A version of this story originally appeared in *DreamSeeker Magazine* (Autumn, 2001) and is available online at http://www.cascadiapublishing house.com/dsm/autumn01/mclabr.htm.

3. For more on this compassionate practice of blessing, which is closely related to intercession, see John O'Donohue's masterpiece, *To Bless the Space Between Us* (New York: Doubleday, 2008).

4. In this regard, see the inspiring prayer by Serbian Orthodox bishop Nikolai Velimirovic available at http://brianmclaren.net/archives/prayer-regarding-critics-and-ene-1.html.

5. Two additional comments on this section of the Lord's Prayer seem appropriate to add here. First, the word "debt," used in Matthew's version of the Lord's Prayer (6:12), suggests "a failure to go far enough" in repaying an obligation. It might evoke the problem of indebtedness common in Galilee, where wealthy Judeans from the south would give loans to their hard-pressed northern neighbors, so they could pay their taxes to the Romans. Mutual forgiveness would signal reconciliation among people separated by class and political affiliation in Jesus's Jewish community. In contrast, the word "trespasses" is used in the commentary on the prayer (6:14). It suggests "going too far," crossing a boundary of rightness or propriety. It may be a special reference to the Romans, whose occupation of Israel was an ultimate act of trespass. For the oppressed to forgive their foreign oppressors would be even more radical than for Judeans and Galileans to reconcile. Taken together, the words suggest radical reconciliation both among "us" and with "them."

6. Not insignificantly, this teaching against revenge is one of the most frequently repeated imperatives in the New Testament.

7. See, for example, C. S. Lewis's classic *The Problem of Pain* (San Francisco: HarperSanFrancisco, 2001), and Yancey, *Prayer.*

8. The issues of suffering, God's agency, miracles, and unanswered prayer come up in my *The Story We Find Ourselves In* (San Francisco: Jossey-Bass, 2008), *Finding Faith: A Search for What Makes Sense* (Grand Rapids, MI: Zondervan, 2007), and *A New Kind of Christianity* (San Francisco: Harper-One, 2010).

9. A song, "With Kindness," adapted from St. Teresa, on my *Songs for a Revolution of Hope,* vol. 1, available at www.brianmclaren.net.

CHAPTER 16: *WHEN:* HOW LONG CAN I LAST?

1. Philip Yancey, *Prayer: Does It Make Any Difference?* (Grand Rapids, MI: Zondervan, 2006), p. 32.

2. For more information on Kent Annan, see his first book, *Following Jesus Through the Eye of the Needle* (Downers Grove, IL: InterVarsity, 2009), and go to http://www.haitipartners.org. His new book, *After Shock* (Downers Grove, IL: InterVarsity, 2011), recounts his experiences in Haiti since the earthquake.

3. Sadly, many, including some Wesleyans, interpreted entire sanctification to mean technical perfection, as if one could begin scoring a perfect ten morally day after day. This kind of immature scorekeeping sadly subverts Wesley's project, which aimed for something far greater and more challenging than avoiding a list of sins. His goal was maturity, a habitual state of living in love for God and others. The best description of Wesley's project that I've read is Thomas Oord and Michael Lodahl's *Relational Holiness: Responding to the Call of Love* (Kansas City, MO: Beacon Hill, 2005).

4. The three examples given here come from an old hymnal found by a friend in a used bookshop in London, *The Methodist Hymn-Book* (London: Wesleyan Conference Office). Although the edition is undated, it was commissioned in 1901. They are found in a section entitled "Aspiration and Hope," in the subsections "For Believers Praying" and "For Believers Seeking Full Redemption." However one may criticize the details of Wesley's doctrine of entire sanctification, and putting aside the spiritual pathologies one can perhaps trace back to it, one can't deny the spiritual fervor—the anticomplacency and anti-apathy—evoked by these hymns. Nor can one deny their honesty. By expressing what they desire, the poets are frankly admitting what they do not yet have or feel or experience. One can't help but lament how few hymns and songs in use today ring true with either this fervency or this honesty.

CHAPTER 17: *WHEN:* SURVIVAL IS UNDERRATED

1. Thanks to Erroll Narain for this reference.

2. Lucretius, *On the Nature of Things,* available online at http://classics.mit .edu/Carus/nature_things.1.i.html.

CHAPTER 18: *NO:* THE VOID EXPANDS

1. Quoted in Sam Keen, *In the Absence of God* (New York: Harmony, 2010), p. 3.

2. Even faith communities that try to exclude doubters repeatedly have to acknowledge the place of skeptics among them. Biblical characters like Elijah and Job can be saintly one day and skeptical the next. And today's true believers can have children who, when they come of age, raise tough questions in the community of faith.

3. C. S. Lewis, *The Problem of Pain* (San Francisco: HarperSanFrancisco, 2001).

CHAPTER 19: *NO:* MAD WITH GOD

1. Quoted in Kenneth Leech, *True Prayer* (Harrisburg, PA: Morehouse, 1995), p. 84.

2. In this light, as Gustavo Gutiérrez says (*On Job: God-Talk and the Suffering of the Innocent* [Maryknoll, NY: Orbis Books, 1987]), the book of Job isn't primarily about explaining the existence of evil, as is commonly assumed. Instead, it grapples with a far more practical question: *How can we wisely speak of and with God in the midst of evil?* (p. 13). See also Jane Redmont, *When in Doubt, Sing* (Notre Dame, IN: Sorin, 2008), p. 390.

3. It might be said that Palestinians face a related agony today. They repeatedly hear both Jewish and Christian Zionists minimize Palestinian anguish under Jewish occupation, and although they cry "No!" few seem to take notice, and things go from bad to worse.

4. Duane Shank, "Never Again," at http://blog.beliefnet.com/godspolitics /2008/05/never-again-by-duane-shank.html.

5. Richard Rohr captures it well in *Job and the Mystery of Suffering* (New York: Crossroad, 1996): "An awful lot of religion is an excuse for not facing our fears, our self, and our doubts. True religion is not denial of doubt but a transformation of it; and often, to be honest, a temporary deepening of our doubt and darkness to get us there. God walks with us into our fears, to feel them, to own them, to let them teach us. During that time we are often in darkness and cannot uphold ourselves. It even feels like a loss of faith. It is then that we slowly learn to let Someone Else hold us, and we come out enlarged and more hopeful. As long as I have lived, I cannot explain the chemistry of this transformation, but those who have gone through *know* it to be true" (pp. 20–21).

6. The questions, significantly, are about creation, which is God's original "word" or self-expression. God's creation, in all its mystery, dynamism, and complexity, deconstructs the feeble and simplistic moralisms and theological theories of Job's friends. And Job himself recognizes that God's frame of reference is far bigger than his own, which reduces him to the same silence that his friends have been reduced to. Something similar seems to have happened, by the way, in recent years, when Darwin, Freud, Einstein, Hubble, and others similarly brought the "logos" of creation to bear on many theological assumptions. The one once again deconstructed the other, much to the chagrin of many religious people.

7. Bruce Cockburn, from "Understanding Nothing," on the album *Big Circumstance* (Rounder, 1988).

CHAPTER 20: *WHY:* WHEN YOU HAVE COME TO ZERO

1. Ruth Haley Barton, *Invitation to Solitude and Silence* (Downer's Grove, IL: InterVarsity, 2004), p. 82.

2. One of the best definitions of "orthodoxy" I've read comes from Kenneth Leech: "Orthodoxy is about being consumed by glory: the word means not 'right belief' (as dictionaries tell us) but right *doxa,* right glory. To be

orthodox is to be set alight by the fire of God" (*True Prayer* [Harrisburg, PA: Morehouse, 1995], p. 11).

3. Walter Brueggemann, *Spirituality of the Psalms* (Minneapolis: Augsburg Fortress, 2001).

4. Little is said about the possibility that the venom and violence of funda- mentalists of various religions is a projection outward of their own inner turmoil and grief—turmoil and grief about a theology that is failing them individually and as a community.

## CHAPTER 21: *WHY:* HOLDING THE QUESTION OPEN

1. From a song by the author, "Why, God, Why?"

2. This is Matthew's wording (26:39). Luke's is similar (22:42). Mark's, which we might presume to be less edited, is even stronger (14:36): "Father, for you all things are possible; remove this cup from me."

3. My Jewish friends might similarly say that during the Holocaust, G-d was on the trains, in the camps, even in the gas chambers.

## PART 4: HARMONY: THE SEASON OF SPIRITUAL DEEPENING

1. In *Finding Our Way Again* (Nashville, TN: Thomas Nelson, 2008), I ex- pressed a similar idea with similar imagery: "You can't take an epidural shot to ease the pain of giving birth to character. In a sense, every day of your life is labor: the rhythmic agony of producing the person who will wake up in your body tomorrow, creating your reputation, continuing your legacy, and influencing your family, friends, colleagues, neighbors, and countless strangers, for better or worse" (p. 11).

## CHAPTER 22: *BEHOLD:* THE EMERGENCE OF THE MEDITATIVE MIND

1. Sam Keen, *In the Absence of God* (New York: Harmony, 2010), p. 85.

2. See Richard Rohr, *The Naked Now: Learning to See as the Mystics See* (New York: Crossroad, 2009). Richard uses the term "contemplative" more broadly to include what I'm calling meditative seeing. I'm going to apply the word "contemplation" more narrowly in our last chapter.

3. The word "behold" plays a fascinating structural role in the Genesis text in those translations that retain it (e.g., KJV, RSV). Note its significance in 1:29; 1:31; 3:22; 4:14; 6:12.

4. This is not to deny that in Simplicity, Complexity, and Perplexity we were also seeing with God. When we learned to identify good and evil, we were seeing (imperfectly) moral realities that God sees. When we learned to cope with difficulty and complexity—to identify ways and means—we were seeing pragmatic realities that God sees. When we learned to decon- struct human constructions, we were seeing (and seeing through) social and conceptual realities that God sees (and sees through). Even when we

learned to doubt human constructions about God, we were coming closer to what only G-d knows about G-d. But if G-d is love, as the New Testament affirms, then to see in love is to see most truly with G-d.

5. Sadly, modern translations of 2 Cor. 5:17 for some reason tend to drop the "behold," Greek *idou,* which means "Look!" "Open your eyes!" "See!" "Perceive!" "Be aware!"

6. The word "holy" in this sentence deserves a brief additional comment here. In dual thinking, holiness suggests purity, according to which those who consider themselves pure judge, condemn, and exclude the impure, often with remarkable harshness. Beyond dual thinking, "holiness" suggests wholly otherness, which means, among other things, to be other than unkind and other than judgmental. So this wholly otherness means holy otherliness, or perfect love. Nondual holiness, then, is an even greater purity that includes being purified from harshness, rejection, and exclusion. It is a purity that always includes and exudes pure compassion. It is a holiness so holy that it loves the unholy, recalling Matt. 6:43–48, especially as compared with Luke 6:27–36.

7. Roland Bainton, *Here I Stand: A Life of Martin Luther* (New York: Mentor, 1955), p. 168.

8. Step 3: "Made a decision to turn our will and our lives over to the care of God *as we understood Him.*" Step 11: "Sought through prayer and meditation to improve our conscious contact with God *as we understood Him,* praying only for knowledge of His will for us and the power to carry that out."

9. The distinction can be felt in contrasting Isa. 40:9 with 1 Kings 12:28. In the former the people are invited to behold G-d, but in the latter, two politically useful idols are proposed as a substitute. Isa. 40, by the way, is certainly one of scripture's most extravagant attempts at conveying the grandeur of God in words, employing vivid simile, metaphor, and rhetorical question. But even there, awe-inspiring words give way to awestruck sight, as Isaiah points to the sky and says, finally: "Take a look at that!" (40:25–26).

10. Peter Rollins explores this theme energetically and brilliantly in his *How (Not) to Speak of God* (London: Paraclete, 2006).

## CHAPTER 23: *BEHOLD:* FAITH BEYOND BELIEF

1. Two cinematic moments also capture this moment of beholding especially well. In *Jurassic Park,* two paleontologists step out of a jeep to see a landscape in which brontosaurs, stegosaurs, and other dinosaurs roam free. Creatures that were accessible to them only as fossils, traces of a lost past, have come to life here and now. In *Contact,* another scientist travels through a wormhole and sees a "celestial event." "Indescribable," she gasps. "They should have sent a poet." Beholding renders all of us dumbstruck, awestruck. We are prose-bound scientists suddenly confronted by transcendent, poetic beauty.

2. I don't think I was reading Thomas Aquinas (1225–74) that day, but I arrived at the same conclusion he did. Years later I came across this quote: "What God is always remains hidden from us. And this is the highest knowledge one can have of God in this life, that we know him to be above every thought we are able to think of him" (quoted in Kenneth Leech, *True Prayer* [Harrisburg, PA: Morehouse, 1995], p. 12).

## CHAPTER 24: *YES:* A UNIVERSAL SPIRITUAL VOCATION

1. Quoted in Jane Redmont, *When in Doubt, Sing* (Notre Dame, IN: Sorin, 2008), p. 258.

2. Interestingly, some translations add to v. 6 the word "although," to say, "Although he was in the form of God, [he] did not regard . . ." The text would more naturally read, "Because he was in the form of God, [he] did not regard . . ." His descent reveals God's true nature—humble and self-giving, not detached and dominating.

3. "Getting saved," "being born again," "praying the sinner's prayer," "making a decision for Christ," and "accepting Christ" are various terms Evangelicals use for the first yes to God.

## CHAPTER 25: *YES:* DO YOU LOVE ME?

1. From Jane Redmont, *When in Doubt, Sing* (Notre Dame, IN: Sorin, 2008), p. 371.

2. Adapted from Richard Rohr, *Everything Belongs* (New York: Crossroad, 2003), p. 31.

3. For a fascinating analysis of the four Gospels, see Alexander Shaia with Michelle Gaugy, *The Hidden Power of the Gospels: Four Questions, Four Paths, One Journey* (San Francisco: HarperOne, 2010).

4. Matthew agrees with John and locates the disciples' encounters with the risen Christ in Galilee. By contrast, in Luke's Gospel, the disciples are explicitly told to stay in Jerusalem. Taken together, the accounts may suggest that the risen Christ is to be encountered both at the margins and in the center of society.

## CHAPTER 26: *[ . . . ]:* NAKED, CLOTHED IN SILENCE

1. Richard Rohr, *Simplicity: The Freedom of Letting Go* (New York: Crossroad, 2004), p. 97.

2. Quoted in Jane Redmont, *When in Doubt, Sing* (Notre Dame, IN: Sorin, 2008), p. 76.

3. Mother Teresa's posthumously published diaries reveal that she spent much time in Stage Three, Perplexity, where God's presence seemed unavailable to her. That reality in no way undermines the validity and beauty of her life with God, but rather intensifies them.

4. Jim Wallis, *Faith Works: Lessons from the Life of an Activist Preacher* (New York: Random House, 2000), pp. 254–55.

5. Also quoted in Wallis, *Faith Works*, pp. 254–55.

6. For more about Steve—and to order his music—check out www.stevebell .com.

7. I believe it was my friend Jim Henderson from whom I first heard the word "otherly."

8. Mikhail Epstein, Alexander Genis, and Slobodanka Vladiv-Glover, *Russian Postmodernism: New Perspectives on Post-Soviet Culture* (New York: Berghahn, 1999), pp. 169–70.

9. Epstein, Genis, and Vladiv-Glover, *Russian Postmodernism*, p. 170.

## CHAPTER 27: [ . . . ]: FULL CIRCLE

1. Barbara Fiand, *Prayer and the Quest for Healing* (New York: Crossroad, 1999), p. 20.

2. We might also say that contemplation is simply the next step beyond normalcy. Eventually all the Pentecostal noise and activity become normal—as do the normal routines of liturgy—and so we move beyond them to silence and rest.

## AFTERWORD

1. Quoted in Kenneth Leech, *True Prayer* (Harrisburg, PA: Morehouse, 1995), p. 39.

2. This beautiful term, "regenerative community of creation," is from a conversation with Dr. Randy Woodley, a Native American and Christian theologian who suggests that "community of creation" is a good contemporary translation of "kingdom of God." "Creation" in this case doesn't simply mean the thing—the created universe. It means the process of creation—a process in which God and creation collaborate. This term, like the "kingdom of God," encompasses both the infinite God and God's finite creation.

3. For Jesus, the greatest commandment was love (Matt. 22:37–40). For Paul, the only thing that matters is faith expressing itself through love (Gal. 5:6). For John, the age-old message we have heard from the beginning is to love one another (1 John 3:11). For the Buddha, each element of the Eightfold Path is an expression of love or compassion. And the Beatles, of course, sang, "All You Need Is Love."

4. In Jeremiah 22:16, God says that showing love to the poor and needy is "what it means to know me."

## APPENDIX A: GROUP PRACTICE

1. I explore this concept in some detail in *Finding Our Way Again: The Return of the Ancient Practices* (Nashville, TN: Thomas Nelson, 2008).

2. Ian S. Markham in *Liturgical Life Principles* (Harrisburg, PA: Morehouse, 2009) offers a needed primer in how liturgy works.

## APPENDIX B: BODY PRAYERS

1. For much more on this subject, see Doug Pagitt and Kathryn Prill, *Body Prayer* (Colorado Springs, CO: WaterBrook, 2005).

# ACKNOWLEDGMENTS

Thanks to pastor and fly fisherman Jeff Petersen for reading an early draft of this book and offering helpful input. Thanks to seasoned editors Mickey Maudlin (at HarperOne in the United States) and Katherine Venn (at Hodder & Stoughton in the United Kingdom) for their sage guidance in shaping this book. Thanks to Ann Moru for her unmatched editorial assistance. Thanks to my talented literary agent, Kathryn Helmers, for the many ways she helps me navigate the fascinating world of publishing, and to Laci Scott, who has deftly and graciously managed my work as a traveling speaker for as long as I can remember. Thanks, as always, to my many mentors and friends, whose contributions are woven into every word I write and who have blessed my life beyond words. Deepest thanks to Grace, our kids, and my parents and extended family, in whose love I live. I am blessed indeed.

This book is dedicated to my grandchildren, born and unborn, in hopes that it will someday be a resource for their spiritual journey.

# Reading and Discussion Guide

PREFACE AND INTRODUCTION

1. In the preface, the author talks about the meaning of clothing and nakedness. How do you respond to the word "naked," especially when it's linked with the word "spirituality"?

2. In what ways have you experienced a "dressed-up" spirituality, and in what ways have you experienced a stripped-down spirituality?

3. The author recalls the story in Genesis of Adam and Eve being "naked and not ashamed." What role has shame played in your spiritual life?

4. What do you hope to get out of this book, based on this preface?

5. In the introduction, the author describes possible situations of his readers using the words "you may" or "you might." Which of these descriptions come closest to your experience right now? Can you think of friends or family members who fit one or more of his descriptions?

CHAPTER 1: SPIRITUAL EXPERIENCES AND SPIRITUAL EXPERIENCE

1. Compare your own religious upbringing with the author's. Do you remember having "an innate spirituality" in your childhood?

2. What people and churches have had a positive and negative effect on your spiritual life through the years?

3. How did the author's telling of his spiritual experience in this chapter affect you? Were there elements of the story you could relate to, or elements that made you uncomfortable?

4. Have you ever had a spiritual experience that you never told anyone about? Why did you want to keep it a secret? Have you ever shared a spiritual experience with others, and what were the results—positive and negative—of sharing that experience?

5. What is your reaction to the book so far? How are you feeling at this point as an engaged reader? What questions have arisen for you? What concerns or objections are being raised?

CHAPTER 2: "BUT I'M SPIRITUAL"

1. How would you restate in your own words the four meanings behind "I'm spiritual" presented by the author in this chapter? Where have you seen or experienced these four elements recently?

2. The author makes up a word: "de-ligion." Define in your own words "religion" and "de-ligion," and point to examples of both.

3. Retell the three stories from the Gospel of John that the author explores in this chapter. Did he offer any insights on these stories that seemed especially helpful for you?

4. The author concludes, "The Spirit, then, is bigger than any particular religion or religion in general. Nobody has a monopoly on Spirit." Do you agree? Why? Why might this statement be hard for some people to accept?

5. Wine, wind, and water . . . talk about what these images say to you about the spiritual life.

CHAPTER 3: TWELVE SIMPLE WORDS

1. The author compares developing a spiritual life to learning a language, running a marathon, and playing a musical instrument. Respond to those comparisons.

2. In what ways does a spiritual life require individual, private, personal practice and in what ways does it require a group or community?

3. How have you experience "the tyranny of *not enough*" in your spiritual life?

4. "Complexity was overrated," the author says. Have you ever grown disillusioned with the complexities of religion? If so, when and how? What happened as a result? If not, what do you enjoy about complexity in religion?

5. Briefly summarize the four stages introduced in this chapter: Simplicity, Complexity, Perplexity, and Harmony. What does the term "naked spirituality" mean to you now, in relation to these four stages?

CHAPTER 4: *HERE:* STARTING RIGHT NOW

1. The author describes the haunting experience of hearing his name called while out in the woods. In what way might you be metaphorically out in the woods, hearing your name called?

2. The author explains that he chose the word "here" to avoid having to name or address God too soon. Why is he concerned about naming God? When you say the word "God," what mental images are in your mind, and in what ways might they be helpful and unhelpful?

3. Is there a place—a particular *here*—where you predictably feel the presence of God? What makes that place special for you?

4. "Presenting yourself to the Presence"—respond to this phrase in your own words.

CHAPTER 5: *HERE:* NAMING THE MYSTERY

1. Try to put yourself in the story of Moses and the bush. How would you have responded?

2. If you had to name one thing or experience in your life that has been the most like your burning bush, what would it be?

3. The author talks about an essential balance between accessibility and mystery in our approach to God. Where do you struggle to maintain this balance? Which leaning comes more naturally to you?

4. Describe your own habits in naming the Divine. What are the strengths and weaknesses of the ways you normally refer to the Almighty? How could you expand your repertoire of names for the Holy One? Did any of the names in this chapter especially resonate with you?

5. Share your experiences in practicing with *here, who,* and *home.*

CHAPTER 6: *THANKS:* THE HAPPINESS OF APPRECIATION

1. Respond to this statement—and give some examples of it: *It's not how much you have that brings happiness; it's how much you appreciate however much or little you have.*

2. Talk about the relationship between gratitude, consumerism, and addiction.

3. Try the author's "treatment" for the Big Yellow Taxi Syndrome, starting with your body, possessions, family, other people, and so on. What stands out from this practice of gratitude? What have you been most taking for granted lately?

4. Has there ever been a time when you experienced the kind of ecstatic gratitude the author describes at the end of this chapter?

CHAPTER 7: *THANKS: DAYENU*—ENOUGH AND MORE, AND MORE

1. What new insights can you offer about that phrase from the Lord's Prayer: *Give us this day our daily bread?*

2. The author speaks of the advantages of disadvantages. Can you think of some of those advantages that you're grateful for right now?

3. Share your experiences of practicing with *thanks, again, this,* or *dayenu.*

4. What would your life be like if you were more grateful for the rest of your days? What most keeps you from practicing gratitude?

5. What questions do you still have about gratitude?

CHAPTER 8: *O:* PRACTICING JUBILATION

1. Have you ever had an especially meaningful experience of joyful celebration (what the author later calls a TAZ—Temporary Autonomous Zone)? If so, share that experience. If not, can you recall a time when, looking back, you wish you would have celebrated more joyfully?

2. What, in your opinion, might help poor people be so freely exuberant, and rich people so typically restrained, in their worship?

3. Is joy the primary emotion you associate with God? If not, what emotion or condition do you primarily associate with God? What would be the effects in our lives and faith communities if we understood God to be an essentially joyful being?

4. Respond to the author's discussion of worship and the brain.

## CHAPTER 9: *O:* NOT JUST A WORD—A WAY OF LIFE

1. What words, songs, sounds, visual images, and experiences most evoke joyful worship for you?

2. Respond to the author's overview of Paul's letter to the Romans, and especially to Paul's use of the word "O!" at the end of Romans 11.

3. The author offers several "firsts" that can help us worship God in our daily lives. Which of those firsts do you already practice? Which would you like to experiment with?

4. Consider visiting some different faith communities to explore their ways of worship. How would you be changed by becoming a more whole-hearted worshiper of God?

5. Share your experiences with "O," "how," or other expressions of jubilation and worship.

## CHAPTER 10: *SORRY:* HOLIER THAN MYSELF?

1. Respond to this statement: *A secret to the spiritual life is desiring to actually be more spiritual than you appear to be. The secret to hypocrisy is desiring to appear more spiritual than you actually are.*

2. Why do you think pretending is so popular—inside and outside of religious circles? Can you think of a person in your life who stands out by not pretending?

3. The author describes the conscience as a moral nerve for the soul. How would you describe your conscience? Too sensitive? Too calloused? About right?

4. How do you feel about the term "naked spirituality" now, in light of this chapter's emphasis on confession and coming out or coming clean?

## CHAPTER 11: *SORRY:* UNLEASHING OUR OWN BECOMING

1. Think of your nation, political party, faith community, or family. If they were to engage in corporate confession, what would they need to address? Why do you think corporate confession is so unpopular, and what are the consequences of its unpopularity?

2. How might you encourage corporate confession in the groups of which you are a part?

3. The author suggests that an atmosphere of grace actually helps us change more than an atmosphere of pressure does. Why?

4. Talk about the dangers of what the author calls a "status mind-set," and the advantages of a "becoming mind-set."

5. Share your experiences of practicing with *sorry* and *mercy*.

## CHAPTER 12: *HELP:* SPIRITUAL JUJITSU

1. The author speaks of sabotaging our failures and our weaknesses. Describe how this sabotage works.

2. Petition is linked with the idea of expanding beyond our limitations. Talk about how this practice of petition could have an effect on you in relation to one of your real-life weaknesses.

3. Contrast immature with mature petition, and relate both to a situation in your life.

4. The author says that the book of Genesis and the theory of evolution teach us the same lessons. Explain.

5. Offer your own reflections on Jesus's prayer in the garden.

6. How do you respond to the idea of being a friend to yourself? What kind of friend are you to yourself?

## CHAPTER 13: *HELP:* TAPPING INTO THE CURRENT OF POWER

1. In what ways have you experienced labeling like the character Jabez? How could you respond to this labeling in a "bless me to be a blessing" way?

2. Talk about some limitations or weaknesses in your life, and how you could better deal with them, based on this chapter.

3. Name some current big and little anxieties in your life, and translate them into requests.

4. Name some common big and little wounds in your life, and translate them into requests.

5. Name some common big and little disappointments in your life, and translate them into requests.

6. Share your experiences with the simple word "help."

## CHAPTER 14: *PLEASE:* AT LEAST TWO HEARTS CARE

1. Have you ever had an experience like the author's in the kitchen, when you were touched deeply with an overwhelming sense of compassion?

2. The author lists several alternatives to compassionate intercession when we are faced with the sufferings of others. Which of these alternatives are most habitual for you?

3. The author uses the image of magnetizing a nail to suggest that by "rubbing up against" God's compassion, we ourselves become more compassionate.

If that's the case, why do you think some religious people and communities seem to lack compassion?

4. Of the many ways that Jesus modeled compassion, which are most meaningful for you, and why?

## CHAPTER 15: *PLEASE:* BEARING THE STRETCHER

1. When have you been on the stretcher? Who was bearing the stretcher for you? When have you been a stretcher bearer for others? Share a story or two.

2. The author recounts a story about a dying animal that evoked compassion in him. Do you have a similar experience? How did it affect you?

3. What story of human suffering has seized your attention in recent days? What words would translate your concern into a request or blessing for these people, such as *peace, protection, strength, hope, comfort, stamina, patience*?

4. Who is persecuting you or causing you pain these days? Experiment with the author's counsel on praying for these "enemies," and share your experience.

5. The author talks about our intellectual problems and unanswered questions regarding prayer. Which issues or questions most trouble you? How has this chapter helped you deal with those questions or issues?

6. Share your experiences practicing with "please" and related words.

## CHAPTER 16: *WHEN:* HOW LONG CAN I LAST?

1. Do you feel you have hit this stage of Perplexity yet? Or would you locate yourself more in Simplicity or Complexity?

2. When do you recall feeling the agony of *when* or *how long* most acutely in your life? Have you ever felt the fear that your faith wouldn't last or survive a touch time, as described by the author?

3. Which line from the hymns in this chapter most resonates with you?

4. How would you describe the strongest spiritual aspiration in your life these days? Are there prayers of exasperation and desperation arising within you too?

## CHAPTER 17: *WHEN:* SURVIVAL IS UNDERRATED

1. How would you describe the gap between your dreams and your present reality at this stage in your life? What kind of desire can grow in this gap?

2. What pressures—of aspiration, exasperation, and desperation—can you acknowledge building within your soul in recent months? On a scale of one to ten, how would you describe the pressure level?

3. Where do you feel a void in your life? What could this void be making space for?

4. Share your experience practicing *when* or *how long*.

CHAPTER 18: *NO:* THE VOID EXPANDS

1. The author presents four possible resolutions to the problem of evil. How do you respond to these four options? Do you know people who have chosen each one?

2. Have you ever experienced a period of spiritual rage and refusal? What initiated it? What did it feel like? How did it end?

3. How do you respond to the Psalms presented in this chapter? What surprised you in them, and what comforted you?

4. If a friend was feeling *No!* but was afraid to express it, what would you say?

5. What would you want a friend to say or do—or not say or do—to help you if you were in a place of rage and refusal?

CHAPTER 19: *NO:* MAD WITH GOD

1. Can you put yourself in the place of people reading the Megillat Hashoah? What would this liturgy do for you?

2. How easy is it for you to distinguish, as this chapter asks you to do, between "the G-d we hope exists" and "the G-d who apparently exists"?

3. What's the closest you've experienced to *peripeteia*? What temptations did you face in that "zone"?

4. What in the recounting of the Job story most touched, intrigued, or bothered you?

5. Have you ever written a poem or prayer of "lament and fury"? If not, why not, and if so, what was the experience like?

6. If you know that you would enter a zone of *peripeteia* six months from now, what would you write in a letter to yourself to help you cope?

CHAPTER 20: *WHY:* WHEN YOU HAVE COME TO ZERO

1. Talk about the ironies and tensions in the simple word "why."

2. Describe how the Bible would look to a person in Stage One, Stage Two, and now at the end of Stage Three.

3. What line or image from the Lamentations passage most touches, inspires, helps, or frustrates you?

4. The author says, "To be abandoned is to find out how real you are." How would you express this statement in your own words? Does it resonate with your own experience in any way?

CHAPTER 21: *WHY:* HOLDING THE QUESTION OPEN

1. Are you surprised that Jesus would use the words "abandoned" or "forsaken" with God? Why?

2. The author distinguishes between two meanings of the word "reason"—cause (referring to a plan in the past) and possibility (referring to good that can be pursued in the present and future). Try to explain what this distinction means and why it's important.

3. The author speaks of naked honesty in this chapter; how is naked honesty important to naked spirituality? Why do we often feel a tension between naked honesty and spirituality?

4. The author speaks of "falling into the G-d below you." What happens when you shift your thinking from God being exclusively above you to God also being below you?

5. Experiment with the "expanding circle of empathy" described by the author near the end of the chapter. Share your experiences of practicing *why*.

## CHAPTER 22: *BEHOLD:* THE EMERGENCE OF THE MEDITATIVE MIND

1. Describe an experience of resurrection or a *behold* moment in your life.

2. Describe the four kinds of seeing mentioned in this chapter—dualistic, multiplex, relativistic, and meditative.

3. The author returns to a theme he has touched on previously: making a distinction between the God "out there" in reality and the image of God "in here" in our thoughts. Why do you think this theme is so important in his exploration of naked spirituality?

4. The author says, "I can't explain how the transfer of trust from God to G-d happened, only that it was messy, slow, reiterative and terrifying. And wonderful." Does this statement make sense to you? Have you experienced anything like this in your spiritual life?

5. Go back and re-read the epigrams that begin each chapter. Pause on one that grabs your attention and practice the slow, meditative, receptive seeing described in this chapter.

## CHAPTER 23: *BEHOLD:* FAITH BEYOND BELIEF

1. The author repeats the terms "slow" and "reverent" and keeps referring to "wonder." Why are these words so important in relation to meditative beholding? What makes this kind of beholding so rare among us?

2. The author playfully invents a word: "wonderstanding." What does that word say to you?

3. Respond to the story recounted by the author about beholding the goodness of God. What feelings and thoughts are evoked within you from this story?

4. Try one or all of the three beholding experiments proposed in this chapter—a public place, a natural place, and an uncomfortable place. Share your experiences.

5. Did you have any *behold* moments while reading this chapter? Were you tempted to hurry through them? Were you able to slow down and savor them?

CHAPTER 24. *YES: A UNIVERSAL SPIRITUAL VOCATION*

1. This chapter begins with the idea of moving downward, descending from meditation to service. How do you respond to this idea of downward mobility?

2. Have you had decisive moments of commitment and consecration in your spiritual life? Describe what led up to them, what they involved, and what they led to.

3. The author says, " . . . our *yes* must become, not simply an event, but a practice." In some ways, that is a primary theme of this book. Talk about the relationship between events (or decisive spiritual *experiences*) and practices (leading to ongoing spiritual *experience*) in your life.

4. How have public worship gatherings and special rituals, days, and seasons helped you in practicing the *yes* of consecration? Have other practices helped you more?

CHAPTER 25: *YES: DO YOU LOVE ME?*

1. What most struck you in the story of Peter and Jesus on the shore?

2. Peter evades Jesus's call by referring to a fellow disciple: "What about him?" In what ways are you most tempted to evade your callings to growth, sacrifice, and service?

3. The author links the *yes* of consecration and surrender to an acceptance of death. Reflect on this linkage, and on your own attitudes to death.

4. *Yes* is a response to a particular invitation: *to join God*. What does it mean to you *to join God*?

5. Share your experience practicing *yes*.

CHAPTER 26: *[ . . . ]: NAKED, CLOTHED IN SILENCE*

1. *Blank canvas, empty space, silence*—the author describes these as good and precious. Describe in your own words why silence would have such a special value in the spiritual life.

2. What person in your life has been a great listener? What role in your life has this person's listening played? In what ways can you see God as Listener?

3. The author describes his frustration with contemplative silence, especially in his younger years. Have you shared that frustration? Why or why not?

4. Reflect on the experience of the guitarist and pianist described in this chapter. What does this story tell you or help you understand?

5. The author concludes this chapter: "And could it be that contemplation is the pause button that freezes time so that we listen to the Listening and witness the Witness?" Respond to this question.

CHAPTER 27: *[ . . . ]: FULL CIRCLE*

1. Follow the spiritual director's advice in this chapter. Share your experience.

2. Try holding in your imagination the image of the resting child from Psalm 131. As you hold this image, with you as the child and God as the mother, what emotions arise within you?

3. Restate the author's description of the contemplative and charismatic approaches to experiencing God. Which of those approaches comes more naturally to you, and why? What might you gain by exposing yourself to the alternative approach?

4. Respond to this statement: "There is nothing more radically activist than a truly spiritual life, and there is nothing more truly spiritual than a radically activist life."

5. Why do you think the author concludes this chapter with the image of diving naked into a river? How does that image affect you?

## AFTERWORD: THE SEA TOWARD WHICH ALL RIVERS RUN

1. "Love is the last word," the author says. Looking back over the hours you have invested reading this book, how has your understanding of the word "love" been enriched?

2. Respond to the statement, "Spirituality is love."

3. What have been the highlights of this book for you? How has it affected you? What do you think you will do differently as a result of reading it?

4. Who do you think would enjoy reading this book? Why would you recommend it to them?

5. In an online interview about the book, the author said, "My prayer and hope for this book is that it will render readers more vulnerable to God's presence in their daily lives." Why do you think he used the word "vulnerable"? To what degree has his hope been fulfilled for you as a reader?

6. If you have a schedule or a calendar program on your computer, pick a date about one month, three months, six months, and one year from today. Choose four passages from this book that you would like to remind yourself to go back and read at each date, and enter a reminder to read the relevant page number on those four dates. What pages did you choose, and why do you want to be reminded of them?

## APPENDICES

1. Who would you like to invite to form a reading group to practice the twelve simple words?

2. How could you make use of the body prayers in Appendix B socially in a small group, class, church service, retreat, or privately in your home?

3. How could the twelve simple prayers be incorporated into a small group, class, church service, retreat, or family time?

4. Have you checked out the additional resources on the author's website? What resources were helpful to you, and why?